The Global Debt Crisis and Its Socioeconomic Implications

Mohamed Rabie

The Global Debt Crisis and Its Socioeconomic Implications

Creating Conditions for a Sustainable, Peaceful, and Just World

palgrave
macmillan

Mohamed Rabie
Georgetown University
Washington, District of Columbia
USA

ISBN 978-3-319-66214-5 ISBN 978-3-319-66215-2 (eBook)
https://doi.org/10.1007/978-3-319-66215-2

Library of Congress Control Number: 2017950559

Cover image © Maurusasdf / Getty Images
Cover design by Samantha Johnson

Printed on acid-free paper

This Palgrave Macmillan imprint is published by Springer Nature
The registered company is Springer International Publishing AG
The registered company address is: Gewerbestrasse 11, 6330 Cham, Switzerland

To my daughters Aseel and Haneen and son Kareem, who enriched my life and made me proud of their life accomplishments

Preface

The near collapse of the international banking system in September 2008, and the Great Recession that followed, have exposed the seriousness of the financial and economic problems facing Europe, the United States and many other countries. They also revealed that these problems are due not to economic and political mismanagement only, but also to European and American loss of economic competitiveness and lack of business ethics by many financial institutions and insurance and mortgage companies. Since the roots of these problems are deep, addressing them requires thoughtful thinking, sound economic and financial reforms, political changes in policy and structure, and, above all, sociocultural transformation.

Owing to the financial crisis, many states in the world were forced to bail out troubled banks and failing corporations, thus adopting expansionist policies to stimulate contracting economies. Consequently, state borrowing increased substantially and caused the public debt and budget deficits of most nations to rise rapidly and reach, in many cases, unsustainable levels. Some troubled states, however, moved to cut spending in order to contain budget deficits and reduce borrowing as they tried to restructure their economies in the hope of regaining competitiveness and reviving their struggling economies. But neither approach has succeeded in correcting the structural deficiencies and achieving the desired goals.

Today, many states in the West and East, North and South are facing a dilemma: how to reduce budget deficits to contain the ever-increasing debt and, at the same time, stimulate stagnating or hardly growing economies to create jobs for the unemployed. All indebted nations subscribing to the free market system are in a bind; the goals they seek to accomplish are contradictory; and the actions they must take are incompatible. While reducing budget deficits to contain the public debt requires reducing government spending and raising taxes, stimulating economies to create new jobs requires increased government spending and tax reductions. Since there is no formula in our classical economic books to achieve these contradictory objectives, something new has to be envisioned. The formula this book tries to invent is called the "Ramo Plan." Its role is to enable nations to resume healthy economic growth and create jobs for the unemployed, without widening budget deficits or increasing the debt burden.

While current economic thinking is no longer able to help, the financial policies implemented since 2008 have proven to be largely counterproductive: they have increased poverty, widened the income and wealth gaps in every society, and failed to stop debt from growing. In fact, without the schemes invented by the American and European central banks to reduce interest rates to near zero, the global debt would by now have reached at least 150% its current size. In order to justify the proposed Ramo Plan and explain the need for it, I shall place it in its proper societal and historical perspectives, a task that includes reviewing the state of the American economy in view of its stimulus plan, as well as the Spanish and Greek economies in view of their austerity plans.

To deal with the public debt crisis, we need to understand that debt is a consequence of budget deficits, which are a consequence of fiscal policies that fail to raise enough revenues to meet a state's spending targets; and failure to raise enough revenues to finance state spending is a consequence of economic policies that fail to grow national economies. In rich countries, such as the United States and Britain, the failure to raise enough revenues is primarily due to unfair social policies that favor the rich at the expense of the poor. This means that solving the debt crisis requires action that includes growing the economies of indebted nations; putting an end to political and economic corruption; and transforming the political and economic systems and cultures of nations. On the other hand, growing the national economies of nations has become a function of the dynamics of the global economy and how it is managed.

This book intends to articulate a plan to liberate all rich and poor nations from the debt burden, restructure the international monetary system and create the necessary conditions for sustainable global sociocultural and economic development, while helping the world's poor and protecting the environment. The plan has come as a result of deep thinking about the woes of our times; the duty to help poor people and desperate children climb out of poverty; the need to save college students from debt and inadequate education; and a moral responsibility to liberate oppressed and undereducated young women and men from economic and social enslavement and radicalization. The plan also aims to save future generations from having to pay a debt incurred by current and previous political leaders.

Since the intention of the Ramo Plan is to help everyone, it does not ask banks, investors or bond holders to sacrifice anything; and it does not call for the redistribution of income or wealth or seek to raise taxes. The plan is a program to free the poor from need and create new investment opportunities for the rich to exploit. As a consequence, it lends a helping hand to everyone and penalizes no one.

But before outlining this plan, I shall explain in the next few pages where I come from; how I view the world and our place as human beings in it; and what kind of lessons we are able to learn from history. This will help to explain why I thought of this plan, and how I am able to reach the conclusions outlined hereunder. Meanwhile, placing the major economic, financial and sociocultural challenges facing all nations in their proper historical context, which will be done in the first chapter, will help us to view the challenges of our times with clarity, and approach them with fair-mindedness and confidence.

People, who believe in God as being the creator of all things, also believe that all humans are the descendents of one man (Adam) and one woman (Eve). Since we have the same mother and the same father, we must be one people belonging to the same and only race; people who believe in evolution also believe that we all came from animals that look like apes that appeared in Africa many thousands of years ago. As a consequence, each theory says that all of us came from one source. In fact, whenever we define ourselves, we unconsciously say the human race, not the human races.

But on our way to populate earth, we were exposed to three powerful forces that shaped our life experiences and greatly influenced the ways we look, think and behave, causing us to develop different traditions, languages and religions. These forces are: natural selection or the law of the survival of the fittest; random mutation that gave us the diversified colors and features we have today; and an unpredictable environment that forced man and animal to continue moving and discovering new places, adapting to nature's dictates and developing different habits and traditions. Some humans and animals were able to survive and flourish, but many vanished because they failed to adapt to harsh environments. Although our life experience moving from one place to another throughout history has enabled us to gain cultural and religious diversity, we have encountered no other race to acquire racial diversity. Embracing cultural diversity strengthens our unity and enriches our lives; embracing racial diversity divides us into savage tribes and destroys the essence of our lives.

On the other hand, religion is an accident of birth: everyone knows that no man or woman was able to choose his or her religion at birth, parents or place or time of birth, name or color or social class at birth. Therefore, no one should be punished or rewarded because of things that were inherited at birth. And since religion is an accident of birth, everyone must have the right to stay in his inherited religion or change it. It is the duty of society to respect everyone's religious choice, and the state's responsibility to protect everyone's religious and nonreligious rights.

People who believe in God also often believe that whatever they inherit at birth reflects God's will. God chooses for each of us our parents and religion, the time, place and life conditions at birth. This means that every religion is legitimate because it was inspired by God; therefore, every religion must be respected by all believers and states. Anyone who refuses to accept the religious beliefs of other people as legitimate and equal to his own religion is in fact rejecting the will of the God he claims to believe in. You cannot accept what God chooses for you and, at the same time, reject what God chooses for your fellow human beings.

As for my life experience, I am fortunate to have experienced the development of human societies over time, and witness firsthand the evolution of civilizations. And because civilizations go through transitional periods before transformations are completed, living the life I have lived has given me a unique, probably unprecedented, opportunity to witness transitional periods in history and feel the agonies and hopes of people living through them. My writings are thus based on real life, and are not a matter of imagination or intellectual curiosity.

I was born into an agricultural community where neither electricity nor running water nor modern sanitation systems were available. Every family in our town owned a house and a piece of land to farm; there were no poor families or landlords practicing feudalism. But as I was growing up and becoming aware of my social and economic environment, war erupted suddenly in my country, causing my family and generation to become refugees. The refugee camp in which I spent about five years of my youth was outside an agricultural town at the edge of a desolate, hot and dry desert. The first two years were lived in shacks rather than in tents because no international organization paid attention to our plight. During this time, my older sister and I were assigned the task of roaming the neighboring desert and mountains to collect vegetables and dry and dying bushes to make fires for cooking; it was a boyhood living the life of a hunter-gatherer who hunted no animals but gathered a lot of vegetables and wood.

Other circumstances led me to share food with nomads, listening to their songs and stories, spending time in their tents, observing their daily life and being with shepherds as they went about their daily tasks in the desert. Walking and talking with sheep herders, and listening to the music of primitive lutes in the company of herds of sheep and well-trained dogs helped me gain a deep understanding of tribal man's culture and purpose in life. By the time I entered high school, my family had moved to Jericho, which is believed to be the world's oldest city. All nine of us lived in a one-bedroom apartment that had none of the basic amenities. We rented and cultivated a small piece of land on which we lived and whose produce provided most of the food we needed to support a subsistence living. All children who were able to help cultivate the produce were required to do so. Domesticated turkeys, chickens, pigeons and rabbits provided meat to supplement our diet.

Upon graduation from high school, I received a grant from the United Nations to study in Cairo, one of the largest and most vibrant cities of the Third World at the time. The trip to Egypt gave me my first opportunity to fly in a plane and spend a night in a hotel, in Beirut, Lebanon. Living in Cairo gave me a chance to observe affluence and abject poverty coexisting peacefully, and to watch modern and primitive cultures living their separate, estranged lives in one place. In the meantime, Third World nationalism and socialism were thriving in Cairo along with anti-imperialism, in an atmosphere that inspired young people and gave hope to the deprived. It was only there that I was able to live in a house with electricity, running cold and hot water, and even a phone that worked. Life in Cairo at this time represented what I call the transitional period separating two civilizations, the agricultural and industrial ones.

Five years later, I received a grant from Germany, where I witnessed the so-called German Economic Miracle, which pulled Germany from the devastation of World War Two to become one of the leading economic powers of the world. I was able to study closely the development of the country's economy and observe the work ethic of the German people, and for almost two years I lived in a mature industrial society. While I was in

Germany, I pursued a graduate degree and worked for a few months in a publishing house. Most of my free time was spent visiting as many cities, villages and historical sites as possible and immersing myself in the culture of the land. Life in Germany gave me a priceless opportunity to move in my thoughts, life conditions and awareness from those of a traditional tribal and agricultural society to those of an industrial, highly organized society. In 1965, I moved to the United States where I completed my higher education, received a Ph.D. degree in economics and taught at two American universities. While living in the United States, I witnessed two of the most important social and political movements in US history: the civil rights movement and the anti-war movement that opposed US actions in Vietnam.

In 1970, I left the United States to teach at Kuwait University; and while I was there I managed to change the educational system and the curriculum, introducing coeducation for the first time in the history of the Arab Gulf states. And through my participation in the cultural life of this society, I learned how immigrant workers lived and how they viewed life conditions in that part of the world. For six consecutive years, I witnessed a semi-tribal society lose the major characteristics of its way of life as oil wealth transformed it into what I call a "petroleum society." It was a society whose roots were anchored in the fifteenth century, while its aspirations were reaching the twenty-first century. Most Kuwaiti people thought and behaved at the time as if they could buy anything with money, and as if they could employ anyone they pleased, offering no rights except the right to get paid. Since those societies had not experienced the agricultural age, the availability of money caused the culture of production to be separated from the culture of consumption.

In 1976, I returned to the United States, where I taught first at Georgetown University in Washington DC and then at three other universities. In addition to teaching, I was involved in business and research, and wrote and published books covering several topics. While living in Washington, I witnessed the transformational impact of the Reagan and Clinton years on American society, culture and politics; it was an opportunity to witness civilizational changes for the third time, and live through the transitional period that led a mature industrial society to enter a new age, whose core systems are based on knowledge. This new age was caused by a knowledge revolution that began in the mid-1990s and is still unfolding.

Between 1998 and 2000, I spent my time shuttling between Washington and Germany, giving lectures at German universities and research institutes, and advising Erfurt University which reopened after more than two centuries, having been closed because of the religious wars of the seventeenth century. In 2002, I went to Morocco where I spent more than two years teaching at Al Akhawayn University and two more years living in Jordan. So for the second time in forty years, I had the opportunity to observe how life conditions and cultures change during a transitional period that separates the agricultural from the industrial age, where globalization has caused traditional cultures to lose many old-age traits and characteristics and to become deformed beyond recognition.

Since boyhood, my life has been an ever-evolving and fascinating story. It has taken me to numerous places in Asia, Europe, the Middle East, North Africa, and North and South America, which has enabled me to look back at my primitive roots and to explore the unknown future in my thoughts and ways of living. Ever since I graduated from college, I have continued to travel, give lectures, write articles for newspapers and publish books. Thus my perspective goes beyond the ups and downs of ordinary life in one society or one civilization, and my connections to places, civilizations and historical phases I have experienced have continued to fascinate me and to challenge my intellectual capacities.

Therefore, I can say with confidence that I have experienced, within my lifetime, starting with the pre-tribal age, the life experience of more than 600 generations. I believe that no other person has lived my life; and no one will ever live such a life because some of the times I have lived have come and gone and will never return. Going through this rough but fascinating experience, I have been able to learn something new from each generation and to gain valuable wisdom from each civilization, causing my perspective on life, culture and history to be unique. And because of the loss of my childhood, home and livelihood, my intellectual curiosity, awareness and love for knowledge were awakened at a very early age, helping me to become what I am today.

Washington DC, USA
September, 2017

Mohamed Rabie

Contents

List of Tables

CHAPTER 1

Evolution of Civilizations

The purpose of this chapter is to explain how human societies have developed over time; and how the movement from one civilization to another has caused each society to go through a transitional period. During these transitional periods, older civilizations lose the major characteristics of their cultures, economies and societies, causing the new civilization to be fundamentally different from the older one; the transition also causes the older civilization and its people to become dependent on the new one and its people.

Social scientists seem to agree that the greatest revolutions in human history were the Agricultural and Industrial revolutions, which gave birth to the agricultural and industrial civilizations. There is also an agreement on three major civilizations: tribal, agricultural and industrial. Nevertheless, a growing number of scholars believe that the twin revolutions of information and communications represent another historical revolution that is destined to transform the totality of life conditions everywhere. This new stage is often referred to as the information age or the globalization age; I call it the knowledge age, because it is knowledge that includes the twin revolutions and recent innovations and scientific discoveries that launched the Knowledge Revolution in the mid-1990s, causing all aspects of life to go through fundamental transformation. Analyzing how these stages developed and how they relate to each other should enable us to place all changes in their proper historical contexts and track the course of transformation over time. It should also enable us to depict the major trends of change and to put us in a good position to make sound predictions.

M. Rabie, *The Global Debt Crisis and Its Socioeconomic Implications*,
https://doi.org/10.1007/978-3-319-66215-2_1

Historical records suggest that long before the development of agriculture human beings were able to get enough food and attain sufficient security to survive and grow. Familial ties, customs and traditions served as the social glue that held early societies together and gave meaning to people's lives. This means that the roots of civilization came into existence probably 30,000 years ago. However, this was a primitive civilization, in which society depended primarily on the hunting of animals and fish and the collecting of wild fruits and vegetables. However, at the end of this stage, man was able to domesticate many animals, and that enabled the tribal society to fully develop and become sustainable; and in some instances semi-settled tribal societies appeared, paving the way for the development of agriculture.

With the development of agriculture some 10,000 years ago, the economic base began to change, causing culture and social and economic structures of society to change fundamentally. "Plant and animal domestication meant much more food and hence much denser human populations. The resulting food surpluses and the animal-based means of transporting those surpluses, were a prerequisite for the development of settled, politically centralized, socially stratified, economically complex, technologically innovative societies."[1] But after agriculture was established and its culture fully developed, the pace of change slowed, causing socioeconomic and sociocultural conditions to stabilize. Nevertheless, the later centuries of the agricultural era witnessed the birth of organized religion, the development of writing, the formation of states and empires, expansion of trade and the incorporation of merchant life into the life of society.

In the second half of the eighteenth century, the production of manufactured goods emerged in England as the most important economic activity. This development heralded the coming of a new era, the industrial age, and the dawn of rapid change in all aspects of life. The coming together of major social, cultural, scientific, and particularly economic and technological developments is what we call the Industrial Revolution. It was a revolution that changed the mode of production and production relations, forcing all aspects of life to change drastically. "Our fathers started the revolution and we are still living it. We could not stop it even if we wanted to."[2] In the early 1990s, industrial society in general began to experience a new wave of drastic change driven by knowledge, the information and communications revolutions and globalization. In the mid-1990s, the knowledge age began to impose its logic on the prevailing ways and states of living, causing all aspects of life to undergo fundamental change.

The Tribal Age

This age lasted longer, but experienced less change than any other age. Its roots go back to the hunter-gatherer era, probably 100,000 years ago, and continued until the development of agriculture 10,000 years ago. People during this age lived in small families that survived through the hunting of animals and the gathering of fruits and vegetables. About 30,000 years ago, tribal society emerged, causing small families to become part of a larger family, while enabling the new society to organize life in ways that made it more secure and dynamic. The domestication of animals some 11,000 years ago enabled nomads to strengthen their economic base and to further develop their way of life. Domesticated animals made tribal life easier and sustainable; the meat of some animals was used for food, while the skin and fur of others was used for clothing and the bones of some served as tools, weapons, musical instruments and ornaments. In addition, people employed some animals, such as the camel, horse and elephant, as means of transportation, which enabled them to move across difficult terrains and interact peacefully and otherwise with other tribes. The intellectual horizon of tribal people, however, remained "limited to their allegiance to the tribe and its traditions and legacy."[3] Culture in this age was in essence a way of life based on inherited norms and a history of feuding with other tribes. The social and cultural aspects of life, or what I call the *sociocultural process*, governed the pace of change and influenced its nature for many generations thereafter.

Since economic conditions were basically the same everywhere, the environment became the primary force influencing the course of change. And because environmental conditions were similar in most inhabited places, they produced similar patterns of living. Consequently, tribal cultures displayed almost identical characteristics in content, attitude, character and outlook; all had the same internal and external dynamics. "Many events in human history seem to correlate very remarkably with environmental controls ... The historical theory that ascribes many events in the human record to environmental causes thus receives powerful support from geology."[4]

But since the places where tribes lived were different in geography and topography and the distribution of plants and animals, different tribes domesticated different animals and developed slightly different cultures. Because of this diversity, argues Jared Diamond, some regions were able to develop faster and make more progress than others. "Hence the availability of domestic plants and animals ultimately explains why empires, literacy, and steel weapons developed earlier in Eurasia and later, or not at all, on other continents."[5] In addition, nature and the dictates of a nomadic life denied people the opportunity to establish roots in one place, leading them to have no attachment to a country or nation. The family house was the place to which tribal people exhibited most attachment, and the tribe was the nation to which they belonged.

The Agricultural Age

About 10,000 years ago, man began to domesticate plants and develop agriculture. Although no one knows how this discovery came about, historical records strongly suggest that agriculture was first practiced in present-day Palestine, Syria, Lebanon and Egypt. From there, it traveled to other Asian, African and European countries. It is also believed that agriculture may have developed independently in other regions, particularly in China and New Guinea. It is significant that "the long transition from foraging to agricultural life … happened in several places seemingly independently, yet within a few thousand years of one another."[6] Year-round warm weather and the abundance of water and fertile land made a semi-nomadic life possible. And this enabled man to observe nature closely and follow its course, and ultimately to discover the lifecycle of plants and develop agriculture.

Since tribal men were forced by nature and culture to spend most of their time foraging, I believe that women were responsible for the discovery of the lifecycle of plants and thus the development of agriculture. In fact, women in many agricultural societies have continued to spend most of their time cultivating the land, tending plants, preparing produce for food, and preserving vegetables and fruits for cold seasons and hard times. Therefore, women should be given credit for causing the most important revolution in human history.

The development of agriculture changed the way in which societies and economies were organized and transformed cultures and people's relationships to each other and to their environment. Agriculture brought about a new civilization, with its own society, economy, culture, social and economic structures, and political organization. "The change from hunting and gathering to agriculture involved more than a mere change in subsistence pattern; it represented a complete change in the social and cultural fabric of life."[7] As a consequence, the old way of life had to recede and the building of a different way of life had to begin. And as agriculture became an established way of life, permanent settlements began to appear and grow in size, leading people to build houses and communities, and to make roots in scattered hamlets and villages. As a result, land acquired a new meaning that forced societies to reorganize their social and economic life around it. "Compared with the thousands of years humans spent foraging, the construction of villages represented another revolutionary change in culture, subsistence, technology, social organization and history. In many respects, humans still have not successfully completed this major transition."[8] The importance of land to people led eventually to private ownership of land, causing society to be divided into two social classes separated mainly by land ownership.

The farming of the land from permanent bases caused people to develop a strong attachment to their environment, which led individuals and families to acquire a sense of belonging to a place and community, and later to a society and state. As a result, people were forced to develop new traditions, initiate new internal and external relationships, and compete to improve the quality of their lives. And as communities grew in size and number, trade appeared and began to play an increasing role in societal life, leading economies to grow and diversity. And with the expansion of trade, a need for a superstructure or state was created to regulate access to water and land resources, and to protect agricultural communities and traders from roaming tribesmen. Subsequently, politics and political institutions, or what I call the *political process*, emerged to play an important role in societal life.

Learning from their experience and environment, people began to develop knowledge and make tools, causing land and labor productivity to rise and needs and desires to grow in ways that affected people's ways of living and social relations. In the meantime, the accumulation of knowledge, the institutionalization of private property and the ability to produce a food surplus worked together to introduce the idea of progress to human life. One of the new forces that played a pivotal role in the development of both state and culture was organized religion. This emerged in response to certain human needs, particularly man's inability to explain nature, its workings and many of its manifestations. Religion was also needed to provide ethical and moral codes of conduct and regulate social relations, especially during the formative stages of agricultural communities. Since some of the questions raised by man thousands of years ago continue to elude science even today, religions have continued to play a major role in individual and group lives, influencing social relationships and people's worldviews.

Since the means of survival during the agricultural age were almost the same everywhere, cultures were similar in content and character. The little change that cultures exhibited during these times came largely as a result of external rather than internal forces, which compelled some groups to interact with each other through travel, trade, migration, war and conquest. "The ways in which different societies responded to challenges distinguished Chinese civilization from that of the Aztecs, or Egyptian civilization from that of India. Problems produced unique responses and further differentiated one culture from another."[9] Nevertheless, the production and consumption of food continued to be the focal point of the life of agricultural society. As a result, *agricultural man ate to live and lived to eat*, making food production and consumption the essence of the culture of the agricultural age both past and present.

With the building of empires, cultures began to play a more active role in life, viewing external forces not only as threats to be avoided, but also as challenges to be faced and potential opportunities to be harnessed. Cultures that viewed external forces as challenges and possible opportunities were able to change faster and make more progress. In contrast, cultures that viewed external challenges as threats to be avoided became suspicious and inward-looking, and thus less able to change and make meaningful progress. Consequently, culture emerged as a force that shaped people's ways of thinking and attitudes, defining individual and community identities and goals, setting priorities and influencing the nature of responses to varied challenges. Nevertheless, cultures, regardless of place and time, have always shown little enthusiasm for change, especially change introduced from the outside.

The Industrial Age

Until the fifteenth century, no nation anywhere in the world had experienced profound change to distinguish itself from other nations. "The world formed a single, albeit large, social system that operated at a much slower pace than that to which we have become accustomed."[10] But around the middle of the fifteenth century, the pace of social, cultural, political, economic, and technological change began to accelerate, causing social systems to enter a period of transformation. Trade, which by then had become an important economic activity, led the ensuing change and paved the way for the economic transformations, scientific discoveries and technological innovations that were to follow, giving birth to what I call, the *economic process.*

Other developments occurred subsequently and played decisive roles in promoting change and accelerating its pace; they included improvements in navigation tools and maps, building better ships, producing potent arms, the development of the printing press, growing competition between the major European cities and states, and the discovery of the New World. Owing to these developments, manufacturing expanded; financial services were legitimized; and scientific and philosophical inquiry multiplied. Three centuries later, the Industrial Revolution took place in England, and from there traveled to other European and North American countries, transforming agricultural life to an extent previously unknown. "Agricultural societies were transformed into urban industrial societies within the space of perhaps a hundred years, and all the accumulated norms, social habits and customs that had characterized rural village life were replaced by the rhythms of the factory and the city."[11]

For example, workers were no longer free to determine their working hours and how to perform their work; tasks were assigned, working hours were specified, regulations were imposed, and hierarchical relationships within the workplace were enforced. Income was tied to work, making survival a function of work availability and worker's capacity to work long hours. Industrial man, as a result, was transformed through manufacturing into a machine, causing work to become the focal point of life. *Industrial man works to live and lives to work*, causing life to start and end with work, even for the majority of rich capitalists. Karl Marx, writing some 80 years after the birth of the Industrial Revolution, observed that "man's ideas, views and conceptions, in one word, man's consciousness, changes with every change in the conditions of his material existence, in his social relations, and in his social life, or in the state of his living."[12]

In the meantime, the concentration of workers living in crowded slums caused things to change, and slowly a new social class emerged and began to form labor unions to facilitate collective bargaining and apply collective economic and political pressure on the industrial state. Intellectuals, seeing the intolerable living and working conditions in and around factories, and the enormity of exploitation of children and women by capitalists, supported the demands of the working class. Gradually, industrial workers developed a class consciousness that made them look and behave as a distinct social class. And as the Industrial Revolution advanced, it expanded and diversified economic and financial activities, causing new jobs to be created and more people to be involved in manufacturing. And this in turn created need for people to perform related tasks such as plant supervisors, sales persons, accountants, banking and investment officers and innovators. Consequently, a new class of largely urban dwellers was born; it was neither rich nor poor but in between. Because of its unique social position and functions, the new class shared neither interests nor traditions with either the rich or poor; it has to develop its own way of life and claim its place in society as a middle class.

On the other hand, people migrating from the countryside to urban centers in search of jobs caused the extended agricultural family and its traditions to disappear. The new communities that emerged in the industrial cities were composed of nucleus families sharing smaller living spaces and facing differentiated life challenges. Traditions and kinship ties that provided the social glue that held traditional agricultural communities together for centuries were no longer workable in the new environment. And because neither tribes nor clans could function in the new society, the state became more dominant and allegiance to it was strengthened.

The age of industry did not only expand manufacturing, it also helped agriculture grow and become more productive; it also expanded trade in agricultural products. As a consequence, agriculture became dependent on industry; it could not grow on its own to meet the growing demand for food without the machines, fertilizers, improved seeds, and the irrigation systems industry and its technological base had developed. Rendering agriculture dependent on industry caused its society to become dependent on industrial society. The natural dependency of agricultural society on industrial society renders the *dependency theory* articulated by Latin American intellectuals largely baseless; it can neither explain lack of development in so many states nor help a nation transform its economy and culture and overcome underdevelopment.[13] There is no doubt, however, that the western capitalist nations and their colonialist enterprise have worked hard to deepen the dependency of Third World economies on their own and, because of that, colonialism did contribute to hindering the development of Third World economies and societies.

The fundamental change in the state and way of human living ushered in by the Industrial Revolution was so profound that it made the history and the wisdom of all previous civilizations largely irrelevant. "The physical and mental world we inhabit has changed more—and faster and more often—in the past 200 years than it did in the previous 20,000 years."[14] Changing the state of human living as described above caused previous history to come to an end; it no longer had valid experiences to share, or proven wisdom to give. Nations that failed to understand this lesson were dwarfed by history and made to pay a heavy price in squandered resources, lost opportunities, and increased dependency on others.

The Knowledge Age

The communications and information revolutions have changed reality in all places, particularly in industrial societies. These revolutions are linked together and dependent on each other, and because of that, they form one societal process, *the infomedia process.* The twin revolutions have transformed the media, leading it to become a powerful tool with the capacity to manipulate the forces of the other three processes and influence the course of change in society. In fact, the infomedia process paved the way for the evolvement of the knowledge age, which began to transform our social, cultural and economic lives in the mid-1990s.

The age of agriculture lasted about 10,000 years before the Industrial Revolution occurred. Because of its long duration, it was able to transform the cultures and economic conditions of most tribal societies in the world. When the Industrial Revolution arrived in the eighteenth century, probably 80 % of the world's population was living in the agricultural age. But when the Knowledge Revolution announced its arrival around the middle of the 1990s, the age of industry was hardly 200 years old. Because of that, only about 30 % of the world's population was living in the industrial age. Owing to the complexity and knowledge requirements of the new age, it is not expected to transform the culture or economic conditions or society of an entire nation at any time in the future; every nation will continue to need people to be engaged in activities that are rooted in the industrial and agricultural civilizations.

As the knowledge age advances, the infomedia process has become more powerful and influential because its services are essential to the proper functioning of all institutions and organizations. Knowledge is expected to make the creation, commercialization and utilization of ideas, services and information the focal point of economic activity. As a consequence, the major source of wealth and power is expected to shift gradually from the domain of capital to the domain of knowledge, and a new person whose job is to create and process knowledge will soon emerge. Because of that, *knowledge man learns to live and lives to learn*, which means his life starts and ends with learning. Since knowledge is associated with individuals more than with groups, the individual will ultimately become the basic unit of the new knowledge society, replacing the nucleus family of the industrial society, which replaced the clan of the agricultural society, which replaced the tribe of the tribal society.

Reactions to developments instigated by the advancement of the knowledge age are deep everywhere. People are overwhelmed by strange currents of change, and there is a feeling of a general loss of direction and control over unfolding events. Reactions to this change range from denial to bewilderment, from political conservatism and religious fundamentalism to radical nationalism and extremism, from embracing the emerging values and lifestyles to cultural particularism, from universalism and globalism to tribalism, from tolerance to racism. All these reactions cause conflict and instigate change and, in the process, create new realities that transform cultures and perspectives to make events more dynamic and irreversible. In fact, the knowledge age promises to make the future a *world in a permanent state of transition.*

Societal Processes of Change

In the not-so-distant past, natural resources, the environment, states, gifted individuals and ideas played important roles as agents of change and forces of transformation. Lately, however, the roles of all such agents have been vastly diminished, and the roles of the societal processes of change have been enhanced at their expense. These processes are the sociocultural, political, economic and infomedia processes. They represent social mechanisms that have evolved over time to facilitate the introduction of change and the management of its consequences. And unlike social systems, societal processes do not abide by certain rules or laws, and are not subject to control by any authority. Together, they form the larger framework within which all social systems and institutions function, and through which all change is introduced and managed.

The sociocultural process includes the social forces, institutions, ideas, values and belief systems that shape and manage the social and cultural affairs of nations. It performs tasks by sponsoring activities to preserve the cultural heritage of nations, emphasizing values and belief systems; clarifying the lines separating sectarian, cultural and religious groups; and responding to external and internal challenges. Since the major organizing principles of this process are values, traditions and religious convictions, it represents the forces of stability and continuity.

The political process includes the forces, activities, ideas and institutions that shape and manage the political affairs of nations. It performs its tasks by responding to political needs at the local level, defining goals at the national level and dealing with trade, financial and security issues at the international level. Usually political decisions are taken by the state, most political activities are carried out by national institutions and goals are defined by the nation's need to advance the national interest, which reflects the views of the political and economic elites.

The economic process includes the forces, ideas, institutions and goals that shape and manage the economic and financial affairs of nations. It performs its tasks by responding to market forces that reflect the preferences of consumers and the interests of businesspeople. Opportunities created by new technologies and changed domestic and international conditions provide strong incentives for this process to expand globally and diversify its activities. Because profits are made by producing and selling goods and services, and since demand for goods and services exists everywhere, the economic process functions at all levels, in all places.

The infomedia process includes the forces, organizations and groups that produce and control the flow of information and news and manage entertainment programs. The infomedia performs its tasks by responding to events and crises, analyzing official policies while giving priority to certain issues over others, providing educational and entertainment programs, collecting and disseminating information and facilitating the flow of ideas worldwide. And for a price, the infomedia provides political and business leaders with the means to promote their causes and reach targeted audiences in a timely manner. The ability of the infomedia to reach everyone, everywhere, at all times; and its willingness to provide information and entertainment programs continuously has given it the power to influence people's attitudes, mold and remold public opinions, and transform cultures. And since all information passes through its channels, it is able to manipulate facts and people's hopes and fears, and influence business decisions.

The sociocultural process was the first societal process to emerge in history, followed by the political process. These two processes, concentrating primarily on continuity and stability, worked together to dominate life for generations. The economic process emerged slowly during the agricultural age and gained momentum after the Industrial Revolution; but before it matured the infomedia process emerged to challenge its dominance. These two processes have concentrated on change rather than continuity and stability. On the other hand, the sociocultural process produced great ideas and ideologies, of which religion is the notable one. The political process produced great leaders, empires and philosophies, of which nationalism, colonialism and democracy are most notable. The economic process produced great technologies, entrepreneurs, inventors, capitalism and communism. The infomedia process is producing great innovations and virtual communities, while systematically destroying many of the old ideological and cultural barriers.

In each age, the societal process that enjoyed most authority in society claimed most of its talent. During the agricultural age, the sociocultural process attracted talented people to serve religion and spread the faith. As the political process became dominant, it attracted talented individuals to become bureaucrats, military commanders and tax collectors. As a result, the sociocultural and political processes denied society the opportunity to use its talent to develop life and economy, directing talent instead to ensuring continuity and stability. Today, economic and infomedia processes attract almost all the talent available in the world; they employ them in scientific research, the development of telecommunications and information technology, finance and marketing. As the economic and infomedia processes employ world talent to develop economic and financial services, they cause socioeconomic gaps to widen, sociocultural divides to deepen and knowledge to become more materialistic and less humanistic.

In concluding this chapter, it is important to reiterate that each societal stage represents a unique civilization with its particular society, economy and culture. Since each civilization comes after a difficult transitional period, every transitional period, viewed from a wide angle, represents a *historical discontinuity* that causes history of the passing era to come to an end, while paving the way for the new era to make its own history. And as one history ends, its logic becomes irrelevant and the wisdom of the past becomes of little value to the people of the new age. Transitional periods tend to be workshops for destructive creativity, where creativity is a tool of destruction and destruction is a condition for further creativity. As history approaches the end of a transitional period, nations of the world tend to feel, as Matthew Arnold once remarked, as if they are "wandering between two worlds, one dead, the other unable to be born."[15]

The experience of a society passing through a civilizational transition is similar to that of a driver entering rough mountainous terrain. As he takes a long curve on a winding road, he loses sight of the landscape that lies behind, while the mountains he negotiates block the view that lies ahead. As his speed and control of the vehicle become subject to the rough terrain, his expectations and confidence become subject to the ups and downs of the road. The familiar landscape that lies behind no longer helps; the horizon that lies along the road is so obscured it provides few clues about what lies ahead. As a result, the driver becomes disoriented and less able to avoid mishaps and serious accidents.[16]

The transition from the tribal age to the agricultural age lasted about 3000 years, and the transition from the agricultural to the industrial age lasted about 300 years, making the second transitional period about one-tenth of the first. Based on this observation, the transition from the industrial to the knowledge age is expected to last about thirty years; it is expected to end in about 2025 and to make our world into one that is in a permanent state of transition, because every subsequent transitional period will be shorter than the preceding one. Since no change is neutral, it causes pain and gain. These tend to be unevenly distributed within and between societies. While some people get most of the gain, others feel most of the pain.

Notes

1. Jared Diamond, Gun, Germs and Steel: the Fate of Human Societies (W.W. Norton, 1999): 92.
2. Charles Van Doren, *A History of Knowledge*, 1991, 263.
3. J. L. Sadie, "The Social Anthropology of Underdevelopment," The Economic Journal 70, no. 278 (June 1960): 294–303.
4. John A. Garraty and Peter Gay, The Columbia History of the World, (172 23).
5. Jared Diamond, Guns, Germs and Steel, 92.
6. Jack Weatherford, "Savages and Civilization," (Ballantine Books, 1994) 46.
7. Jack Weatherford, Savages and Civilization, 49.
8. Garraty and Gay, The Columbia History of the World, 52.
9. Weatherford, Savages and Civilization, 50–51.
10. Ibid., 26.
11. Francis Fukuyama, the Great Disruption, *The Atlantic*, May 1994, 46.
12. Karl Marx and Friedrich Engels, the Communist Manifesto, 51.
13. Mohamed Rabie, A Theory of Sustainable Sociocultural and Economic Development, Palgrave Macmillan, 2016, pp. 104–7.
14. Curt Suplee, Imagine This, *the Washington Post*, January 2, 2000, B1.
15. Lenichi Ohmae, The End of the Nation State, 1994, 10.
16. Mohamed Rabie: Global Economic and Cultural Transformation, Palgrave Macmillan, 2013, chapter 3.

CHAPTER 2

Global Change

Since the mid-1990s, change caused by the information and communications revolutions has transformed the way in which individuals, groups, societies and states view themselves and the world around them; it has also transformed traditional cultures and life conditions and how economic and financial systems function. As a result, most assumptions that underpin social, political and economic theories have been largely invalidated, causing old theories and road maps of the near past to lose their usefulness. Since transitional periods cause confusion and lead people to lose their sense of direction, no new theories and road maps could be developed in time to replace the old ones and manage the consequences of change. This chapter tries to identify and briefly analyze the most important socioeconomic transformations the world has witnessed since the middle of the 1990s.

Economic globalization has transformed national economies in ways previously unknown, creating a very complex and integrated global economy that functions outside the parameters of the past; in fact, no state or collection of states is able today to control or even manage the new economy. As a result, economic structures and production relations have been forced to change, causing the nation state to lose most of its power to control its economy. It has also caused societies in general and the industrialized ones in particular to enter a transitional period leading to a new, much complex society, having its own unique culture and economy, as well as its social and economic structures that differ from those of the industrial and agricultural societies.

M. Rabie, *The Global Debt Crisis and Its Socioeconomic Implications*,
https://doi.org/10.1007/978-3-319-66215-2_2

During transitional periods, it is always easier to identify change and describe some of its manifestations than identify its root causes, influence its course or predict its ultimate outcome. On the other hand, as transitional periods cause existing economic, social and political structures to lose validity and start crumbling, they create a trust deficit that feeds corruption, hypocrisy and opportunism in every society; and this in turn creates need for new ideas and laws and regulations to guide societies, economies and politics into a largely uncharted future no one can escape.

The financial crisis of 2008 was one of the consequences of a trust deficit caused by the transition of American society from the industrial age to the knowledge age. People in banking and finance, in mortgage lending and insurance, driven by greed and lack of social responsibility and accountability, were able to exploit the outdated financial regulations and create new, highly complicated financial products, manipulate clients and regulations, and take unwarranted risks that caused the mortgage bubble of 2007 which led to the 2008 financial crisis and the Great Recession. The financial reform bill passed by the US Congress in 2010 is an attempt to close that trust deficit. But since in my view this is yet to be recognized and understood by Western economists and political leaders, the reform bill would not be able to prevent another financial crisis and a deeper recession in the near future. At the time of writing, President Trump, supported by a Republican majority in both the Senate and the House of Representatives, is trying to abolish these regulations.

Every society in the world has two types of trust: traditional trust and social trust. The first prevails in small circles such as families, villages and communities of faith; the second prevails in larger cities and within business and civil society organizations. Traditional trust is a function of cultures that seldom change in one's lifetime, particularly in traditional agricultural societies; social trust is a function of laws, regulations and interests that never stop changing, particularly in industrial societies. As societies move from one civilization to another, social and business relationships become more complex, while interests become more relevant, causing existing laws and traditions to become less able to control change and regulate its many manifestations. As a consequence, societies in transition experience *trust deficits*; while traditional trust loses ground as its space shrinks, social trust is still weak because its legal base is yet to be developed, and wherever trust deficits exist, corruption, manipulation and eroding business ethics spread and deepen their roots in society.[1]

The rapid industrialization of South Korea, China, India, Brazil and a few other nations has caused the global capacity to produce most essential goods and services to exceed the global capacity to absorb such goods and services. As a result, economic growth has slowed down, exposing the global economy to the dangers of recurring recessions, financial crises and high unemployment rates. The global steel industry, being one of the industries burdened by excess capacity, is teetering between failure and bankruptcy. This creates an urgent need to expand existing markets and develop new ones to keep pace with the growing production capacity. Since the absorption capacity of the industrialized states in general is fast approaching its limits, in part because of the shrinking middle classes, aging populations, low population growth rates and widening wealth and income gaps between rich and poor, efforts to develop new markets must therefore concentrate on states where economies are still underdeveloped. And this is a task that market capitalism appears unwilling to take on, because its captains seem to feel comfortable exploiting existing opportunities and accumulating more wealth and power.

The internationalization of major trade, investment and financial markets has caused national economies to become integrated, creating a global economy where its many economic and financial components compete and collaborate with each other as a matter of need; it has also caused the economies, politics and security matters of most nations to become interdependent. As a result, there is no national problem anywhere today without an international dimension, and no international problem without a national root. As a consequence, the ability of states to deal with major economic, financial and security challenges on their own has been vastly weakened. The debt crisis is one example that demonstrates the intricate relationships that tie national and international institutions and states' interests together; and even regional approaches to deal with such issues have failed. In addition, labor is able to move with ease from one place to another, causing clusters of industries and pockets of poverty to spread everywhere. This "contains unifying capacities across national borders and sharpening conflicts within such boundaries. The global capital and the immigrant workforce are two major instances of transnationalized categories that have unifying properties internally and find themselves in contestation with each other inside global cities."[2]

Free trade and open investment markets have changed the rules that govern traditional relationships between jobs and job-seekers, particularly industrial and knowledge jobs. Beginning three decades or so ago, many job-seekers have to leave their towns and sometimes countries and risk dying to reach a foreign country where decent jobs are available to improve their life conditions. While this economic migration continues today, most immigrants lack the right education and skills to excel in a knowledge-based economy; and therefore the jobs available to most economic immigrants are low paying, which leaves them disadvantaged. This creates tension and heightens fear on all sides of the nationality and cultural lines in societies that are attractive to economic immigrants. Wars in Syria, Iraq, Libya, Yemen and Afghanistan on the one hand, and poverty, drought, terrorism and ethnic conflict in several African and Asian states on the other have caused millions of people to flee their homelands and seek refuge in Europe. In the meantime, poverty, lack of opportunity, political instability and drug wars in a few Latin American states have caused a stream of migrants seeking freedom and a better life in the United States. This stream of political refugees cannot be stopped until hope is restored and economic and life conditions in the conflict-ridden countries are transformed, which the Ramo Plan, to be articulated in the next chapter, is designed to do.

In contrast, knowledge and industrial jobs in the new age are continuously searching for cheap but highly qualified and motivated workers to employ. Industrial jobs travel from one state to another, looking for disciplined labor with the right skills and attitudes, while knowledge jobs are traveling, often virtually, looking for inexpensive but well-educated workers with exceptional talents. As a result, highly qualified and motivated people no longer need to leave their home towns or countries to obtain rewarding jobs with corporations that reside in faraway places. Since multinational corporations abandoned their traditional commitments to labor, community and country years ago, they are willing to hire anyone and invest in any country in order to maximize profits and enlarge market share. Therefore, any state that is ready for such corporations will find them ready to bring their capital, technology, culture and management systems to create new jobs for its skilled labor, and to help it industrialize.

Sociologist Saskia Sassen argues that globalization has caused the creation of global cities, in addition to creating a global economy. Global cities, according to Sassen, "accumulate immense concentrations of economic power while cities that once were major manufacturing centers suffer inordinate declines; the downtowns of cities and business centers in metropolitan areas receive massive investments in real estate and telecommunications while low-income urban and metropolitan areas are starved for resources; highly educated workers in the corporate sector see their incomes rise to unusually high levels while low- or medium-skilled workers see theirs sink. Financial services produce super profits while industrial services barely survive."[3] As a consequence, manufacturing centers of the past have declined and lost their glory and pride; some have become ghost towns. This in turn has caused old towns and communities to become homes for poor, largely hopeless and helpless people.

"The presence of a critical mass of firms with extremely high profit-making capabilities contributes to bid up the prices of commercial space, industrial services and other business needs, and thereby makes survival for firms with moderate profit-making capabilities increasingly precarious."[4] This in turn, encourages businesses with low profit-making capabilities to become informal, operating in the shadows, paying low wages and offering little or no social benefits to their employees, causing inequality to spread, deepen its roots in society and become structural. And though income, wealth and power inequalities are as old as human history itself, the new age of knowledge is witnessing the emergence of a global super-rich class owning more than 50 % of the global wealth and controlling the political, economic and infomedia processes and therefore influencing the direction of change everywhere.

Back in 1991, I argued in *The New World Order* that the US social philosophy and systems of economic management and political organization have led to "creating and perpetuating three types of socioeconomic and sociocultural islands in the United States. The first type in generally characterized by affluence and security; the second is characterized by poverty and violence; both of these types, however, are urban islands; and the third type, which dominates rural America, is generally less affluent than the first and largely more peaceful than the second."[5] As a result, the rural type tends to be culturally different from both urban types. This simply means that socioeconomic and sociopolitical inequalities and sociocultural differences are not new but deeply rooted in every society. However, economic and cultural globalization has served to normalize these differences and inequalities, and to legitimize them in the eyes of most people, particularly the eyes of the controlling political, economic and media elites. But as wealth and power are more concentrated in fewer hands poverty and ignorance spread, inequalities become structural and economic growth rates decline.

The transition from the industrial age to the knowledge age that started in the mid-1990s has disrupted life as we knew it; it has dissolved the connection between the immediate past and the near future, causing the industrial economy and society to lose their main characteristics and sense of direction. But as the industrial age comes to an end, the knowledge age is still being born, leaving the present waiting for the unknown. The present we are living in today has been reduced to a mere port where the past is ending its long journey, as the future gets ready to begin its voyage into a new world that no one knows much about. Consequently, people and the systems through which they function and manage their life affairs have begun to experience one crisis after another without much hope of regaining balance in the near future. Regaining balance and confidence requires two basic things: understanding the nature of the transition; and articulating new ideas and systems to manage change and facilitate the construction of new cultures, economies and societies.

All of the above developments have caused most economic, social and cultural conditions of decades ago to change drastically in a short time, causing the assumptions upon which old economic and financial theories are based to be invalidated. Such assumptions include the notions that national economies are largely closed, trade is subject to restrictions, foreign investment is subject to regulations, investment requires domestic savings, the nation state is in control of its economy, and neither labor nor money is free to cross state borders. Since all such restrictions have been fully or partially removed, the traditional tools for managing national economies and dealing with issues such as recessions, unemployment and trade have become ineffective. Consequently, the **traditional economic theory** has become largely dysfunctional. This is why the US government has failed to create good paying jobs for the overwhelming majority of unemployed Americans and to restore higher economic growth rates; and why European efforts to deal with the Greek debt crisis have failed to solve or even ease the debt problem, or to create jobs for the unemployed millions in Europe.

Failure to acknowledge the declining relevance of traditional economic and financial tools will cause most economists and politicians to think inside a largely empty box and fail to realize the need for new tools. While traditional economic thinking may continue for a few more years, it can neither explain the nature of change nor can it deal with its consequences. Even the law of supply and demand, which represents the core of the classical economic theory, has become partially dysfunctional. For example, owing to the large increase in oil prices in the late 1970s, demand for oil declined by 17 %; however, the almost tripling of oil prices in 2005–6 failed to cause even a small decline in demand. Rising prices of smartphones do not seem to discourage anyone from using them; on the contrary, they seem to have encouraged young people to spend more on upgrading their phones and adding new apps. This change is largely due to the deep sociocultural transformations that world society has witnessed since the advent of the Knowledge Revolution in the mid-1990s. The Great Recession does not represent another business cycle, as many economists have claimed; it signifies the end of an era.

There is no doubt that the traditional economic theory has had a solid record of success in managing the economic and financial affairs of nations in good times and bad during the second half of the twentieth century. Economists have also played and continue to play a major role in debating economic policy, political decisions, the distribution of wealth and income, and the impact of these issues on fairness, poverty, employment, the middle class, equality and social mobility. However, the moment a theory's assumptions become unrealistic, the theory loses its relevance and becomes useless.

Building a theory is like building a house: you start with the foundations, which is the equivalent of making assumptions. If the foundations are good, the house will last for a long time, but not forever; if the assumptions are realistic, the theory will last for as long as situations remain the same or experience little change. Nevertheless, foundations exposed to earthquakes and floods are unlikely to live long or stay solid for a long time; and so are assumptions that try to reflect human behavior and living conditions that never stop changing, particularly during transitional periods that take societies from one civilization to another.

Notes

1. Mohamed Rabie; A Theory of Sustainable Sociocultural and Economic Development; Palgrave Macmillan, 2016, chapter 9; 169–72.
2. Saskia Sassen, The Global City; Strategic Site/New Frontier, American Studies, Sumer/Fall 2000 p. 90.
3. Ibid., p. 82.
4. Ibid., p. 84.
5. Mohamed Rabie; The New World Order, Vantage Press, 1992; 78–9.

CHAPTER 3

The Global Debt Crisis

Without going into details, public records indicate that the US public debt was 73% of the American gross domestic product (GDP) in 2008; it rose to 102% in 2012 and reached 105% in 2016. As for Japan, the debt to GDP was 171% in 2008, 216% in 2012 and 232% in 2015. China's debt was 32% of GDP in 2008, 37% in 2012 and 43% in 2015. In the United Kingdom, the debt ratio to GDP was 57% in 2008, 101% in 2012 and 103% in 2015. In France, the debt ratio was 79% in 2008, 109% in 2012 and 116% in 2015. In Germany, the debt ratio was 70% in 2008, 86% in 2012 and 80% in 2015. As for states of the Organization of Economic Cooperation and Development (OECD), the debt to their combined GDP was 80% in 2008, 107% in 2012 and 111% in 2015.

As a percentage of GDP, the debt estimates for some of the major economic powers and highly indebted states are as follows; Belgium 106%, Brazil 59%, Canada 95%, Cyprus 110%, Egypt 95%, Greece 180%, India 66%, Ireland 126%, Italy 132%, Jordan 90%, Lebanon 134%, Portugal 125%, South Africa 45%, Spain 101% and Turkey 36. For the Eurozone as a whole, Eurostat says the public debt to GDP ratio passed 92% in 2015. On the other hand, the combined GDP of all nations, according to the International Monetary Fund (IMF), has reached $75.5 trillion in 2015, and the total public debt, according to my estimates, is about $69 trillion, or 90% of global GDP. About $53 trillion or 78% of this debt is owed by the OECD member states, whose combined GDP is estimated at $48 trillion. China's GDP is estimated to have reached $11.4 trillion in 2016, which makes its debt about $5 trillion. Since the combined GDP of other states, including

M. Rabie, *The Global Debt Crisis and Its Socioeconomic Implications*,
https://doi.org/10.1007/978-3-319-66215-2_3

Brazil, India and Russia, is about $16.5 trillion, their debt would be about $10 trillion, or 61% of their GDP.

As a percentage of the global GDP, the debt of the OECD nations is about 78%, China's debt is about 7% and the debt of the rest of the world's nations would be about 15%. (Numbers and ratios are based on information obtained from seven major sources; the World Bank, the IMF, the OECD, European Council, Eurostat, the CIA World Factbook, Global Finance and Trading Economics websites and the different debt clocks.)

While the global debt is estimated at $69 trillion, interest due on this debt until maturity is estimated at $19 trillion. As a consequence, the total debt obligations of all nations until maturity would be about $88 trillion, of which about $69 trillion is owed by the OECD states, including Japan, about $13 trillion is owed by developing nations and about $6 trillion is owed by China. These numbers and ratios clearly indicate that the current debt crisis, unlike the crisis of the early 1980s, is the rich nations' problem. Nevertheless, I believe that when and if all states reveal their actual debt obligations, the total will exceed $100 trillion.

The Ramo Plan

Today, most nations face mountains of debt and huge budget deficits that hinder their abilities to grow their economies, create jobs for the unemployed, and help their needy and university students burdened by debt. As a consequence, poverty and unemployment rates remain high in most countries, and a sense of hopelessness and helplessness overwhelms a majority of people in many parts of the world. Since the debt problem is not limited to ten or twenty states, it must be viewed as a global issue. To address this issue and the social ills it has precipitated, I present below the Ramo Plan. This is a creative plan that defies conventional economic wisdom; yet it has the capacity to liberate all states from the debt burden, restructure the international monetary system, restore global financial stability and create the necessary conditions for sustainable global development and international peace. The plan is as follows:

1. To designate the International Monetary Fund (IMF) as a global central bank, with powers to issue a new international currency to be called Ramo, divided into 100 zents, and to issue bonds in Ramos, in addition to its current functions;

2. To set the value of the Ramo at the rate of the IMF Special Drawing Rights unit, which means converting the virtual IMF currency to a real one that could be used by banks, states and people;
3. To give each state the opportunity to repay its entire debt obligations, including interest due until maturity, by issuing money notes and credit certificates in its own national currency payable to the IMF;
4. To authorize the IMF to open a trust account or an escrow account in which all such funds would be deposited and kept for the sole purpose of meeting the debt obligations of the IMF member states; the IMF would pay all debt notes on behalf of its members as they become due, not before or after;
5. To ask each state to pay an amount equivalent to 10% of its total debt obligations as management fees; these fees, expected to be about \$10 trillion, would be deposited in a special fund managed by an international board of renowned personalities to finance programs outlined hereunder and compensate the initiators and administrators of this proposal;
6. To establish a \$1 trillion educational fund to build fifty new universities, with a mission to promote peace, cultural diversity, tolerance, critical thinking, creativity and innovation, and develop environmentally friendly technologies; all universities would be strategically located to serve as many regions of the world as possible;
7. To establish a \$1 trillion humanitarian fund to help victims of war and natural disasters such as hurricanes, tsunamis, earthquakes, serious diseases and refugees worldwide;
8. To establish a \$1 trillion environmental fund to restore the global environment to its past glory with its blue skies, rivers and seas, as well as beautiful forests, plants and animals;
9. To use the remainder of the management fees, estimated at \$7 trillion, to establish a sustainable development fund (SDF) to assist all developing and underdeveloped nations to transform their traditional cultures, grow their economies, reduce poverty, create jobs for the unemployed and join the industrialized world;
10. To create a few international corporations and institutes in coordination with the World Bank to facilitate the articulation and implementation of plans to help poor nations develop their economies, transform their cultures and industrialize.

The moment a nation pays its debt and the management fees as outlined above, it becomes free of debt and the IMF assumes full responsibility for its debt obligations. Since a global economy needs a global central bank to function properly, the new role assigned to the IMF and the issuance of the Ramo would serve to restructure the international monetary system, basing it on a new "gold standard." Since the IMF does not have enough gold, a golden Ramo, backed by the good faith and currencies of all member states, would become the international standard currency against which all other currencies would be pegged, making all currencies more stable and less susceptible to manipulation by traders and politicians. Exporters of oil, natural gas, food products and other strategic commodities would be able to price their exports in dollars or Ramos, enabling them to forecast future incomes and spending plans more accurately. Meanwhile, using the Ramo to price major export commodities would guarantee fairness; no nation would pay less as the value of its currency appreciates against the US dollar; no nation would pay more as its currency depreciates against the dollar. The issuance of the Ramo would mark a new era in history in which all states will finally acknowledge that all economies have become not just interdependent but largely integrated.

Since budget deficits include interest payments to service the debt, many states would see their deficits vastly reduced the moment they paid their debt. Some states such as Germany would likely see their deficits disappear overnight. Such a development would calm global financial anxiety, restore investor and consumer confidence, strengthen banks, and give all states a decade or so to restructure their spending and tax policies and balance their budgets.

Concerns and Fear of Inflation

Some economists will argue that repaying the public debt in this fashion amounts to printing money and issuing credit not backed by solid assets such as gold and silver. This is true, but so is the printing today of dollars, euros, pounds and other currencies; these are currencies backed by the good faith of the states issuing them, not by gold or other assets. Compared with these currencies, the Ramo would be backed not by one state but by all IMF member states. Furthermore, if the debt is not paid as proposed, any debt repayment in the future would be made in dollars or euros or another currency. In fact, all loans would be made and repaid in regular currencies that lack material backing. Therefore, the means to pay today as well as later are the same; the only difference is paying today and freeing all nations from the debt burden and revitalizing the world economy, or waiting until the highly indebted states begin to default one after the other and the banking, credit and international trading systems stop functioning.

Other economists might argue that creating so much money would ignite inflation and hurt consumers everywhere. This is simply incorrect. The IMF has no mandate to spend any portion of the money it would receive except as outlined above. The proposed arrangement for debt repayment changes the identity of the payer only, not the amount to be paid or when it is paid. Though the IMF is required to pay all debt notes as they become due on behalf of its member states, it could arrange, in coordination with concerned beneficiaries, to roll over some loans and keep the money for as long as needed to maintain financial stability.

There is no doubt that repaying some $100 trillion over twenty to twenty-five years is a cause for concern; however, existing needs and available monetary tools are capable of managing this money and easing all concerns. Trillions of dollars are needed to strengthen European and American banks and enable them to repay loans to central banks. And since paying the debt does not eliminate the budget deficits of all states, borrowing will resume immediately after the debt is paid, but at a much slower pace. Moreover, states can issue bonds to reduce financial liquidity when the need arises, and central banks have the power and tools to tighten money supplies. In addition, the Ramo Plan gives the IMF authority to play a role in managing international financial liquidity.

On the other hand, the plan to help poor nations to develop their economies and transform their national cultures could create millions of investment opportunities annually for decades to come; the SDF, to be outlined in the next section, would facilitate the creation of millions of jobs in developed and developing countries. Moreover, as the IMF pays back loans, it should give lenders the option of being paid in the same currencies of the loans or in Ramos. This action alone would limit the increase in the supply of all national currencies, while paving the way for the Ramo to play its intended role as a major reserve currency.

Inflation, which means higher than usual rates of increase in the general price level, has lost most of its power; it has been brought under control in most parts of the world. The belief that increasing the supply of money causes prices to rise rapidly and ignites inflation is based on assumptions that have long been invalidated. Such assumptions include the notions that national economies are largely closed, money is not able to cross state borders freely and that trade is subject to restrictions and tariffs. The major cause of inflation today is supply shortages of essential goods, not excess supply of money. Many people have money but have no desire or need to spend more; therefore, money alone cannot ignite inflation. If demand for essential goods increases rapidly or supply shortages of such goods are suddenly felt, inflation will be ignited, even in situations of tight money supply. Since the world's capacity to produce most goods and services exceeds its capacity to absorb such goods and services, no shortages are expected to occur and cause inflation. Food products are probably the only exception, and their prices are beyond anyone's control because shortages are often caused by bad weather, political instability, monopoly, price manipulation and hoarding. In fact, one of the reasons for slow economic growth today is the decline of major commodity prices such as oil.

In the late 1990s Alan Greenspan, the chairman of the Federal Reserve at the time, began to raise interest rates as he feared inflation. Since I saw no inflation coming, I wrote a short article under the title "The Ghost of Inflation," in which I argued that inflation no longer presents a real threat to industrialized states; it has become a ghost that is feared but not seen. There are many forces that have transformed inflation from a threat to a ghost; these include the internationalization of capital and investment markets, free trade and the growing industrial capacity of Asia. While it may be unwise to declare that inflation is dead, it has lost most of its teeth; it may be able to bite, but it can no longer hurt. Unfortunately, none of the newspapers that received the article bothered to publish it. Had it been circulated, the unintentionally engineered US recession of 2000 might have been avoided; and the situation we are in today might have been different.[1]

Germany, which fears inflation more than any other state, spent hundreds of billions of dollars within a few years during the 1990s on political reunification and economic integration without igniting inflation. Moreover, in response to the Great Recession, the US government and the Federal Reserve increased the supply of money by some $4 trillion within a few years, also without igniting inflation. In fact, the overwhelming fear since the financial crisis of 2008 has been of possible deflation, not inflation; deflation is a gradual reduction in general price levels that threatens the values of fixed assets such as land and homes.

Nonetheless, inflation remains a threat to poor countries where the economy is not free, currencies are not convertible, state intervention in economic management is substantial, protectionism is pursued as a state policy, and where states are largely corrupt and essential commodities are monopolized by greedy traders and speculators. Inflation also presents a problem in a few former communist and industrializing countries where the state is weak, the economy is in transition, relevant laws and regulations are still being developed, financial institutions are shaky, and political and economic corruption is widespread. However, the Ramo Plan would also deal with the threat of serious inflation; it provides all developing states with the capital, knowledge and technical assistance to develop their economies, improve labor productivity and food security, transform their societies and cultures, and strengthen business ethics. Nonetheless, no plan can guarantee that corruption or greed or manipulation of prices will disappear any time soon; the issue of moral hazard will stay with us for as long as we live. No rich or poor, developed or developing, Western or Eastern nation is immune to it.

It is now widely accepted that the cost of bailing out any state will be shared by the banks and investment funds that made the loans, as well as bondholders: "Germany is calling for imposing stiffer restrictions on euro zone banks, and shifting some of the burden of future bailouts to holders of governments' bonds issued by indebted states."[2] This makes all lenders fear losing a portion of their assets and discourages many of them to lend more money without sufficient guarantees. If Germany's proposals were to be implemented, the debt crisis would more likely be reignited, with consequences no one is able to predict. In such a case, it is likely that one or more European indebted state would default, some European banks might fail and many bondholders would revolt, causing strife and conflict to overwhelm a few Eurozone countries.

The German proposals reflect a condescending mentality that says in words rather than deeds that politicians are free to make serious mistakes, and the public has no choice but to pay for these mistakes without holding politicians accountable. In fact, I believe that our world has never had a collective Western leadership that is so politically and economically corrupt, and morally and intellectually bankrupt. This political and economic corruption has encouraged most large American and European corporations to ignore business ethics and abandon their social responsibilities and commitments to the common good, instead adopting policies to maximize profits without regard to the consequences of their actions on the lives of people and the world economy. As a consequence, they have begun to cut costs, reduce healthcare and social benefits to employees, and provide fewer services to their customers, cheating them whenever they can, causing business ethics to deteriorate beyond recognition. It has become hard for any American to find a corporation he can trust.

The issuance of the Ramo and the arrangements to pay all nations' public debt remove all risks associated with possible state defaults and bank failures. Meanwhile, the establishment of the SDF and the educational, humanitarian and environmental funds has the potential to double international trade in a few years and stimulate all economies; it would also create millions of new investment opportunities for investors, in addition to creating tens of millions of new jobs worldwide.

Would the repaying of the debt and the creation of the Ramo have a negative impact on the US dollar, the euro and other reserve currencies? The answer to this is yes and no. Issuing the Ramo as an international reference currency would stabilize all currencies, including the dollar and the euro, and would enable such currencies to play their traditional economic and monetary roles; it would also undermine the capacity of politicians and traders to play one currency against another. With the Ramo being the world's reference currency, each state, including the United States, would be able to revalue and devalue its currency at any time to manage its trade balance and influence prices of major exports and imports. Nonetheless, the Ramo could be expected to slightly weaken the attractiveness of the US dollar and the euro as reserve currencies. Since both currencies have been weakened and made less stable by the financial and debt crises and the slow growth of the American and European economies, the Ramo is needed to supplement them and to foster the international monetary system.

Sustainable Development Fund

The rapid economic development of several Asian states, especially South Korea, China and India, has caused the industrial production capacity of the world economies to surpass its absorption capacity, creating a wide gap between the global supply of and the global demand for most industrial products, electronic and textile goods and services. Without expanding global demand to narrow this gap substantially, the average rate of the world's economic growth will decline further, and the world community of nations will fail to address the economic, financial and social challenges it faces today. Such challenges include how to enable Western economies to resume healthy growth, create enough jobs for the unemployed millions in Europe and America, contain growing trade deficits, meet the needs of poor nations and stabilize the world economy. Challenges also include how to end regional wars and ease political turmoil in many parts of the world, as well as dealing effectively with the roots of radicalism and terrorism and human trafficking. Without growing the economies of developing nations and making the global economy fair, it will become increasingly more difficult to produce enough food to feed the growing numbers of the world's poor in Africa, Asia and Latin America, create jobs for the youth of those regions, and ease economic and war migrations to industrialized Western states from the less developed and poorer countries that are plagued by war and conflict.

If helping poor nations was a luxury in the near past, it is a global security and human necessity today. World political stability cannot be sustained and radicalism cannot be contained without economic growth and a fairer distribution of wealth and income among social classes and nations. Economic aid and charity cannot create enough jobs for the unemployed to undermine radicalism or to increase global demand for goods and services to enable the American and European economies to resume healthy growth and deal with social challenges at home. Since our world has become a global village, no nation is able to live in peace and affluence for long unless other nations feel at least financially comfortable and politically stable; and no nation will feel secure unless its neighbors feel secure as well.

The spread of poverty in many parts of the world, coupled with the rising awareness of life conditions on the other side of the global economic and cultural divides, has created several groups of angry, often alienated and radicalized young people in several parts of the world, particularly in the Middle East, Africa and some European states. These are people who feel betrayed by their political leaders as well as by the American, British and French leaders. And because their grievances continue to be ignored, their anger rises as their numbers grow and their targets spread. Since these groups grew out of frustration and despair, the idea that they can change the world in line with their beliefs has become an ideology that unites them and motivates them to act, often on their own.

Radicalized Islamic organizations, of which al-Qaeda and ISIS are examples, cause most people who belong to them to believe that it is their duty to do what it takes to destroy the enemy. In fact, most members of such organizations tend to believe they do not need to belong to an organization in order to participate in the "holy war" against the enemies of God and "true" Islam. This means that the elimination of ISIS and other radical groups from Syria, Iraq, Yemen, Libya, Somalia, Nigeria, Afghanistan, Pakistan, Egypt and other states will not end religious radicalism. As long as the sociopolitical, socioeconomic and sociocultural conditions that caused the creation of this murderous ideology are not changed, the radicalization of young people will continue, and so will the killing of innocent women, men and children, and the destruction of cities and mankind's historical treasures.

On the other hand, despite the fantastic increase in the industrial capacity of both China and India, both states still have millions of people without work. Every new industrial job created in those countries will further aggravate the imbalance between the global supply of and the global demand for industrial goods and services. Failure to acknowledge this fact and act accordingly will heighten the vulnerability of the world economy to recurring recessions and financial crises; it will also worsen trade imbalances, increase budget deficits and deepen sociocultural and sociopolitical problems everywhere.

As mentioned earlier, the debt obligations of all nations are estimated at $89 trillion, however, I expect debt by the time this plan is considered and debt obligations are revealed to reach $100 trillion. The 10% management fees would generate about $10 trillion; $3 trillion of these fees would be used to launch the educational, humanitarian and environmental funds, and $7 trillion would be used to launch an SDF. A special societal development plan would be developed by the World Bank for each country, and money would be spent over twenty to twenty-five years to purchase whatever is needed to launch and foster national development plans that include economic restructuring and the sociocultural transformation of societies. The following goals define the mission of SDF:

1. Help all developing and underdeveloped countries build modern roads and railroads, ports and airports, bridges and dams, as well as electrical grids and water and sewage systems, and basic industries;
2. Modernize agricultural farming machinery and techniques and irrigation systems, as well as water and financial management systems; train farmers and farm workers, develop rural communities and revive traditional industries;
3. Build enough schools and universities, hospitals and clinics, and train enough school teachers, university professors, physicians, nurses, engineers, lawyers and technicians to meet the educational and healthcare needs of growing urban and rural populations;
4. Design special training programs for workers to enable them to acquire the right skills and attitudes to perform efficiently; all

workers must be taught how to appreciate time, work and money in order to keep the national economy growing and state institutions functioning properly;

5. Support national universities, establish technical schools and fund specialized research institutes committed to identifying local, national and regional problems, and to finding home-grown solutions sensitive to traditional customs and cultural values and beliefs;
6. Help civil society organizations to grow in size and effectiveness, and train judges and media professionals to empower the courts to fight corruption, enforce the rule of law and protect the environment as well as people's and animals' rights;
7. Raise public awareness of the utter importance of changing attitudes toward science, work, time, life and other people, while improving the quality of education and healthcare and the means to protect the environment. Public schools and religious institutions and the media are capable of doing this job if given the right education, training and funding;
8. Facilitate the creation of a fairly large middle class aware of its social role, and train a new, professionally qualified and socially responsible entrepreneurial and managerial class;
9. Strengthen food security programs and energy supplies at national and regional levels; and
10. Launch a genuine sociocultural transformation process in every country, according to its needs in the present and prospects in the future.

Two points need to be emphasized in this context. First, all educational and healthcare systems in the Third World lack modern management systems to enable them to do the job they are supposed to do. Second, most members of existing business and entrepreneurial classes in poor and rich countries alike tend to be corrupt and lack social responsibility. Therefore, the creation of a new ethical entrepreneurial and business class is a must; otherwise, most money will be wasted and the desired socioeconomic and sociopolitical goals will fail to materialize.

Educational Fund

As the people of the world become more and more connected, forming a global village, the leadership of this village has proven to be neither ready nor qualified to lead collectively and ensure the protection of the environment and the safety of people. The educational fund is intended to train future leaders for our global village, where cultures and life conditions are becoming progressively more complicated. Though our world has become one large but highly diversified community, our village still lacks a leadership committed to the welfare of its inhabitants and aware of its place in history. What we have today is a largely narrow-minded leadership that thinks small and works to divide rather than unite the world peoples, to dehumanize some and glorify others rather than humanizing everyone and dehumanizing no one. As a consequence, our leadership has failed to convince the village's many tribes and clans to stop fighting each other, and to concentrate instead on building their economies and preserving their cultural heritage. Therefore, the world needs a new, more educated and enlightened, leadership.

Students attending the global university system, which would have fifty campuses, would be chosen on the bases of their grades and aptitude tests, and the educational fund would pay for their education. To enable students to gain a global outlook and learn about other cultures and peoples through living, all students would be required to spend their college life at two or more campuses. Universities would try to have equal numbers of undergraduate and graduate students, as well as males and females. And while undergraduate programs would concentrate on educating young people to be global citizens committed to peace, equal opportunity, social justice, environmental protection, cultural and religious diversity, and tolerance, graduate programs would concentrate on research in all technical and social fields, with an emphasis on developing innovations to make our lives more enjoyable, our global economy sustainable, our world secure and peaceful, and our global village more lovable and enjoyable.

As the educational fund tried to recruit the smartest students available in the world, it would also try to hire the best and most committed professors; it would also try to design study programs that meet the current and future needs of the peoples of the world in general and the Third World in particular. There is no doubt that there are many great universities in the United States, Western Europe and Asia that continue to lead in technical innovations and research in humanities and social science; however, their work has largely been dedicated to serving the needs of the industrialized countries and their economies and societies, as well as the world's largest corporations. As a result, less-developed countries have become dependent on educational systems and programs that are less able to identify with their particular cultures and socioeconomic needs, which differ from those of the industrialized societies.

For example, the World Bank, after more than seventy years of working in the development field and investing hundreds of billions of dollars, has failed to help a single country develop and industrialize; as a consequence, almost all theories of development written between the 1950s and 1980s have been abandoned. Because of this, new books on development have begun to focus on issues rather than process; issues such as freedom, corruption, poverty, inequality, education, economic management, environmental awareness, the empowerment of women, the role of government in society and the like; thus avoiding the complicated, but badly needed, tools to construct comprehensive development processes. There is no doubt that these issues are important because they affect the direction of development and its chances of success; but since all such issues are connected to each other, they cannot be addressed separately.

In the summer of 1991, I was invited by the Swedish government to participate in the "European Conversations" conference. The invitation, signed by Mr. Odd Engstrom, then deputy prime minister of Sweden, included the following paragraph: "I would like to arrange a meeting between **leading thinkers and thinking leaders** to discuss how we are to succeed in reconciling political legitimacy and economic rationality in a Europe where national borders have lost more and more of their significance. Can we establish a democracy at a new, regional level? How can the new Europe create welfare for so many? Is there a common identity which embraces all this multiplicity of mutually intertwined national destinies—and, if so, is this something we want?"

There were about thirty participants at the conference. Eighteen of them were invited from outside Sweden, the British economist Amartya Sen and I being among them. On the second day of our discussion, Professor Sen spoke to me: "I have a puzzling, troubling question for which I have no answer: Can you tell me why most people in the Third World lie?" After giving that challenging question some thought, I found that the answer was simple; it did not need research institutes or special conferences, or even much thinking, to arrive at it.

I told my colleague that day that most people of the Third World lie because they lack freedom. When young men and women have no social freedom, every time they do something that violates traditional customs they lie to their parents and teachers; when ordinary people have no religious freedom, every time they ignore a religious duty they lie to everyone who takes religious rituals seriously; when educated people and intellectuals have no freedom of speech, every time they are asked about their views and opinions they lie in public or to the police; when merchants and bankers have no economic freedom, every time they violate or manipulate established regulations they lie to the government. Therefore, lack of freedom, be it social, religious, political or economic, or of speech, is the major force that motivates, at times compels, most Third World people to lie.

In addition, I replied that when lying becomes an acceptable habit that few people challenge, it causes social, political, economic and religious corruption to spread and deepen its roots in society, cultural trust and honesty disappear, social responsibility crumbles, business ethics vanish and prospects of societal development become very slim indeed. Therefore, no one should expect economic development to succeed in any society that lacks freedom, particularly social and religious freedoms. To succeed, development requires two basic steps: economic restructuring and sociocultural transformation; and while economic restructuring is easy, sociocultural transformation cannot be accomplished without modernizing and humanizing the educational system.[3] In 1999, Amartya Sen, who was later awarded the Nobel Memorial Prize in Economic Sciences, published his highly regarded book entitled *Development as Freedom*.

I believe that the concept of economic development was misconceived from the beginning. The assumption that economic development is possible without developing human resources, cultures, institutions and the politics of nations amounts to treating the economy and society as two separate facets of life; ignoring the fact that no economy can function without people, and no people can survive without an economy capable of meeting, at the very least, their basic needs. The failure of development thinking in the West to identify the root causes of underdevelopment of Third World countries in general, and to articulate feasible approaches to development, is largely responsible for wasting trillions of dollars and countless opportunities and valuable time, while causing billions of people to needlessly suffer poverty and indignation for decades. This means that there is a need for a new approach to deal with the complex issues of development and underdevelopment in most parts of the world. In my book *A Theory of Sustainable*

Sociocultural and Economic Development, published by Palgrave Macmillan in 2016, I articulate a new theory of societal development that views development as a bird. It says that a bird, to fly and stay healthy, needs two wings. With one wing, the bird might be able to jump and run but it cannot fly or stay healthy for long. This is like development: to succeed and achieve its objectives, it needs both economic restructuring and sociocultural transformation.[4]

David Landes argues that the major key to wealth is openness, which means openness to new ideas and to borrowing from other nations the technologies that are more productive or more capable of enhancing the quality of life. Francis Bacon, writing in about 1600, suggested that the compass, gunpowder and the printing press, which were borrowed from China, were the major forces that transformed European life. No borrowing of ideas and technologies, however, can create fundamental change in society unless its social, cultural, religious and political environments are hospitable to the introduction of new ideas and technologies. People in charge of the economic and political processes need to have enough awareness to see the potential contributions of new ideas and technologies to their fortunes as well as to the welfare of society, and need to convince the general public of their utility. Europe at the time of Francis Bacon had been experiencing the deepest social, cultural, religious, political and scientific transformations in its entire history, covering all aspects of life. As a consequence, the doors were wide open for new ideas to be considered, new technologies to be borrowed and invented, and change to be accepted.

While openness to new technologies is important to economic development, openness to new ideas is important to political change and sociocultural transformation, and thus to moving society from feudalism and totalitarianism to freedom and democracy. This, in turn, helps restore the dignity of the poor and weak and protect their meager resources from the greedy rich and powerful. Therefore, no fundamental economic or political change is possible unless the social, cultural and religious environments of society are transformed. To make all these environments hospitable to change and transformation, we need first to build a creative and innovative educational system, and create an educated and largely enlightened class of men and women to manage it.

Humanitarian Fund

The humanitarian fund is intended to meet the emergency needs of all regions and peoples affected by natural disasters such as tsunamis, hurricanes, earthquakes, floods, starvation and epidemics, as well as man-made disasters such as war. War and conflict cause people to suffer and live in miserable conditions as refugees in need of food, medicine, jobs, education and hope. The humanitarian fund would have staff and a system in place to swiftly deliver assistance wherever it was needed, as well as the necessary supplies to respond immediately and comprehensively to major emergencies. The fund would work with similar national and international organizations to meet the urgent needs of suffering people everywhere; it would also act as an international accreditation agency to evaluate and accredit not-for-profit organizations working in the field of international relief and humanitarian assistance.

With the manner in which past catastrophes such as hurricanes, tsunamis and war victims have been dealt with seems to indicate that no organization has the capacity to deal with the large-scale destruction that is caused by such incidents. While Katrina exposed the limitations and impotency of US government agencies, the 2010 earthquakes in Haiti, the 2015 earthquake in Nepal and the 2011 floods in Pakistan have also proved that neither national nor international organizations have the capacity to provide timely assistance to help desperate people in need; in fact, some of the victims' needs are yet to be met.

On January 12, 2010, a devastating earthquake struck Haiti, killing more than 160,000 and displacing close to 1.5 million people. Five years later, scars of the tragedy remain in Port-au-Prince. "When you walk around the country's capital Port-au-Prince, you still see half-destroyed buildings around town," says photographer Gael Turine who spent ten years photographing in the country. "The wounds are still here, and everyone says that they're living in worse conditions than before." He describes the situation: "When you look at the history of humanitarian relief, there's never been a situation when such a small country has been the target of such a massive influx of money and assistance in such a short span of time . . . On paper, with that much money in a territory the size of Haiti, we should have witnessed miracles; there should have been results." And yet the situation was still dire five years after the earthquake.[5]

In 2011 Pakistan was inundated with heavy monsoon rains. Rain continued for more than a month, causing unprecedented floods, and this in turn caused considerable damage to property, affecting the lives of millions. According to Wikipedia, it is estimated that the floods killed approximately 434 Pakistani civilians, damaged or destroyed more than 1.5 million homes and affected the lives of some 5.3 million people. At least 1.7 million acres of arable land was damaged as a result of the flooding. The 2011 floods had followed the historic 2010 floods, which devastated the entire country.[6] Despite the tens of millions of dollars donated by the world community to help the survivors of the floods, and the participation of several international aid agencies and organizations in the construction process, the scars of the floods remain today.

As for Nepal's earthquake: "Throughout Nepal, water has become a pressing concern. The earthquake destroyed nearly 5,200 water supply systems and 220,000 personal toilets ... The shifting earth changed groundwater levels, causing water sources to suddenly disappear. Around 1.14 million people are now in need of safe supply of drinking water, and 1.04 million do not have access to usable toilets. The financial requirements to fix these problems nationwide might be insurmountable. According to a Post-Disaster Needs Assessment prepared by Nepal's National Planning Commission, the amount required to fully recover and rebuild is estimated to be $6.6 billion—about one-third the annual gross domestic product of Nepal."[7]

If the money from the proposed humanitarian fund were to be invested in US government bonds with a 2.5% annual interest rate, the annual income would be $25 billion a year; more than enough to meet the challenges of global emergences year after year, probably for eternity. As a consequence, the need for donor conferences to raise money for victims of natural disasters and man-made wars, and for pledges of help that do not usually get paid in full, would be eliminated, not just for years to come but for centuries. Victims' needs would be met without fuss, while using financial aid as an economic or political tool to pressure or coerce poor states and needy people would stop, thus respecting the dignity of the poor and weak and honoring their rights. In fact, every time I think of this fund and the role it could have played in the past, I wonder why no one has come up with the idea before, thereby saving tens of millions of lives, rebuilding millions of homes and villages, and preventing dreams from being shattered by grief and loss of hope.

Sustainable Environmental Fund

Since the 1970s, the world has become progressively more aware of the damage caused to the environment by neglect and misuse, particularly by the manufacturing, mining and oil industries. As a consequence, the need to protect the environment has become a priority in most parts of the world. However, despite the substantive work that has been done in this field, no environmentalist, government official or international organization is able to confirm whether we are approaching environmental sustainability or still moving away from it. However, If the $1 trillion that I propose is devoted to this fund were to be invested in US government bonds at an annual interest rate of 2.5%, its annual income would be about $25 billion, enough to hire more than a million scientists, engineers, workers and other personnel, who could be engaged in cleaning and restoring our global environment and protecting it from abuse and misuse. As this fund worked to protect our environment, it would work to make global sustainability a reality.

The Brundtland Commission Report issued in 1987 defines sustainability as "development that meets the needs of the present without compromising the ability of future generations to meet their own needs states"[8] It states further: "The environment does not exist as a sphere separate from human actions, ambitions, and needs, and attempts to defend it in isolation from human concerns have given the very word 'environment' a connotation of naivety in some political circles. The word 'development' has also been narrowed by some into a very limited focus, along the lines of 'what poor nations should do to become richer.' But the 'environment' is where we live; and 'development' is what we all do in attempting to improve our lot within that abode. The two are inseparable."[9]

Though this report provided a clear definition of sustainable development, it could not answer questions about how to achieve this goal, nor could the experts who tried to do so later. No one seems able to say with confidence how to reach a state of sustainability or what the needs of future generations will be that we must consider. Moreover, no one knows how many people there will be at any time in the future, what percentage of our resources will be available or what the state of technology will be years from now. We also do not know how much progress we are making towards the state of sustainability. But despite the complicated nature of these questions, we cannot ignore them; we need to keep on thinking, organizing and working to reach our goals.[10]

As national development agencies strive to achieve sustainable development, they tend to treat sustainability as a largely domestic rather than global endeavor. But sustainability, both economic and environmental, is unattainable except at the global level, because many nations have access to nonrenewable resources such as natural gas, and rivers and seas, which they can waste or pollute without giving much consideration to the needs and interests of the other nations that depend on the same resources. Therefore, fairness and reality dictate that sustainability must be treated as a global endeavor, and that the sacrifices needed to accomplish it and the benefits generated by it should be shared by all nations. "In order to be sustainable, development must also be harmonious. At least a certain amount of social cohesion must exist on a planetary scale in order to create the conditions for the peace we need,"[11] and for the human environment we seek to secure for all.

Since development is a comprehensive societal process, no economic development plan can succeed in a traditional society without being preceded or accompanied by a plan to transform the sociocultural environment of society.[12] Economic restructuring, investment in education, sociocultural transformation, healthcare and infrastructure development, and environmental preservation and protection, which the SDF and the other funds intend to address, would increase women's awareness and free most of them from the chains of ignorance and traditions, and thus empower them to gain self-confidence and become more active workers and respected members of society. As a consequence, population growth rates would decline gradually, leading the demographics of most developing nations to approach those of European nations by the end of this development phase.

Therefore, the full implementation of the Ramo Plan should reduce world population growth rates to near 1% within twenty to twenty-five years, place the global economy on a truly sustainable growth path, protect our mother earth, create a new spirit of equality and fraternity among all peoples and nations, and vastly weaken the power of and rationale behind the ideologies of racism, radicalism and terrorism, exposing their futility, falsehood, criminality and inhumanity. Our global village, as a result, would become a place to love and in which we could enjoy living.

Notes

1. Mohamed Rabie; The Making of History; Authors Choice Press, 2001, 142–3.
2. Fudging the revolution, *The Economist*, February 20, 2016, 27.
3. Mohamed Rabie, A Theory of Sustainable Sociocultural and Economic Development, chapter 11.
4. Ibid; chapter 13, pp. 185–207.
5. Olivier Laurent, *Time*, Haiti Earthquake: Five Years After, January 12, 2015.
6. 2011 Sindh Floods; Wikipedia; https://en.wikipedia.org/wiki/2011_Sindh_floods
7. Elijah Wolfson, One year after a devastating earthquake, Nepal is still in ruins, News Week, April 21, 2016.
8. NGO Committee on Education, Report of the World Commission on Environment and Development: Our Common Future, chapter 2, "Towards Sustainable Development," http://www.un-documents.net/ocf-02.htm
9. Ibid.
10. Mohamed Rabie, A Theory of Sustainable Sociocultural and Economic Development, chapter 3.
11. http://www.legrand.com/EN/sustainable-development-description_12847.html
12. Mohamed Rabie, A Theory of Sustainable Sociocultural and Economic Development, chapter 3.

CHAPTER 4

A View of the Global Scene

The following is a general look at the major forces that are shaping the economics and politics of most nations and regions of the world. During most of the twentieth century, only two great powers were able to dominate the fields of politics and economics and effectively influence the direction of global change. However, as the number of centers of economic and political power has grown, the rules of the old game have changed, giving emerging markets and a few nations a role to play in shaping the future. As a result, more players are involved in shaping politics and influencing economics, particularly at regional level.

Nevertheless, the dynamic relationship that ties politics to economics and economics to politics, and both to people's cultures and living conditions, has given rise to new non-state actors and enabled them to greatly influence the outcomes of global change. These actors include the World Bank, the International Monetary Fund (IMF), the World Trade Organization, multinational corporations, civil society organizations and terrorist organizations. But no matter how many powers emerge, the United States, being the world's dominant political, economic and military power, remains the power to fear and respect, to watch and listen to. And because of its tremendous power and influence, the United States must be held accountable for its actions and inactions.

On the other hand, we need to recognize that the corporation has become the most active player in the sphere of economic and financial affairs, because most corporations are better equipped than most states to make investment decisions based on economic considerations.

M. Rabie, *The Global Debt Crisis and Its Socioeconomic Implications*,
https://doi.org/10.1007/978-3-319-66215-2_4

Corporations are also able to assemble the required capital, technology and manpower, and bring their business cultures, management teams and technical expertise to manufacture and market internationally; and in the process create jobs that ease unemployment in the states they invest in. And since corporations represent sixty-nine of the largest 100 economies of the world, they must also be held accountable for their actions and the consequences of their actions on people's lives and the global economy. "The number of businesses in the top 100 economic entities jumped to 69 in 2015 from 63 in the previous year."[1] We also need to understand that if corporations were to be left alone, they are likely to concentrate on exploiting the resources of host states, rather than helping them to develop their economies, transform their cultures, protect their environments and improve the quality of life of their citizens. Corporate actions are the major factor causing income and wealth gaps within and between societies to widen, leading to slower economic growth rates and the spread of conflict and poverty worldwide.

The invisible hand, which Adam Smith discovered and analyzed almost 250 years ago, became visible in the late nineteenth century as Western economies grew and capital began to play an increasingly significant role in the economic and political life of industrial societies. Following the end of World War One, the economic process emerged as an influential societal process in industrialized and industrializing countries, affecting all aspects of human life, including the environment. As a consequence, the political process felt that its powers were threatened; and this led the state to take action to constrain the freedom of the economic process, enacting new laws to regulate big banks and mortgage and insurance companies, and guarantee government oversight over major economic and financial activities.

Meanwhile, facing a serious challenge from Marxism, Western states felt a need to develop the welfare state in their countries to help the poor and the elderly, and to ensure a decent life for people who could not work and others who retired from work without adequate savings to live comfortably. This action was particularly important to Western societies in order to undermine the appeal of socialism, and to protect themselves from the threat of communist ideology, its premise of class conflict and its promise of classless society. As a consequence, several European states witnessed the formation of social democratic parties that were able to control politics and regulate economics, and to implement welfare programs that proved to be helpful in defending Europe against communism and providing high-quality services to the public at large, without undermining economic growth or competitiveness.

As the appeal of socialism weakened in the early 1980s, the US government, Britain and Germany moved to restore freedom to the market's invisible hand. Financial regulations were relaxed, giving big banks more freedom to set interest rates and conditions for lending, and corporations were allowed to slowly but methodically dismantle labor unions and disavow commitments to the general welfare of their employees and local communities. The writings of economist Milton Friedman, who supposedly said that "There is one and only one social responsibility of business—to use its resources and engage in activities designed to increase its profits," provided the rationale that enabled corporations to ignore everything workers and society care about, and concentrate instead on creating financial products and service that enabled them to manipulate consumers, minimize risk and maximize profits.[2]

Today, business greed and economic and political corruption have enabled capital to buy politicians and corrupt politics, manipulate existing laws, cause legislators to enact new laws and gain enough power to become ruthless and often heartless as well, exploiting every opportunity and everyone for the sake of money. But every step toward more materialism is a step away from the values of equality, social justice, business ethics, and respect for human rights and the dignity of man. With the loss of social responsibility, the knowledge man and the capitalist of the twenty-first century has become the modern nomad of the tribal age; he has a residence everywhere, but no home anywhere, belongs to no particular society or nation, believes in no ideology and is committed to no special cause, except making more money.

Research regarding the concentration of wealth and power in fewer hands suggests that such actions and attitudes hurt the rich as well as the poor, though the poor suffer much more than the rich. People usually feel poorer when their incomes and wealth are substantially less than their neighbors and relatives and friends, even in situations where their living conditions improve. Consider the case of bonuses given by companies to employees: when some employees get more than others, those who get less feel unhappy and protest, not because they are denied a share of what is being given, but becaue of the way bonuses are divided. Wealth and poverty, fairness and unfairness, happiness and unhappiness, justice and injustice are relative terms; therefore, most people tend to feel jealous and resentful when they realize that their wealth and incomes are lagging behind their colleagues who work as much as they do, or less. Therefore, to make people feel happy and cause social peace to prevail, income and power in society should be divided in ways that reflect people's contributions and needs.

The Political Scene

In a lecture I delivered on March 30, 2016 in Germany, I was asked if conflict and war hurt the interests of large corporations that function globally. Not all corporations, I answered; some corporations do get hurt because their business requires peace and stability. For example, those engaged in farming and food production or oil exploration in areas plagued by conflict are exposed to substantial losses owing to war; in contrast, corporations that manufacture weapons and warplanes and ammunition, or provide logistical support and security services to armies tend to make more money from war. War does not only suit such corporations, but it often entices them to participate in war and to justify their involvement in it, claiming that they are helping the "good guys." In fact, military and security industries throughout the world would be in deep financial trouble if conflict and war were to stop, and peace and stability were to prevail. The military industry, including companies that provide security services and logistical support, ranks among the most profitable industries in the United States; and in states such as Russia and Israel, weapons exports represent a major source of income for governments. They also enhance military and political ties between sellers and buyers of weapons at the expense of the lives and well-being of the poor and powerless everywhere.

Today, most states suffer from conflict, and its economic, political, social and psychological consequences. While some peoples suffer more economically, others suffer more politically and socially. War and conflict tend to destroy the social and cultural fabrics of warring societies, causing peace, harmony and tolerance to be undermined; they also make reconstruction and peace-building difficult to initiate and sustain. In fact, fighting wars has become easier and less expensive than building peace and ensuring the stability that is supposed to follow. "the wars America will fight in the foreseeable future will be protracted, low-intensity struggles with no clear victories. There will be no raising American flags over a vanquished enemy's capital, no parades."[3] Just consider Afghanistan. How much money did the United States spend over the last sixteen years fighting the war there, and trying to build a modern state? All US efforts seem to have failed to bring peace, stabilize the political situation or build a functioning government.

South East Asia is a region that suffers from a low-level conflict, which makes the region's environment less conducive to political stability and economic progress. Instability forces some states such as China, Vietnam, Philippines and South Korea to spend more money upgrading their armies and preparing their peoples for possible war. Economic cooperation and free trade areas—when fairly structured—represent major forces in creating new economic opportunities, and promoting peace and cultural diversity. In contrast, conflict causes potential economic growth rates to decline as it weakens political stability and security. For example, the roots of conflict in the Korean peninsula go back to World War Two, when in 1945 the United States and the Soviet Union decided to partition Korea into two parts. In 1948 both parts became independent states; and in 1950 a bloody war erupted between North and South Korea. This lasted three years and caused millions of casualities on both sides.

According to the United Nations (UN), the South Koreans and their Western allies "suffered over 559,000 casualties during the war, including approximately 94,000 dead. America's share of this human loss totaled 36,516 dead and 103,284 wounded."[4] As for the North Koreans and their Eastern allies, the "UN estimated that Communist military casualties exceeded two million dead, wounded, and prisoners. Civilian losses were even more appalling-approximately one million South Korean and up to two million North Korean civilians either died, disappeared, or were injured during the course of the war, while millions more became refugees."[5] Despite this huge loss in human life and material assets, neither the United States nor the Soviet Union learned their lesson. In the 1960s, the United States initiated a bloody and costly war in Vietnam, and in the 1970s, the Soviet Union initiated a similar bloody war in Afghanistan. Both superpowers lost their wars again.

In 1916, the Middle East region was divided by the British and French governments into several states and protectorates in order to facilitate its occupation and colonization. As a result, Arabs were denied their legitimate right to self-determination and the establishment of an independent Arab state; They were therefore prevented from achieving their political, economic or security objectives, and the region entered a period of conflict and instability that caused its peoples to remain divided and underdeveloped. And while some people were allowed later to form nation states, such as the Jordanians and Lebanese, the Palestinians were denied the right to self-determination and the formation of a state. In the meantime, political instability and underdevelopment encouraged the military to intervene in the political process and to launch several coups in Syria, Iraq, Egypt, Libya and Yemen. In Algeria, a popular revolution was launched against French colonization; it lasted several years and claimed the lives of some 1.5 million Algerians.[6] On the other hand, British colonialism and control of Palestine was instrumental in creating Israel and causing several wars between Israel and its Arab neighbors, which continue to feed regional instability and radicalism.

Meanwhile, the discovery of oil in Iran, Iraq and the Gulf Arab states in the first half of the twentieth century heightened competition between the great powers, and instigated political and ethnic conflict in the region. As a consequence, religious tension spread and deepened its roots in most societies, leading to religious fundamentalism. The creation of Israel in 1948, the division of Arab states into two ideological camps because of the Cold War and Iran's 1979 Islamic Revolution have caused the Middle East to witness one crisis after another without interruption. America's proxy war against the Soviet Union in Afghanistan during the 1980s precipitated the birth of Islamic radicalism, which led two decades later to terrorism and the 9/11 attack on New York and Washington, which in turn provoked the United States to launch a war against Afghanistan in 2001 and invade Iraq in 2003. These two wars in particular, and the US determination to undermine Russia's interests in the region, have caused civil and regional wars that continue to claim the lives of hundreds of innocent people every day, and to destroy the social and cultural fabrics of the societies involved.

Owing to these developments, conflict in the Middle East has become an unremarkable facet of everyday life. War in Iraq, Syria, Yemen and Libya has destroyed the economies of these states, undermined peace and stability, and caused all states to become failed states; it has also damaged the already struggling economies of Jordan, Lebanon and Egypt. Moreover, religious radicalism and terrorism have made life intolerable for many people, killing more than a million in Syria and Iraq since 2011 and precipitating the largest refugee crisis in our times. The number of Syrians, Iraqis, Yemenis and Libyans living in Jordan, Lebanon, Egypt and Turkey alone is estimated to have exceeded 10 million; in fact, it is estimated that by 2016 about half of the Syrian people were living in refugee camps in Syria and the neighboring states.

Conflict and war is not limited to the Middle East and parts of Asia; it covers most parts of the world. Many states in Latin America, Africa and Europe are witnessing conflict; Nigeria, Mali, Somalia, South Sudan and other African states are fighting each other or fighting terrorists to protect themselves. While conflict in most parts of Latin America is related to drug trafficking and smuggling people to the United States, almost every election in Africa has led to conflict or civil war. Azerbaijan and Armenia are fighting each other over Nagorno Karabakh, and Ukraine is in turmoil owing to its geography, which places it between the West and Russia. Western Europe is facing an unprecedented refugee crisis and a vicious wave of terrorism, which is threatening European unity and causing the largely racist forces on the right to disrupt normal life in Europe and undermine its liberal, humane image. Turkey is fighting with its Kurdish minority, who are seeking equal civil and cultural rights; it is also deeply involved in the war in Syria.

While territorial claims have almost vanished from the political map of the world, war and conflict in the twenty-first century are being shaped by poverty and lack of economic opportunity as well as social justice and political freedom. In addition, several religious and cultural minorities in Europe, Asia, Africa and the Middle East are seeking independence, some by peaceful means and others by force, as in Ukraine, Georgia and Philippines. The US policy to maintain control of the Arab oil resources has led America to intervene in the domestic affairs of most Arab states with the intention of destroying the social and cultural fabrics of their societies, thereby causing them to become failed states. The ultimate goal of this policy is to divide each state into smaller states along ethnic and religious lines, rendering them easy to manipulate and control. Adolf Berle, advisor to President Franklin Roosevelt, said that control of the incomparable energy resources of the Middle East would yield "substantial control of the world." Noam Chomsky adds that American rulers "believe that the loss of control would threaten the project of American global dominance that was clearly articulated during World War II."[7]

Rowena Hammal says that if "there is one issue on which historians should be able to agree, it is that the artificial division of a country usually creates more problems than it solves. The twentieth century is full of examples: Ireland in 1921, Germany after each of the two world wars, the partition of India in 1947, the creation of Israel in 1948. Korea's division led to a war which proved as serious as any of the difficulties encountered by those nations. A unique set of internal and external factors combined to create a conflict which almost precipitated a nuclear war."[8] What happened in Iraq after it was invaded and occupied by the United States in 2003, what happened in Sudan after it was partitioned in 2011 and what has been happening in Syria since 2011 validates this point.

"The creation of South Sudan as an independent country was 'hailed as a triumph' mainly because very few people wanted to think through the implications of creating a new state that seemed bound to become a failed state in a short period of time. South Sudan's independence is a testament to a deeply-ingrained belief in the West and elsewhere that a country's serious problems can and should be addressed by partitioning the country and setting up a new state ... This is worth bearing in mind the next time we hear the calls to divide Iraq, which is once again becoming a more popular option for a 'solution' to the country's current conflict."[9] In fact, this is what the United States calls "Plan B" to solve the Syrian conflict. This means that America, which dictated the partition of Sudan, seems determined to finalize the partition of Iraq and to impose a worse partition plan on Syria. In view of what happened in South Sudan, it would be foolish to assume that the United States made an honest mistake in Sudan.

Conflict in the Middle East as well as in most other parts of the world is a human tragedy; it is a sociopolitical, socioeconomic and sociocultural catastrophe caused by human actions. Such actions include foreign intervention, decades of colonization; political mismanagement, lack of economic development and cultural misunderstandings. Owing to the particular history of people who were colonized in the past, conflict tends to have a strong foreign factor that complicates every situation, prolongs each conflict and makes compromise solutions hard to reach.

In addition to home grown problems that cause conflict, such as widespread poverty, lack of good education and structural unemployment, the great powers have continued to play an active role in making most situations worse. Their competition for political influence and natural resources has led them to view regional conflicts as opportunities to be exploited and tools to manage their relations with one another. As a result, no great power has shown sincere interest in resolving a single major conflict in the world, causing all conflicts to worsen over time. Major conflicts include the Indian–Pakistani conflict over Kashmir; the Korean crisis between South and North Korea; the Arab–Israeli conflict over Palestine; and the Western Sahara dispute between Morocco and the Polisario, backed by Algeria; the Ukraine conflict; the Syrian and Yemeni civil wars; and the war on ISIS.

This lack of interest in resolving international conflicts has caused the wars in Iraq, Syria, Libya and Yemen to continue to claim the lives of hundreds of people day after day, and destroy historical sites considered by all civilized peoples to be treasures of humanity. Conflicts of this nature and magnitude tend to burden the consciousness of most people, with the exception of merchants of war. Recent migrations from Iraq, Syria, Somalia, Libya, Yemen and Afghanistan have changed the demographics of several Arab and European states; and, in the process cultures, politics and security matters have been affected in all countries concerned. The latest episode in the business of creating and perpetuating conflicts and failed states for the purpose of managing great powers was the transformation of Ukraine in 2014 from a largely stable state plagued by corruption into a failed state that suffers from conflict and faces the threat of partition. While great powers are busy instigating more conflicts and wasting more material and human resources, the only winners are the merchants of weapons; and the major losers are the poor in every rich and poor country.

This means that finding successful solutions to conflicts in general requires putting an end to foreign intervention and addressing the root causes of conflict embedded in social, cultural, political and economic structures. The root causes of conflict in most parts of Africa, South and Central America and the Middle East are to be found in foreign intervention that has not stopped since the eighteenth century; in the dark alleys of abject poverty, ignorance and inequality; and in a lack of quality education, social justice, freedom and hope. This requires transforming educational systems and giving all members of society access to good education with emphasis on tolerance, because traditional social and political structures tend to divide rather than unite people, and suppress their desires to be free and enlightened.

It should be clear from this quick survey that the world is facing serious political and security challenges that require the cooperation of great and regional powers to manage them. To stabilize the global situation, the world needs a new vision with a creative plan to transform the sociocultural and economic conditions on the ground, and an enlightened global leadership committed to peace, social justice, security and development. Since the United States sits in the driver's seat, no new vision is possible without transforming American politics and the country's way of thinking; it needs to abandon its policy of conflict management and adopt instead a policy of conflict resolution. A policy that seeks to manage conflict makes America part of the problem, while a policy that seeks to resolve conflict makes America part of the solution. In fact, a policy to manage conflict makes America the protector of merchants of death who make money as more Americans and non-Americans die fighting senseless wars.

The Ramo Plan, with its six major components—the liberation of all nations from the debt burden, the creation of the Ramo as a reference currency, the establishment of a fund for sustainable development, and the educational, humanitarian and environmental funds—is the only visionary plan to save us and our planet from an impending catastrophe, while transforming our world into a humane and sustainable one. It is also the shortest and safest way to create a shared objective to motivate great and small powers to cooperate and face the many challenges of our times collectively.

The Economic Scene

The outlook for the global economy is not encouraging: economic, financial, unemployment and social reports suggest that the world economy is slowing down, while uncertainty is causing investors and consumers to be cautious. At the same time, neither the World Bank nor the IMF has been able to make credible projections of future growth for years; both institutions have lowered their projections, often more than once every year over the last few years. A lack of accurate measures to predict future economic changes causes all institutions to make different forecasts. For example, the IMF projected that the world economy would grow by 3.2 % in 2016, while the World Bank expected the rate to be 2.9 %. However, in June 2016 the IMF lowered its projection to 3.1 %, while the World Bank lowered its projection to 2.4 %, which matches the UN projections in its "World Economic Situation" report issued May 13, 2016. However, the intelligence unit of *The Economist* predicted just a 2.1 % growth. Now we know it was 2.3 %.

The World Bank says in its *Global Economic Prospects 2016*, "More generally, 2015 growth estimates for more than half of developing countries were further downgraded. Disappointments are concentrated in Latin America and, to a lesser degree, Sub-Saharan Africa, where a number of commodity exporters are struggling to maintain growth."[10] Other sources suggest that the lower economic growth rates are driven by several forces: continued growth deceleration in the emerging markets and developing countries in general, low commodity prices in the post-2008 crisis, weaker capital flows, falling oil prices, economic and political uncertainty, subdued global trade, widening income and wealth gaps, and conflict in the Middle East.

According to the World Bank, more than 40 % of the world's poor live in developing countries that have experienced slower economic growth in 2015. As a consequence, the rates of poverty and unemployment in most Third World states have risen, causing despair and anger to deepen and labor productivity to decline, as well as encouraging radicalism and sometimes violence. If the slowdown of 2015 and 2016 were to continue for a few more years, it could spill over to other states and cause an economic recession worse than the Great Recession. Since this has so far lasted more than eight years, a new recession at this time of political uncertainty and conflict would last more than a decade, with consequences no one is able to predict or avoid. The situations in Greece, where the debt crisis is moving from a serious to a dangerous stage, and in Brazil, Russia and the Middle East, whose economies have sustained substantial damage, make such a possibility more probable.

The World Bank states: "Although it is still a low-probability scenario, a faster-than-expected slowdown in China combined with a more protracted deceleration in other large emerging markets is a risk. Empirical estimates suggest that a sustained 1 percentage point decline in growth in the BRICS (Brazil, Russia, India, China, and South Africa) would reduce growth in other emerging and developing economies by around 0.8 percentage point and global growth by 0.4 percentage point. Compounding this risk is the possibility of a protracted decline in potential growth throughout emerging and developing economies, persistently subdued growth in major high-income countries, and an escalation of geopolitical tensions."[11] Since political tension causes instability and uncertainty, it usually causes economic growth rates to slow down and wealth and income inequalities to widen.

The economic situation in the United States looks quite stable, despite the fact that the rate of growth in 2016 was only 1.9 %. As for the Eurozone, the situation looks less encouraging: low growth rates, persistent high unemployment rates, large public debt, and political and social challenges facing most states are all causes for concern. While acceleration in the number of refugees is creating chaos at political and social levels, forces opposed to foreign migration are gaining popularity and momentum. As a consequence governments are being forced to rethink their policies and priorities. Meanwhile, the high number of refugees coming from the Middle East and Africa is straining the absorption capacity of most states as well as their resources. On the other hand, disagreement about the fate of refugees is undermining solidarity within the European Union (EU), while acts of terrorism in France, Belgium, Germany and Britain have created a general atmosphere that is hostile to refugees in general and Muslims in particular.

Britain's decision to leave the EU has made the economic prospects for both Europe and Britain less promising than before. In fact, the EU has never appeared to be as politically uncertain and economically weak as it appears today; and when combined with the slow growth in the United States, and the prospects for continued growth deceleration in the emerging markets and the developing states, the future of the EU's economy looks rather bleak.

The World Bank says further that Eurozone growth picked up in 2015, as domestic demand strengthened and exports accelerated, partly owing to the lagged effect of the depreciation of the euro. For the year as a whole, "Euro Area growth is estimated at 1.5 percent, in line with previous expectations, with activity firming in Spain, somewhat disappointing in Germany, and still lagging in France and Italy … Since the start of the European Central Bank's (ECB) quantitative easing program, credit conditions have improved and credit growth has resumed following several years of contraction. However, credit remains tight in some countries because of elevated non-performing loans and impaired bank balance sheets."[12] Nevertheless, based on information obtained from Eurostat and the *Guardian*, the French and German economies grew by 0.3 % in the third quarter of 2015 and Italy's economy slowed down to 0.2 %, the Dutch economy barely grew, the Portuguese economy actually stagnated, and Finland's economy contracted by 0.6 %.[13]

The *New York Times* reported that by April 2016 the Eurozone economy had got back to the size it was before the global financial crisis of 2008: "The 19-country currency union, which as a bloc is the world's second-largest economy, enjoyed an unexpected acceleration in the first three months of the year, when it expanded by a quarterly rate of 0.6 percent." Though the Eurozone economy had regained what it had lost over the last eight years, it is hard to say that it has recovered; a few member states may have recovered, but the region as a whole has not. Statistics reveal that the Eurozone has lost a decade of economic growth. In the meantime, the inflation rate in Europe is too low for a healthy economy, and many banks have bad loans that keep them from extending new loans. As a consequence, the ECB is worried because "low or subzero inflation could lead to deflation that can choke the life out of an economy for years."[14]

In fact, the unemployment rate in the Eurozone is over 10 %, three percentage points higher than it was in 2008, and the debt situation, as demonstrated by Greece being salvaged for the third time from default, is still deteriorating.[15] In Greece and Spain, the unemployment rate is still above 20 %, and about half of the young job-seekers cannot find jobs; in France, the unemployment rate among young people has reached 25 %; 34 % in Portugal; 39 % in Italy; 48 % in Spain; and almost 50 % in Greece. As for the nineteen states of the EU, the youth unemployment rate was 19 % in April 2016.[16]

In short, Europe is facing structural unemployment, a largely stagnating economy, a restive population that lacks optimism, a leadership that lacks imagination and a serious debt crisis. Europe is a continent that has lost its optimism and enthusiasm, and faces an unprecedented migrant challenge that threatens its unity, social peace and sociocultural cohesion. In addition, Europe faces a growing conservative, almost chauvinistic movement that threatens its values of liberty, equality and tolerance, and weakens its democratic character as well as its established social order.

As for Japan, World Bank reports say that economic growth "remains fragile, with private consumption and investment failing, [despite] continued policy stimulus. Private consumption contracted in 2015 and investment was stagnant, which was only partially offset by positive but relatively subdued export growth. Rising female participation has boosted employment rates. Long-term inflation expectations remain below the 2 percent target, despite further policy easing by the Bank of Japan."[17] Nevertheless, the World Bank expects the Japanese economy to grow by 1.3 % in 2016, up from the 0.8 % forecast for 2015; it must be noted, however, that the reported 0.8 % growth did not materialize. *Focus Economics* reported that the Japanese 2015 growth rate was 0.5 %; "the economic weaknesses observed in 2015 are far from abating and have likely carried into this year. In February, consumer sentiment continued its downward trend and exports contracted for the fifth consecutive month. Moreover, the recent appreciation of the yen promises to further dampen the all-important external sector:"[18]

In China, state policy is changing as the economy continues to shift from manufacturing to services, which signals slower growth rates in the future. Nevertheless, *Global Economic Prospects 2016* states that "Real incomes have continued to increase, albeit at lower rates, contributing to sustained growth of private consumption. A continued rebalancing from industry to services should support the shift from investment to consumption, whose share in GDP [gross domestic product] is gradually recovering from a post-crisis dip."[19] In view of the slowdown, "the People's Bank of China lowered benchmark interest rates and eased required reserve ratios, while implementing new policies to facilitate refinancing for commercial banks." In addition, the bank continued to inject liquidity into the financial system, causing the deficit to widen to a six-year high of 2.3 % of GDP, and China's foreign reserves to decline in 2015 by an estimated $443 billion.[20]

According to the *Wall Street Journal*, China "recorded a pronounced deceleration in growth last year, affirming that a multiyear slowdown is biting the world's second-largest economy harder and shows little sign of abating."[21] The economic growth rate for 2015 was 6.9 %; though this rate is one of the world's highest, it is the weakest in a quarter century for China, and it signals that the economic momentum of the last twenty-five years is weakening. Chinese Premier Li Keqiang attributed the slowdown to "increasing downward pressure on the economy, complicated by slack global demand."[22] And with growing debt and excess housing and factory capacity, the economy is not expected to maintain previous rates; in fact, the 2016 growth rate was 6.7 % and the projected rate for 2017 is 6.5 %.

On the other hand, UBS Group AG estimates that China's "total debt equals almost 260% of annual economic output, up from less than 160% in 2007".[23] Since bad loans are on the rise, people and companies spend the equivalent of 20 % of GDP on interest payments. And as the economy slows and the yuan weakens, Chinese are moving their money out of the country. "Wealthy families are increasingly trying to move large sums of money out of the country, worried that the value of the currency will fall and their savings will be worth less. If the government cannot keep citizens from rushing to the financial exits, China's outlook could darken. The swell of outflows is a destabilizing force in China's slowing economy, threatening to undermine confidence and hurt a banking system that is struggling to deal with a decade-long lending binge."[24] As a consequence, China finds itself, just like most other states, in a dilemma: "if the government cuts interest rates, more capital flees. If it raises interest rates, more debt-plagued companies risk going bust and fuel joblessness."[25] This means that the coming years are likely to see a decline in productive investment as well as a slowdown in the economy.

Several international institutions and many economists in Europe and the United States have argued that income and wealth inequalities undermine social mobility, and make it hard for members of the middle class and the poor to climb the social ladder. Lack of adequate social mobility causes most people born in poor families to remain poor, and most people born in rich families to remain rich. *Fortune* magazine said: "Economic disadvantage for the overwhelming majority translates into ill health, missed educational opportunity, and—increasingly—the familiar symptoms of depression: alcoholism, obesity, gambling, and minor criminality."[26] Yes: economic disadvantage translates into poverty and lower incomes and social mobility, it also causes inequality to worsen. Economists at the Bank of International Settlements suggest that "rising equity prices have been a driver of inequality … Monetary policy may have added to inequality to the extent that it has boosted equity prices. Unconventional monetary policies [devised by the European and American central banks] might have had the most significant effects on the dynamics of wealth inequality through changes in equity returns and house prices."[27]

Though I agree with this viewpoint, there is more to inequality, especially in America and Europe. The European and American central banks, by reducing interest rates to near zero, have enabled big banks to have access to free money and lend it to big corporations and nation states at relatively high interest rates. Thus, central banks' actions have enabled banks to make easy money without taking the usual risks associated with lending and investment; as a result, they have given commercial banks no incentives to lend money to consumers and small investors, particularly when risk is involved. This is why big American banks have made more profit since the financial crisis of 2008 than at any time in their history. Consequently, presidents of large banks, hedge funds, corporations and major financial institutions have continued to give themselves and members of their management staff obscene salaries and bonuses. In addition, these policies have caused the incomes and savings of the poor and retired people to decline year after year.

Thomas Piketty argues that capital/labor inequality is a serious problem; and though there are no shortages of justification for redistribution of capital and its income, the means used in the capitalist and socialist states have been disastrous. "The case can be made purely in terms of social justice, in order to achieve a true redistribution of income between capital and labor. Or it can be made in terms of economic efficiency, in order to combat the negative effects of capital market imperfections. In practice, efforts at capital/labor redistribution in the twentieth century have been disastrous not only in countries that tried to abolish private ownership of capital, where workers' living standards stagnated while improving rapidly in the capitalist countries, but also in the West, where a very small fraction of the tax burden actually falls on capital."[28]

Because the American and European central banks' misguided monetary policy is still in effect, income and wealth inequalities continue to rise in almost all countries in the world. As the income and wealth gaps widen, the middle class shrinks and the number of the poor rises. In order to meet their basic needs and survive during the recession, many members of the middle class and the elderly were forced to spend a good portion of their wealth, causing many of them to lose their life savings and homes and cars, even ending up living on street corners or in homeless shelters. In Britain, the ruling elite of all parties give orders to remove helpless people sleeping in the streets, while allowing the rich to deposit their millions and billions in tax havens abroad because such actions are legally sanctioned. Trump's proposal to lower tax rates on corporations is expected to aggravate this situation.

The American and European central banks' monetary policy, which enabled commercial banks to borrow at near zero interest rates and lend to states at substantially higher rates, may have had an adverse effect on the world's economy, particularly in the West. When the bulk of profits and income goes to the rich, the poor receive little money to spend; and this causes consumption to decline, which in turn discourages investors from investing and creating new jobs. Since income and wealth gaps continue to widen, there is little hope that the global growth rates will regain momentum any time soon. In fact, I believe that until central banks change their current policies and replace them with new ones designed to narrow income and wealth gaps, the world economy will continue to grow at lower rates. And as the economy slows down, the probability of another global recession will become more likely. Reports issued by the World Bank, the Bank for International Settlements and concerned economists in Europe and America suggest that as income and wealth gaps widen, they cause national economies to lose momentum and slow down, becoming more susceptible to financial and economic crises.[29]

In response to ECB suggestions to move to negative interest rates, Katie Evans wrote: "Negative interest rates could increase inequality. While the experiences of countries who have tried negative rates suggest it wouldn't lead to a boom in mortgage lending, the cost of borrowing would remain at rock bottom for those who could afford to do so. Those with substantial incomes and existing assets could borrow cheaply and invest in assets like property. Those on lower incomes, meanwhile, would find it even harder to save for a deposit and see house prices rising further out of reach."[30]

The facts and opinions expressed here seem to suggest that the economic and monetary policies adopted by most states, particularly the United States and the Eurozone, have become tranquilizers meant to quieten the patient rather than an effective treatment to heal obvious aliments. Tranquilizers usually become less effective as time passes, and have no power to treat any patient or restore his health. The advantages of tranquilizers are fewer than their disadvantages, and therefore they need to be stopped before they kill the patient they are meant to keep alive.

These policies were developed to deal with the 2008 financial crisis, which was caused by the accumulation of public and private debt. Since the debt burden has increased rather than decreased over the last eight years, the situation remains dangerous; it has caused many states and billions of people to be trapped in a vicious circle, crying for a remedy. The Ramo Plan is designed to liberate all rich and poor nations from the debt burden, and help underdeveloped countries develop their economies and transform their traditional cultures, thus revitalizing the global economy, restoring political stability, helping the poor and needy everywhere and making environmental sustainability achievable.

Notes

1. Duncan Green; The world's top 100 economies: 31 countries; 69 corporations, The World Bank; September 20, 2016.
2. Milton Freedman Quotes: http://www.goodreads.com/author/quotes/5001.Milton_Friedman
3. Jeff Stein and Jonathan Broder; Can America Win a War? Newsweek, April 30, 2015. http://www.newsweek.com/2015/05/08/can-america-win-war-326812.html
4. Korean War – Nuclear Weapons. https://www.awesomestories.com/asset/view/NUCLEAR-WEAPONS-Korean-War
5. Ibid.
6. France remembers the Algerian war, 50 years on, France 24, March 19, 2012. http://www.france24.com/en/20120316-commemorations-mark-end-algerian-war-independence-france-evian-accords
7. Noam Chomsky, Who Rules the World? Metropolitan Books, 2016, p. 45.
8. Rowena Hammal, Destined to Fail? How the division of Korea led to the Korean War, *History Review*, September 2010, 67. http://www.historytoday.com/rowena-hammal/destined-fail-how-division-korea-led-korean-war-0#sthash.m3swko1A.dpuflf
9. Daniel Larison, "South Sudan and the Partition "Solution" for Foreign Conflicts," The American Conservative, June 29, 2015.
10. The World Bank; Global Economic Prospects 2016, p. 3.
11. Ibid., pp. 5–6.

12. Ibid., p. 9.
13. Eurozone GDP: Growth slows to just 0.3%, *The Guardian,* Nov. 15, 2015.
14. The New York Times, April 29, 2016 (http://www.nytimes.com/aponline/2016/04/29/world/europe/ap-eu-europe economy.html?ref=world&utm_source=Sailthru&utm_medium=email&utm_campaign=New%20Campaign&utm_term=%2AMorning%20Brief&_r=0).
15. Eurozone Economy Regains Size of 2008 but Remains Shaky, *the Associated Press,* April 29, 2016.
16. OECD Data, Youth unemployment (https://data.oecd.org/unemp/youth-unemployment-rate.htm).
17. Global Economic Prospects 2016, The World Bank, p. 10.
18. Japan Economic Outlook; Focus Economics, April 5, 2016 (http://www.focus-economics.com/countries/japan).
19. Global Economic Prospects 2016, World bank, p. 10.
20. Ibid., p. 10.
21. Mark Magnier; China's Economic Growth in 2015 Is Slowest in 25 Years, The Wall Street Journal, January 19, 2016 (http://www.wsj.com/articles/china-economic-growth-slows-to-6-9-on-year-in-2015-1453169398).
22. Ibid.
23. Ibid.
24. Keith Bradsher; Chinese start to lose confidence in their currency; New York Times, Feb. 13, 2016. https://www.nytimes.com/2016/02/14/business/dealbook/chinese-start-to-lose-confidence-in-their-currency.html
25. Mark Magnier; China's Economic Growth in 2015 Is Slowest in 25 Years, The Wall Street Journal, January 19, 2016.
26. Chris Matthews, Wealth inequality in America: It's worse that you think, Fortune, October 31, 2014.
27. Washingtonsblog, Central Bank Economists: Bad Central Bank Policy Is Increasing Inequality, March 10, 2016 (http://www.washingtonsblog.com/2016/03/central-bank-economists-bad-central-bank-policy-increasing-inequality.html).
28. Thomas Piketty, The Economics of Inequality, The Belknap Press of Harvard University Press, 2015, p. 65.
29. Jeff Voudrie, Past 10 years of US GDP Growth reveal Disturbing Trend; *Jeff's Blog*; March 2, 2015 (http://www.seeitmarket.com/past-10-years-us-gdp-growth-reveal-disturbing-trend-14156/).
30. Washingtonsblog, Central Bank Economists: Bad Central Bank Policy Is Increasing Inequality, March 10, 2016 (http://www.washingtonsblog.com/2016/03/central-bank-economists-bad-central-bank-policy-increasing-inequality.html).

CHAPTER 5

The US Political and Economic Scene

Since the United States is the world's political, economic and military leader, and the only superpower, it deserves special attention. In fact, without understanding the American situation, it would be difficult to read the future and guess what is likely to happen in the world of politics, economics and security matters. In this chapter, an attempt will be made to give an overview of the political and economic situation in America as it looked in the middle of 2017. To plan for what might happen in the future, we need to examine the US political, economic, cultural and ideological transformations of the last three decades; we also need to speculate about what might happen in the coming few years.

The American story of building the greatest political, economic and military power in history has convinced most Americans, particularly white Americans, to believe that they are somehow superior to other peoples, and therefore they are an exception to the rule. Because of this belief, many Americans believe they are entitled to privileges at home and freedom of action abroad that others should not have. Being exceptional also means that Americans must do whatever they can to promote American values, ideals and way of life worldwide. "America was born as an idea, and so it has to carry that idea forward. The American idea is revealed in the country's birth as a "city on a hill," an inspirational notion that resides deep in the American psyche, and by the distinctive spirit of American individualism and enterprise."[1]

As a result of this way of reasoning, a new philosophy emerged slowly to justify American condescending attitude toward other peoples, and a new

M. Rabie, *The Global Debt Crisis and Its Socioeconomic Implications*,
https://doi.org/10.1007/978-3-319-66215-2_5

ideology was articulated to organize American life and guide state behavior. This ideology is made up of three major components: democracy, capitalism and exceptionalism. As we view the political and economic situation, I will explain these concepts and their role in American political, social and economic life.

A View of the Political Scene

The identity of every nation is rooted either in history or ideology. Because the United States had no history prior to its independence in the eighteenth century, its identity had to be invented and anchored in ideology. Since all ideologies tend to be rigid and undemocratic, the American ideology claims to be exceptional because its roots are to be found in the principles of individualism, liberty, equality and opportunity. Emphasis on this claim resulted in adopting "American exceptionalism" as a national ethos.

Pakistan, like the United States, had no history of its own prior to its independence in 1947. Before this date, Pakistan was a part of India; but one of the consequences of World War II was the partition of India into two states: India and Pakistan—the latter of which included Bangladesh. However, Bangladesh and Pakistan were put together by combining two peoples who believed in the same religion but were culturally, linguistically and geographically separate. In 1971, after a short but bloody war with Pakistan, Bangladesh won independence and became a member of the United Nations. Following independence, both Pakistan and Bangladesh adopted Islam as an ideology from which the state derives political legitimacy.

Rationalwiki.com defines American exceptionalism as "a belief that the United States is unique or exceptional when compared with the historical development of other countries."[2] Attempts to perpetuate this claim during election campaigns and every time America finds itself facing a serious challenge has made American exceptionalism a popular ideal held by many Americans on both the right and the left of the political divide.[3] But for US politicians American exceptionalism is a rhetorical slogan to provoke enthusiasm among the largely naive masses during election campaigns and national celebrations. However, the promotion of this slogan has led many believers to become racists and feel proud to be racists.

Being exceptional, the United States as a nation is supposed to assume an activist role on the global stage and to set an example for other nations to follow; it has to be a "shining example" to the world. But since exceptionalism implies looking down at other peoples and cultures, "this sort of presumptive moral superiority is virtually never welcomed by other nations, and is almost always resented, particularly when the United States has a long history of engaging in gunboat diplomacy itself."[4] In fact, Americans' belief in exceptionalism has been one of the reasons for worldwide resentment of American actions overseas and dislike of its foreign policy. To the rest of the world, American exceptionalism "sounds less like "America is Exceptional" and more like "Exceptions should be made for America."[5] Because America feels exceptional, the ruling political and economic elite have given themselves the right to interfere in the internal affairs of most nations, and ignore international norms and laws they do not like.

David Frum, who served in the White House during the George W. Bush administration, says, "As Americans have become more uncertain of their nation's continued hegemony, their leaders have insisted ever more emphatically upon the doctrine of 'American exceptionalism.' The debate over America's relative decline seems to pit those who would absolutely deny the reality of decline and those who welcome it. Yet the lesson of the decline of British power between 1870 and 1914 would seem to be that the post-American world will be a much more dangerous and violent place, as ambitious new contenders seek power in ever more aggressive ways."[6] But an honest review of America's actions since the Monroe declaration of 1823 would reveal that the bad situation we are in today was a result of continued American interference in the affairs of other nations. The Monroe Doctrine, which declared US opposition to European colonialism in the Americas, "stated that further efforts by European nations to take control of any independent state in North or South America would be viewed as the manifestation of an unfriendly disposition toward the United States."[7] Therefore, to say that the post-American world would be a more dangerous and violent place, as Frum claims, amounts to saying that we have no choice but to follow the dictates of the American empire no matter what it does.

In fact, the history of all colonialist and imperialist powers reveals that their intentions have always been to steal the resources of the poor and weak nations and undermine their traditional cultures and future prospects, which made the history of imperialism violent and destructive. I believe that regardless of all probable consequences, all forms of hegemony must be ended; otherwise poor and weak nations are unlikely to see freedom or progress. Therefore, world intellectuals committed to peace, social justice and cultural and religious freedom need to articulate a humane alternative to hegemony capable of ending great powers' self-serving competition.

Public opinion polls taken in America over the last decade suggest that the American people have generally lost confidence in the major institutions of the US government, including the US presidency and Congress, as well as the Supreme Court, the major political parties and the media. However, Americans often tend to differentiate between the political system as a tool of governance and democracy as a cultural value; and therefore, while they continue to criticize the political system and their leaders harshly, they continue to believe in democracy. This is an attitude that reflects a belief in democracy as a great idea to be cherished on the one hand, and a conviction that the American political system has been corrupted on the other. In fact, "the claim of the dominant group to represent the general interest is always more or less fraudulent."[8]

Democracy is commonly defined as "a form of government in which the supreme power is vested in the people or in their elected agents under a free electoral system."[9] In a more general sense, it is "a state of society characterized by formal equality of rights and privileges."[10] This makes democracy a system of governance that regulates the relationship between the state and the public in ways that enable the governed to elect their governors and participate in the making of decisions that affect their lives, while empowering the public to hold their state representatives and government officials accountable for their deeds.

There is no doubt that democracy has had its share of successes and failures. Its greatest success, in my view, is manifested by its ability to transform itself from only a system of governance into a sociocultural value. As a value, democracy reflects an attitude that promotes freedom and believes in equality and social justice. This transformation was made possible by the spread of liberty and respect for human rights, which education systems have facilitated in the industrial nations of the West. As a consequence, democracy has become a mindset that induces people to accept others as equals, respecting their rights and beliefs. Democracy therefore entails more than elections and political participation; it serves also as a cultural value that seeks to establish the principles of mutual recognition, equality, respect for human rights and peaceful coexistence.

Democracy, both as a political system and a sociocultural value, has succeeded to a large extent in all industrialized societies, but failed in almost all pre-industrial societies. For example, despite the appearance of nationalistic movements and largely racist ideologies in Germany and Italy during the early decades of the twentieth century, democracy survived and gradually flourished in both countries. On the other hand, almost every election in Africa is followed by conflict or civil war.

Nevertheless, the American democratic experience shows that members of the political, economic, financial, and military and media elites have been able to gain extra powers and use them to deny many people opportunities to which they are entitled in democratic society; they are also able to use the media to manipulate people's fears and needs, falsify their consciousness and inflame their passions to achieve their objectives. This suggests that the economic, political and military elites have replaced the ruling families of older times in repressing people indirectly and denying them some of their legitimate rights, while the major media organizations have replaced organized religion in brainwashing the general public and justifying absolutism. The language used by a few presidential contenders during the 2016 US elections campaign shows that many politicians and media personalities are ready to use racism to achieve political ends, causing elections to become an exercise in unintentionally undermining democracy itself.

When President Barack Obama was elected in 2008, probably half of the American people thought that his election had finally bridged the racial gap and that he would transform America and the world, making both safer and more humane. But the failure of Obama to devise programs to bridge the racial gap has caused attitudes of many white Americans to become more negative, leading them to become more suspicious and fearful; and this in turn has caused tension to rise between the police and black Americans across the country. As for the world population, Obama's record has been a great disappointment; he failed not only to restore sanity to an American foreign policy that had (in my opinion) gone mad during the Bush administration, but has made the situation worse. In Iraq, Libya, Syria and Yemen, America's actions and inactions suggest that the Obama administration sought to transform those four states into failed states and keep them as such, thus crippling their abilities to restore stability and security. And despite its success, this policy has proven to be self-defeating; it has encouraged radicalism and motivated terrorist groups to target every place within reach.

The 2016 Election Campaign

The presidential election campaign of 2016 has indicated a few trends that continue to influence the thinking of many Americans and shape their attitudes towards themselves, their fellow citizens, particularly minorities living in America, and the world around them. The major trends of change that were revealed are:

1. The replacement of the political orientations of the past by Ideological polarization. While political orientations reflect differences in attitudes toward challenges and opportunities, ideological polarization reflects contradictory religious and philosophical convictions. While different political orientations lend themselves to compromise solutions, ideological polarization does not, causing society to become divided along sociocultural lines that cause conflict and create cultural ghettos; an issue to be explained later.
2. The unprecedented rise of Donald Trump's popularity seems to suggest that he was the only presidential contender to read the mood of blue collar workers, small farmers, the unemployed and churchgoers. And by uttering the forbidden words of racism, Trump was able to appeal to a large segment of white Americans and make them believe in him and his ability to "make America great again". By attacking Latino migrants and calling them rapists and murderers, and promising to prevent Muslims from visiting America, Trump was able to gain added popularity and win the elections.
3. Ideological polarization across party lines has been reinforced by polarization within the parties themselves. While presidential contenders Ted Cruz, Mario Rubio and Ben Carson have deepened the ideological divide within the Republican Party, forcing it to move to the right and be more conservative and closed-minded, Bernie Sanders, in contrast, has deepened the ideological divide within the Democratic Party, forcing it to move to the left and be more liberal and open-minded. Yet the recent history of both parties suggests that neither one is fit to lead America in this turbulent age.
4. Americans who supported Trump and others who supported Sanders have launched a rebellion against the establishment, the social forces that control it and the media. But despite this rebellion's failure to achieve its objectives, both movements are expected to continue to transform the American political and economic cultures and deepen the ideological divides in society. One of the probable outcomes of this change is the split of each party into two. While this possibility is rather weak on the right, it is more probable on the left.

I believe that creating a third party to the left of the Democratic Party will be a good thing for America and the world. Such a development would strengthen democracy at home and make politicians more accountable and less comfortable in their seats of power; it would also make decisions to go to war, waste lives and money and destroy other nations more difficult. In the meantime, market capitalism would lose some of its ability to corrupt politicians, manipulate people and situations, and enrich its captains at the expense of everyone else. This should cause business ethics to improve and the pay gap between managers and workers to narrow.

Following the election of Trump, leaders of the National Rifle Association (NRA) claimed to have been the major force behind Trump's victory. These are people who vote to protect the interests of white Americans, not the interests of America; some of them claim that white Americans are the majority and their culture is the dominant culture; and because of this they are entitled to special rights including the separation of whites from other Americans. By making such claims, white supremacists ignore the fact that they are the ones who confiscated the land from its owners, killing millions of the natives, raping their women and stealing their children; they also ignore the fact that people who have migrated to America over the last two centuries have contributed to making it great. Most whites also forget to acknowledge that the black people who were brought to serve them and farm the plantations were subjected to slavery and exploitation and denial of human rights for a long time; it was this treatment of blacks that caused them to lag behind whites in education and wealth and social status.

Jared Taylor, the president of the American Renaissance Foundation, said in an interview aired by the National Public Radio on November 19, 2016 that whites are a different race and were created to be different, and therefore they need to be separated from the rest of the people of America; he also said that each person should have the right to discriminate against anyone for no reason. The election of Trump has given people like Mr. Taylor an opportunity to be represented in the White House and in other US departments. As a result, racially motivated groups are being empowered to become respected members of society with access to the major centers of power in Washington.

The major media organizations claim that Hillary Clinton's defeat was partially caused by fake news created by Trump supporters, adding that the public should have been able to differentiate between fake news and true news. In so claiming, the media forget that they have been faking news and distorting facts for decades in order to serve the interests of the ruling elite, of which they are an integral part. In fact, they are the ones who knowingly promoted the lies of the George W. Bush administration, when it claimed that Saddam Hussein had weapons of mass destruction in order to justify the invasion of Iraq in 2003. The American media has continued to lie to the American people and the world regarding what is happening in Syria, Iraq, Libya, Yemen and Ukraine; the narrative of the Syrian tragedy in particular has consistently been the opposite of the truth. So it was members of the American mass media that started the game of lying and hiding the truth to support an insane American foreign policy, particularly in the Middle East; and this has come at the expense of their credibility and the credibility of the US government. Thus the media pushed the public to seek other sources of information, giving fake news outlets an opportunity to claim a place for themselves in the maze of falsehood and deception.

When Chris Wallace of Fox News moderated the last presidential debate on October 12, 2016, he said that the size of the public debt is about 79% of the American gross domestic product (GDP), when in actual fact it had already reached 106%. Chris Wallace is not ignorant and has staff to give him the facts; but he is a spokesperson for the conservative elite in America and a promoter of ideas that are designed to falsify the consciousness of the American people. The Republican Party claims that social security payments to retirees are not an entitlement but a government subsidy; although the truth is that payments to retirees have been an entitlement since the program was enacted in 1935. By claiming that social security is a subsidy, conservatives justify reducing payments and legitimize stealing the life savings of the poor to enrich the super rich.

America is a nation that has lost its sense of direction; and because of that, it is no longer able to define its national interest and articulate a rational and humane plan to advance its goals at home or abroad. Ideological polarization and military adventures, and the apparent failure to fight ISIS in Iraq and Syria, has confused the American public, and has complicated the process of developing a set of principles to guide America's domestic and foreign policies.

A View of the Economic and Social Scene

The failure of the American economy to resume normal growth, the loss of millions of manufacturing jobs and the continued widening of income and wealth gaps have all hurt American workers and the poor. Meanwhile, the free market philosophy, which encourages outsourcing and off-shoring, has caused the center of economic power to shift rapidly from the West to the East.

If you consider US energy policy since 2014, it is easy to recognize that the political elite has no problem hurting the energy industry and the American people and causing the bankruptcy of many companies in order to hurt Russia, Venezuela and Iran. Forcing the Arab Gulf states to lower oil prices has not only hurt millions of poor people in Russia and Venezuela, but also millions more in the Middle East, Latin America and Asia; those are people who work in the oil-exporting Gulf States and others who depend on remittances coming from those states. In addition, thousands of American workers have lost their jobs in the energy industry and related activities, which has caused several cities and small towns to suffer badly.

The decline in oil prices, which began in 2014, was welcomed by many oil experts and economists, who predicted that lower prices would boost the global economy and cause growth rates to accelerate; but nothing of the kind has happened. Instead, the impact of lower prices has largely been negative. The oil exporting states lost substantial income, causing many of them to experience large budget deficits instead of surpluses; and importers of oil did not see growth rates rising. For example, the 2014 global growth rate of 3.4% declined to 3.1% in 2015 and to 2.7% in 2016. In projecting a lower rate for 2016, the International Monetary Fund (IMF) cited lower oil prices.

Since national economies have largely become part of an integrated global economy, winners and losers from changes in the prices of commodities have been drawn from individuals, corporations and industries. The oil market provides a good example. In the past three years, oil prices have gone from over $110 a barrel to about $50. The significant price drop has made shale gas extractions less competitive, while penalizing extraction and refining industries and the development of related technologies, causing many US and European companies to suffer. Low oil prices are also a strong disincentive to investment in the green economy.[11] Even India, which imports 75% of its oil, has lost more than it gained from lower oil prices owing to declining Indian labor remittances from the Gulf.

Since the outcome of the 2016 presidential elections does not seem to promise positive change, ambitious nations and foreign leaders are likely to challenge American leadership; and this is a recipe for increased global tension, conflict, radicalism and terrorism. The first thing that America must do is to transform its foreign policy; restructure its economy and rethink its business culture; stop the income and wealth gaps from widening further; and deal fairly with other nations. These actions are needed to cure America from the curse of "exceptionalism," and transform it into a nation that is interested in peace and security for all.

The recent appreciation of the US dollar against all major currencies has caused American exports to become less competitive and thus less able to compete with Chinese, German and Japanese exports. But since the value of the Chinese yuan is pegged to the dollar, the dollar appreciation has not had tangible effects on American exports to China or imports from China. While US exports to China have continued to increase incrementally, China's exports to the United States have continued to increase substantially, causing the American trade deficit with China to rise year on year. US trade in goods with China according to the US Census Bureau may be seen in Table 5.1 (all numbers are rounded in billions of US dollars)[12]

These figures indicate that the competitiveness of the US economy compared to that of China has remained fairly steady from 2000 to 2016; US annual imports from China were close to 4.5 times its exports to China; and American exports to China have increased by approximately 3.5% annually during the same period. As a result, the US trade deficit with China jumped from $84 billion in 2000 to $347 billion in 2016.

According to the World Bank, "United States domestic demand in 2015 was supported by robust consumption and dynamic investment outside the oil sector. In contrast, net exports remained a drag on growth, and industrial activity continued to be subdued in the second half of 2015. The decline in net exports is a principal factor dampening growth at present. This is the result of the strength of the dollar and the softness in external demand, particularly from large emerging markets."[13] Nevertheless, the

Table 5.1 Foreign trade—U.S. trade with China—census

Year	*Exports*	*Imports*	*Deficit*
2000	16	100	84
2002	22	125	103
2004	34	197	162
2006	54	288	234
2008	70	338	268
2010	92	365	273
2012	111	426	315
2014	124	467	343
2015	116	482	366
2016	116	463	347

World Bank expected the American economy to do better in 2016 than in 2015, but the final figures show that it grew by 1.9% as compared to the 2.4% of 2015.

In addition, the World Bank said that "labor participation has continued to trend down, and is unlikely to recover much as the number of baby boomers approaching retirement age increases. Labor productivity has moved downward in recent years, constraining potential output growth."[14] It is true that the rate of unemployment in the United States has fallen to 4.5% in 2016, but the major force behind this apparently positive development is not the growth of the manufacturing sector or exports, but the decline in worker participation in the labor force. In fact, the US active labor force has been shrinking since the Great Recession; in 2007, for example, 66.4% of all Americans had jobs or were actively seeking work; at the end of 2015, the rate was 62.6%—the lowest level since 1978. If the number of workers and potential workers who left the labor force were to be added to the currently unemployed, the unemployment rate would be about 9.2%, not the official rate of 4.5%.

Table 5.2 provides month by month information regarding the decline of American participation in the labor force.[15]

On August 5, 2016, Erica L. Groshen, Commissioner of the Bureau of Labor Statistics, issued a statement in which she provided important information on employment. She reported that "nonfarm employment rose by 255,000 in July, and unemployment rate was unchanged at 4.9 percent. Job gains occurred in professional and business services, health care, and

Table 5.2 Bureau of Labor Statistics data

Year	*Jan*	*Feb*	*Mar*	*Apr*	*May*	*Jun*	*Jul*	*Aug*	*Sep*	*Oct*	*Nov*	*Dec*
2006	66.0	66.1	66.2	66.1	66.1	66.2	66.1	66.2	66.1	66.2	66.3	66.4
2007	66.4	66.3	66.2	65.9	66.0	66.0	66.0	65.8	66.0	65.8	66.0	66.0
2008	66.2	66.0	66.1	65.9	66.1	66.1	66.1	66.1	66.0	66.0	65.9	65.8
2009	65.7	65.8	65.6	65.7	65.7	65.7	65.5	65.4	65.1	65.0	65.0	64.6
2010	64.8	64.9	64.9	65.2	64.9	64.6	64.6	64.7	64.6	64.4	64.6	64.3
2011	64.2	64.1	64.2	64.2	64.1	64.0	64.0	64.1	64.2	64.1	64.1	64.0
2012	63.7	63.8	63.8	63.7	63.7	63.8	63.7	63.5	63.7	63.8	63.6	63.7
2013	63.6	63.4	63.3	63.4	63.4	63.4	63.3	63.2	63.3	62.8	63.0	62.9
2014	62.9	63.0	63.2	62.8	62.8	62.8	62.9	62.9	62.8	62.9	62.9	62.7
2015	62.9	62.8	62.7	62.7	62.8	62.6	62.6	62.6	62.4	62.5	62.5	62.6
2016	62.7	62.9	63.0									

financial activities. Employment in mining continued to trend down."[16] However, a report issued by Groshen in April 2016 had stated that "manufacturing employment fell by 29,000 in March, and durable goods manufacturing has lost 68,000 jobs ... Since a recent peak in September 2014, mining employment has fallen by 185,000. More than three-fourths of the job losses over this period have been in support activities for mining."[17] It is clear that these numbers do not describe a healthy economy; but a fast declining industrial sector that used to be the envy of the world. On the other hand, loss of manufacturing jobs causes the size of the middle class to shrink, while causing poverty to spread in old manufacturing and mining towns.

"Again and again on the campaign trail, Donald Trump made promises he couldn't keep, playing on the ignorance of his base and revealing his own glaring misunderstanding of policy. The GOP candidate repeatedly vowed to strong-arm companies into keeping jobs at home instead of sending them to Mexico, renegotiate NAFTA and impose stiff import taxes on foreign goods. It was a message that appealed widely to Trump supporters, blending the illusion of economic hope with the rubric of 'America First' nationalism. Problem is, nothing about Trump's vision has anything to do with reality, and U.S. jobs continue to be sent across the border."[18]

Criticizing the BLS report of May 2017, Investment Research Dynamics said; "Regardless of how you want to slice and dice the phony numbers, the 'labor force participation rate' fell to 62.7% of the working age population. This means that 37.3% of the entire U.S. population between the ages of 15 and 64 decided that they couldn't be bothered with working or looking for a job. That metric alone completely invalidates anything the BLS reports about the U.S. 'employment situation.'"[19]

Inequality and Social Mobility Income and wealth inequalities are two closely related but different economic concepts; however, both are used to differentiate between the upper, middle and lower classes of society on the basis of how much income people earn and how much assets they own. Income inequality focuses exclusively on the average annual income earned by a member of each class; while wealth inequality focuses on the distribution of national assets among the social classes at a given time. Nevertheless, both measures are needed to give a true picture of how wealth and power is distributed in society and what type of opportunities social classes have open to them at any time. The income and wealth gaps tend to determine the degree of social mobility because they reflect the ease of moving from one social class to a higher one. The more unequal the distribution of income and wealth is, the less social mobility exists; and the narrower the income and wealth gaps are, the more social mobility exists. Since 2008, income and wealth inequalities have widened in all developed and developing countries.

There is more than one reason for the weak social mobility and excessive income and wealth inequality in America; nevertheless, the current economic and social policies of the US government and the prevailing business culture are the major factors that are creating and perpetuating these inequalities. As levels of income and wealth inequalities rise and levels of social mobility decline they cause the capacity of the US economy to grow at rates high enough to fulfill the needs of most people to weaken. According to the Social Security Administration, 53% of all American workers make less than $30,000 a year, which means that the majority of American workers belong to the lower middle class and the poor. Owing to this fact alone, probably over 50% of all American workers are poor and expected to stay poor.[20]

In December 2014, the Pew Research Center issued a report on inequality in America. An analysis of the report says, "The wealth gap between America's high income group and everyone else has reached record high levels since the economic recovery from the Great Recession of 2007–09, with a clear trajectory of increasing wealth for the upper-income families and no wealth growth for the middle- and lower-income families. In 2013, the median wealth of the nation's upper-income families ($639,400) was nearly seven times the median wealth of middle-income families ($96,500), the widest wealth gap seen in 30 years when the Federal Reserve began collecting these data."[21] In addition, the report tells us that American families belonging to the upper-income class have a median net worth that is nearly seventy times that of the country's lower-income families, also the widest wealth gap in thirty years. "The data have also shown a growing gap in wealth along racial and ethnic lines since the recession ended."[22]

Robert Reich says that "kids from low-income families, without much wealth, start out at a huge disadvantage. This is especially true for children of color from low-income families. Such families typically rent rather than own a house, and don't earn enough to have any savings. These structural disadvantages have built up to the point where the median net worth of white families is now more than 10 times greater than that of African-American or Latino families."[23] He talks here about racial inequality, which must be added to the overall income and wealth inequalities to give us a good picture of inequality and social mobility in America.

Matt Bruenig summed up the facts of racial divide in America; "White families hold 90 percent of the national wealth. Hispanic families hold 2.3 percent of the national wealth. Black families hold 2.6 percent of the national wealth."[24] To have a clearer picture of this racial disparity, we need to know that Hispanics who hold 2.3% of the national wealth represent 16.5% of the American population; and African Americans who hold 2.6% of the national wealth represent 12.2% of the American population. According to Slate.com, "the median white family has a net worth of $116,000 dollars. This indicates that 41 million white households across the nation have over $116,000 dollars in net worth. In comparison, nearly 40 percent or 5.6 million African American homes in the U.S. have zero or negative net worth. In addition, when you deduct the family car as an asset, the median black family in America only has a net worth of $1,700 dollars."[25]

Despite claims of economic recovery, the data provided by the Pew Research Center indicate that middle-income families haven't seen any income gains since the Great Recession. "The median wealth among upper-income families increased from $595,300 in 2010 to $639,400 in 2013. The typical wealth of middle-income families was basically unchanged in 2013—it remained at about $96,500 over the same period."[26] As a percentage of the total wealth in America, the wealthiest 1% owns today more than 50% of the wealth, while in 2014 the poorest half of the population owned just 2.5% of the country's wealth.

Moreover, the Great Recession has destroyed a significant portion of the wealth of the middle-income and lower-income families, particularly the wealth of the retired and older people; and the economic "recovery, has yet to arrive at their doors. Middle- and lower-income families' wealth levels in 2013 were comparable to where they were in the early 1990s. On the other hand, while most American families remain financially stuck close to the bottom of the wealth pyramid, the upper-income families have seen their median wealth double between 1983 and 2013; it rose from $318,100 in 1983 to $639,400 in 2013. The typical wealth level of these families increased each decade over the past 30 years."[27] In addition, the financial policy of the US Federal Reserve since 2008 has caused the poor to get poorer and the rich to get richer. As a consequence, the number of Americans on food stamps has gone from 32 to 46 million during the Obama administration.

Fortune magazine said on October 31, 2014, "There is no dispute that income inequality has been on the rise in the United States for the past four decades. The share of the total income earned by the top 1 percent of families was less than 10 percent in the late 1970s but now it exceeds 20 percent as of the end of 2012."[28] Joseph Lawler, quoting a report issued by economist Emmanuel Saez of Berkeley, wrote on June 6, 2015, "The share of total US income earned by the top 1 percent grew from 20.1 percent in 2013 to 21.2 percent in 2014, and that the top 10 percent share also rose, from 48.9 percent of all income in 2013 to 49.9 percent."[29]

On July 13, 2015, AlterNet published an article written by Larry Schwartz in which he lists what he calls "35 mind-blowing facts about inequality." In the following few paragraphs, I shall summarize the major facts and ideas contained in this article.[30]

Owing to the Arab oil embargo of 1973 and the Iranian Revolution of 1979, the international oil markets were interrupted and the world economy suffered a setback; as a consequence, the expansion of the American middle class was halted. And with the rise of Ronald Reagan's conservative revolution, argues Larry Schwartz, the long and painful contraction of the American middle class was accelerated. Cuts in corporate taxes, stagnant worker wages, the right-wing war on labor unions and corporate outsourcing of work overseas greased the wheels of the middle-class decline and the upper-class elevation. Cuts in taxes on the wealthy have resulted in lower government revenues, which has led to a reduction in budgets for most social programs. All of this has led to the current era of national and international income and wealth inequality that has been unparalleled since the 1920s.

Today, Schwartz says, "In 81 percent of the counties in America, the median income, about $52,000, is less than it was 15 years ago. This is despite the fact that the economy has grown 83 percent in the past quarter-century and corporate profits have doubled. And though American workers produce twice the amount of goods and services they produced 25 years ago, they get less of the economic pie."[31] According to the US Bureau of Labor Statistics, "77.2 million workers age 16 and older in the United States were paid at hourly rates, representing 58.7 percent of all wage and salary workers in 2014."[32] While American corporations paid workers lower wages as they made more profits, the amount of money they gave out in bonuses on Wall Street in 2014 was twice the amount that all minimum-wage workers earned in the country combined. Since the numbers of Wall Street workers is estimated at 168,000, the money these workers have received in bonuses alone is twice what the 77.2 million minimum wage Americans have received.[33]

The super rich Americans who represent .01% of the population take home about 6% of the entire national income, each earning around $23 million a year, some of them receiving over $1 billion a year. And despite the miserable life conditions of the poor, or maybe because of that, the bottom 90% own 73% of the total private debt. And owing to certain laws and policies, the poor are forced to accept the minimum wages paid to them; as a consequence, over 20% of American children live below the poverty line. This rate is higher than in almost all other developed countries.

Changing the economic philosophy and taxation rates during the Reagan and George W Bush administrations was probably the major factor behind these developments. While tax rates for the middle class have remained essentially unchanged since 1960, tax rates on the highest earning Americans have plunged from almost 70% in 1945 to around 35% today. Corporate tax rates have dropped from 30% in the 1950s to under 10% today. As a result, the United States had to borrow about $1 trillion in the first decade of the twenty-first century in order to pay for the tax cuts given to the richest American households who were earning over $250,000 a year, causing US public debt to exceed $19.9 trillion in June 2017.[34] In the middle of September, 2017, the debt reached $20.17 trillion. And with the debt rising, interest payments increase, the budget deficit widens, and allocations for social programs decrease, causing poverty to spread.

On the other hand, in 1965 CEOs earned about twenty-four times the amount of money the average worker earned; in 1980, they earned forty-two times as much; and today, CEOs earn 325 times the average American worker. In addition, the richest 400 Americans have more wealth, estimated at $2 trillion, than half of all Americans combined. At the same time, the average white American's median wealth is now twenty times higher ($113,000) than the average African American's wealth of ($5600) and eighteen times the Hispanic American's ($6300). In addition to these facts, Larry Schwartz says that the median wealth of the top 1% in 1962 was 125 times the average median wealth in America; in 2010, the median wealth of the top 1% reached 288 times the median wealth in America. And while the wealth of the top 1% dropped about 16% during the Great Recession, the wealth of the other 99% of Americans dropped 47%, causing the wealth of the rich to increase substantially compared to the median wealth in America.[35]

In the meantime, the financial industry's 2014 bonuses were double the combined earnings of all Americans who worked full time at the federal minimum wage. "Wall Street banks handed out $28.5 billion in bonuses to their 167,800 employees last year, up 3 percent over 2013. These annual bonuses are an extra reward on top of base salaries in the securities industry, which averaged $190,970 in 2013."[36] Sarah Anderson says, "Wall Street's bonus culture, we learned from the 2008 financial industry meltdown, creates an incentive for high-risk behaviors that endanger the entire economy,"[37] and the welfare of most members of society.

The *Washington Post* reported on May 12, 2016 that "The top five hedge fund managers made more than $1 billion each last year; the top 25 hedge fund managers made a combined $12.94 billion ... the average pay was $517.6 million."[38] Leading the list of those billionaires was Kenneth Griffin of Citadel, and Games Simons of Renaissance Technologies, each of whom made $1.7 billion in 2015. This equals the GDP of the Central African Republic, whose population is over 5 million people.

These data reveal that American inequality has reached the highest level in the world, causing upward mobility to become very difficult indeed. Meanwhile, primarily thanks to the Great Recession and the debt crisis, downward mobility has become easier than before. As the size of the middle class shrinks, more people join the ranks of the poor than those who join the ranks of the rich. In the meantime, racism, which has never left the American scene, is on the rise, causing discrimination to spread and be tolerated, especially against cultural and religious minorities of African, Latin American and Middle Eastern origin. The election of President Trump and his anti-migrants rhetoric is destined to poison intercommunity relations and deepen mutual fear and alienation.

The Washington Post reported on July 16, 2016 that "Pessimism about race relations in America is higher than it has been in nearly a generation ... in the aftermath of the mass shooting of police officers in Dallas and the high-profile police shooting deaths of two black men in Baton Rouge and suburban St. Paul, Minnesota, more than 6 in 10 adults say race relations are generally bad, and a majority say they are getting worse. Professor Peniel Joseph, the founding director of the Center for the Study of Race and Democracy at the Lyndon B. Johnson School of Public Affairs at the University of Texas, said; 'This is certainly the worst political climate that I've seen in my lifetime.'"[39]

As for economic growth, Jeff Voudrie says, "Sometimes we lose sight of the bigger picture when we focus on just one quarterly number. If we zoom out and look at what the actual economic growth [in America] has been going back to 2007, there is a disturbing trend that emerges."[40] Here is the annual GDP growth by year as provided by the above source:

2007	1.8%
2008	−0.3%
2009	−2.8%
2010	2.5%
2011	1.6%
2012	2.3%
2013	2.2%
2014	2.4%
2015	2.4%
2016	1.9% (this figure was published in 2017)

Based on these numbers, the average GDP growth of the US economy over the last ten years has been 1.4% per year. However, if we ignore the years of the Great Recession (2008 and 2009) and consider the last seven years only, the average annual GDP growth would be about 2.1%, hardly enough to create jobs for the new workers who enter the labor market annually. Though the United States is still the world's largest economy, says Trading Economics, "in the last two decades, like in the case of many other developed nations, its growth rates have been decreasing. In the 50's and 60's the average growth rate was above 4 percent, in the 70's and 80's it dropped to around 3 percent. In the last ten years, the average rate has been below 2 percent."[41] The four most important factors causing this decline are the rising public debt, the widening income and wealth inequalities, the decline in productivity, and the slowdown in consumer demand.

The Organizing Principles of American Life

As mentioned earlier, the philosophy that governs American life and culture and influences the attitude of most Americans is made up of three major components: democracy, capitalism, and exceptionalism. This section will focus on the American dream concept embodied in American exceptionalism, leaving democracy and capitalism to the next chapter. However, I believe, as do many other American intellectuals, that American exceptionalism is a fiction, from which a few myths and fallacies have emerged to shape the convictions of most white Americans and lead them to view themselves as different from most other peoples, and superior to them. Here are the major fallacies and myths:

1. America is the land of opportunity;
2. America encourages upward social mobility;
3. America expects personal responsibility;
4. America is a melting pot; and
5. America helps other nations and stands with the weak.

The American Dream The American Dream is "the belief that anyone, regardless of where they were born or what class they were born into, can attain their own version of success in a society where upward mobility is possible for everyone. The American dream is achieved through sacrifice, risk-taking and hard work, not by chance."[42] As for the tenets of the American Dream, the Investopedia says that "they can be found in the Declaration of Independence, which states, 'We hold these truths to be self-evident, that all men are created equal, that they are endowed by their Creator with certain unalienable Rights, that among these are Life, Liberty and the pursuit of Happiness.'"[43]

There is no doubt that America was probably the greatest land of opportunity in human history for almost two centuries; however, opportunities have been on the decline since the 1970s, not because America has become poor or lagging in creativity, but because the American political and economic systems have become less democratic and more corrupt and largely dysfunctional. In addition, the growing income and wealth inequalities have caused social mobility to decline. As a consequence, the number of people who are able to achieve the American dream and the number who still believe in it has decreased. The WashingtonsBlog.com reported in 2010 and again in 2014 that the American Dream has moved abroad. It reported that the President of the Federal Reserve Bank of New York, Bill Dudley, has said: "I don't think the issue of income mobility receives the attention it deserves. It is a foundational element for a well-functioning democratic society and provides evidence about the ability of an economy to provide opportunities for its citizens."[44] This means that lack of income mobility undermines democracy and limits the availability of economic opportunities.

President Reagan thought that one element of the American dream is "the opportunity to grow, create wealth, and build a better life for those who follow;"[45] But, at the time of Reagan, the Washingtonsblog.com says, "no one talked much about income inequality, which is a major determinant to the ability of every American to move up the income ladder and realize the American Dream. Though income mobility in America has remained relatively stable for years, it remains well below several other nations."[46] According to Stanford economist Raj Chetty, "The probability of moving from the bottom quintile to the top quintile is 7.5 percent in the United States, as compared to 11.7 percent in Denmark and 13.5 percent in Canada. So effectively the chance of achieving the American Dream is not the highest for children born in America. Bad government policy is responsible for the medieval, king-and-serf levels of income inequality and social mobility which are destroying our economy."[47]

Michael Snyder wrote on January 30, 2015; "We are the generation that gets to witness the end of the American Dream. For decades, the rest of the planet has regarded the United States as 'the land of opportunity' where almost anyone can be successful if they are willing to work hard. But now that has all changed. The 'American Dream' has been transformed into a very twisted game of musical chairs. With each passing year, more people are falling out of the middle class, and most of the rest of us are scrambling really hard to keep our own places. Something has gone horribly wrong, and yet Americans are very deeply divided when it comes to finding answers to our problems."[48] Snyder provides twenty-two numbers that prove the death of the American Dream; these are some of the important ones;

1. "A recent survey discovered that 55 percent of Americans believe that the American Dream either never existed or that it no longer exists. And while 55 percent of all Republicans still believe in the American Dream, only 33 percent of all Democrats do. Meanwhile, 59 percent of Americans believe that 'the American Dream has become impossible for most people to achieve.'"[49]
2. After adjusting for inflation, median household income has fallen by nearly $5000 since 2007; and the median wealth figure for middle-income families fell from $78,000 in 1983 to $63,800 in 2013. Moreover, figures reveal that 53% of Americans were considered to be middle income in 1967, but in 2015 only 43% of Americans were. According to the *New York Times*, the typical American household is now worth 36% less than a decade ago.
3. Traditionally, owning a home has been one of the key indicators that you belong to the middle class. Unfortunately, the rate of homeownership in the United States has been falling for seven years

in a row. Now, 52% of all Americans cannot even afford the house they live in. In 2008, 53% of Americans considered themselves to be middle class; by 2014, only 44% considered themselves to be middle class.

4. In 2008, 25% of all Americans in the eighteen- to twenty-nine-year-old age bracket considered themselves to be lower class; in 2014, 49% of all Americans in that age range considered themselves to be lower class; which means that the numbers of American youth feeling disadvantaged and neglected has doubled in just six years.
5. The number of Americans on food stamps has gone from 32 million in 2009 to 46 million in 2015. Right now, more than one out of every five children in America is on food stamps. According to the US Census Bureau, 65% of all American children are living in a home that receives some form of aid from the government.
6. More than 50% of all children in US public schools come from low income homes.
7. While 53% of all American workers make less than $30,000 a year, 62% of all Americans are currently living paycheck to paycheck, which means that the majority of Americans are unable to save any money for a house or even for an emergency.

Social Mobility Social mobility means the ability of individuals and families to move from one social class to a higher one. However, there are three types of mobility: upward mobility that leads to a higher social class, downward mobility that leads to a lower social class and horizontal mobility that leads people to move from one place to another. Mobility is a function of several factors; social and economic and political structures, government policies and political freedom, popular culture, and the distribution of income, wealth and power in society. Open, largely democratic societies are usually more conducive to upward mobility. In contrast, undemocratic and socially stratified societies are usually less conducive to upward mobility; people living in such societies are more likely to move downward rather than upward, especially in bad economic times and political instability dominated by conflict and war.

Income and wealth inequalities cause societies to be socially, economically and politically stratified. Owing to racism and the creation of cultural ghettos, American culture has become less open and conducive to social mobility. "In 1946, a child born into poverty had about a 50 percent chance of scaling the income ladder into the middle class. In 1980, the chances were 40 percent. A child born today has about a 33 percent chance."[50] According to *Fortune*, "Though much more productive and generally better educated, most of today's workers are falling farther and farther behind their parents' generation in most measures of economic well-being ... More than half of Americans will experience a year of poverty by the age of 60."[51]

Personal Responsibility Feeling personally responsible for your actions is a good thing to have in any society at any time; but feeling personally responsible for whatever happens to you is a bad thing. Such a feeling of personal responsibility defies rational thinking because it reflects failure to see what happens around you and what others might be doing to take advantage of you. As a result of feeling personally responsible, a large segment of the American people support the notion of having smaller government and favor reducing tax rates and public spending; they also support the right to carry arms. But personal responsibility that means smaller governments and reduced tax rates is a recipe for the perpetuation of the current income and wealth inequality, weak social mobility and loss of hope. Under such conditions, neither the American Dream nor the ideals of liberty, equality and opportunity will be protected.

Melting Pot Many writers and politicians claim that America is a melting pot; a place where all people living in America and others who will come to live in America will eventually meld together into a cohesive society. But neither experience nor reality supports this claim. Traditional values, religious fundamentalism and racism have made the melting pot more of a frying pan than anything else. People in America continue to be divided along ethnic, cultural, religious and ideological lines that run parallel to each other; a trend that causes more conflict than social peace and more exclusion than inclusion. In fact, the invention of the Internet has caused people in America and elsewhere to be divided into sociocultural groups, most of whom have formed cultural ghettos that determine how they live and think.

I coined the cultural ghetto concept in the late 1990s to describe the way most religious groups and minorities live and think and view themselves and others. Like-minded people sharing same ideas and values and convictions are able today to create spaces where they exchange ideas, promote their beliefs and share information they care about, planning action across oceans without having to see each other. The Internet and social media have facilitated the creation of cultural ghettos everywhere, at all levels, in every society. Since Immigrants tend often to be undereducated and living in strange lands, they usually lack adequate knowledge of the language, culture and laws of the land; and that leads most of them to live in small, mostly isolated communities, forming social and cultural ghettos that keep them largely isolated and relatively uninformed, and often poor.

Ghettos are divided into two types; traditional and cultural. A traditional ghetto is a place where people are usually forced to live in isolation owing to racism or discrimination or poverty that separates them from the rest of society. A cultural ghetto is a space rather than a place, where like-minded individuals choose to live socially and intellectually insulated from the rest of the society to which they belong. And while members of traditional ghettos in general work hard to get out of their ghettos as soon as possible, members of cultural ghettos tend to work harder to remain in their self-created ghettos, isolated from the rest of society; they also tend to resist new ideas and refuse to listen to outsiders, regardless of what they have to say.

The more members of cultural ghettos intensify their interactions with each other, the more narrow minded and intellectually isolated, and sometimes dangerously deranged, they become. Members of cultural ghettos are often able to hear themselves and like-minded people only, and listen to the echoes of the voices of their ancestors and heroes who died a long time ago. In America today, not only religious groups and minorities have formed cultural ghettos, but intellectuals on the right and the left have done the same thing; they have become a strange breed of human beings living in virtual communities that seek no advice from others, and have little or no interest in whatever views and ideas come from outside their closed world. Such people do not live in a "bubble" as the American media like to say; instead, they live in virtual ghettos that have no doors to break open.

By enabling alienated and excluded minorities to organize around traditional values and ideologies, modern communications systems and the Internet and social media have facilitated the creation of cultural ghettos in every rich and poor society. Members of such ghettos do not need to live together in one place to form a ghetto. By using modern means of communication, they are able to create virtual communities where a unique ghetto mentality develops and prevails to tie them together through shared values, attitudes, religious convictions and belief in conspiracy theories. All of these characteristics encourage members of cultural ghettos to hate others and to see them as enemies unworthy of trust or empathy. With the election of Donald Trump and the revival of racism, it is expected that the number of cultural ghettos in America will increase substantially and cause intercommunity relations to worsen.

Most religiously conservative groups and culturally narrow-minded ones have formed cultural ghettos in America, where they read books, exchange information, listen to radio talk shows and watch TV programs that deepen their convictions and perpetuate their isolation. Members of most cultural ghettos often feel oppressed and discriminated against, and seem convinced that social and cultural integration with society at large threatens their identities and ways of life, even their very existence as special communities. And this causes them to lose the ability to relate to the rest of society and the world in a rational manner. Since cultural ghettos formed by the political right and left in America are composed of educated people, members tend to feel superior to others; and this is what motivates them to seek no advice from anyone, encouraging them to conspire to remain on the top or regain control of power, while ignoring morality and ethics to achieve their goals.

US public opinion polls seem to suggest that most conservative and racist Americans are increasingly focusing on narrow issues not shared by the general public. Conservatives and the largely naive masses tend to watch TV programs that are biased in favor of what they believe in. A traveler in America's South cannot fail to notice that the culture of people in that region differs from the cultures in the West and the East. Since the South is largely ignored by the mass media, and because people there are subject to the influence of radio and TV talk shows promoting socially, politically and religiously conservative views, more people are becoming narrow minded; and narrow-mindedness is causing sociocultural and sociopolitical divides in America to deepen further.

Today, every state in the world is experiencing sociocultural segmentation; all sociocultural groups tend to be more interested in cultural issues that concern their members most, and less interested in national issues that concern the general public or the world. As a consequence, members of most cultural ghettos are less inclined to revolt against most issues, even issues they perceive as unfair; and this attitude in particular helps the rich and powerful elites to remain in control, thus causing bad situations to get worse day by day.[52]

America Helps Other People and Stands with the Weak The belief in being exceptional has encouraged most white Americans to ignore what is considered "bad" history, such as American involvement in slavery and colonialism, and past inhumane treatment of Native and African Americans.

Instead, white Americans tend to emphasize the positive role played by the Founding Fathers and the Constitution and US involvement in world affairs, especially during World War Two and through the Marshal Plan to rebuild the devastated economies of its European allies, and a few enemies. Based on this belief, Americans tend to view themselves as a nation committed to spreading democracy, freedom and respect for human rights; and providing political support, education and financial aid to strangers in need. As a consequence, most white Americans believe that America can do no wrong no matter what American political and military leaders and corporations do.

Today, American exceptionalism rests on the assumption that the US military is a force for good, when US military involvement in world affairs has largely been driven by imperialistic ambitions to expand US influence and dominate other nations. In fact, American pursuance of economic interests has led its military to commit untold crimes in Latin America, the Middle East and Asia. To view the extent of American imperialism, you need only to look at the magnitude of the crimes that the neoconservatives of the George W. Bush administration committed in Iraq, and review the destruction the hawks of the Bill Clinton and Obama administrations caused and continue to cause in Libya, Syria, Iraq and Yemen, often in coordination with their British and French allies. On May 12, 1996 Madeleine Albright, the first woman to be US secretary of state, was asked on CBS's *60 Minutes* about the 1991 American war on Iraq: "We have heard that half a million children have died. I mean, that's more children than died in Hiroshima. And, you know, is the price worth it?" Albright calmly replied: "I think this is a very hard choice, but the price—we think the price is worth it."[53]

Noam Chomsky reminds us of the results of the WIN/Gallup International poll on the question: "Which country do you think is the greatest threat to peace in the world today?" The United States was the champion by a substantial margin, winning three times the votes of second-place Pakistan. By contrast, says Chomsky, "the debate in American scholarly and media circles is about whether Iran can be contained; in view of the poll, it would seem that there are more pertinent questions: Can the United States be contained and other nations secured in the face of the U.S. threat?"[54] Chomsky says further that the reasons for the world's concerns are sometimes recognized in the United States, as when former CIA director (Michael Hayden), discussing Obama's drone campaign, conceded that "Right now, there isn't a government on the planet that agrees with our legal rationale for these operations, except for Afghanistan and maybe Israel." A normal country would be concerned by how it is viewed in the world. Certainly that would be true of a country committed to "a decent respect to the opinions of mankind. But the United States is far from being a normal country."[55]

Commenting on the results of the same international poll, the Washing tonsblog.com said, "The US has a history of lying to begin unlawful wars of aggression. In fact, this is business as usual when the history is comprehensively and objectively examined. US leaders lie about the above easily-verified facts, and then joke about killing millions. Their behavior is therefore best described as 'psychopathic' threat to world peace."[56] And to spread their lies, the mass media has become an instrument to falsify the consciousness of the masses and make lies sound credible and believable.

There is no doubt that the United States gives billions of dollars annually to other nations and provides grants to needy people and states. But most of the aid is military, not economic or humanitarian; and most US military aid goes to two states only, Israel and Egypt. Nevertheless, if one considers how much US dollars are being held by poor people around the world, tucked in pillows and mattresses rather than kept in savings accounts in banks, forfeited interest on those dollars exceeds all financial aid given by America to poor nations. Honesty is a virtue in short supply in America; politicians lie, the media lie, corporations lie, banks lie and the poor people who still believe in American exceptionalism lie to themselves: they continue to close their eyes, ears and minds in order to feel good about themselves and their country.

Notes

1. Noam Chomsky, Who Rules the World? p. 33.
2. American Exceptionalism; (http://rationalwiki.org/wiki/American_exceptionalism).
3. Ibid.
4. Ibid.
5. Ibid.
6. David From, Requiem for American Exceptionalism, *The Atlantic*. March 21, 2015 (http://www.theatlantic.com/politics/archive/2015/03/requiem-for-american-exceptionalism/388381/).
7. Monroe Doctrine, the Wikipedia.
8. Giovanni Arrighi, The Longest Twentieth Century; Verso, 2010, p. 50.

9. Webster's Encyclopedic Unabridged Dictionary of English Language, 1989, 384.
10. Ibid.
11. See Marco Magnani, Why the fall in oil prices is a problem for everyone, World Economic Forum, March 30, 2015.
12. Trade in Goods with China; United States Census; 2016 (https://www.census.gov/foreign-trade/balance/c5700.html).
13. The World Bank; Global Economic Prospects 2016, p. 8.
14. The World Bank; Global Economic Prospects 2016, p. 8.
15. Bureau of Labor Statistics; Labor force participation in the rate, August 5, 2016 (http://data.bls.gov/timeseries/LNS11300000).
16. Bureau of Labor Statistics, Economic News Release, April 1, 2016.
17. Bureau of Labor Statistics, Economic News Release; August 5, 2016 (http://www.bls.gov/news.release/jec.htm).
18. Kali Holloway; One of Trump's Biggest Campaign Promises Is Already Going in The Flames; AlterNet, April 3, 2017 http://www.alternet.org/news-amp-politics/us-jobs-flee-country-one-trumps-biggest-campaign-promises-already-going-down
19. There IS No B.S. Like The BLS; Investment Research Dynamics, June 2, 2017 http://investmentresearchdynamics.com/there-is-no-b-s-like-the-bls/
20. Michael Snyder, the Death of the American Dream in 22 Numbers, Washingtonsblog, January 30, 2015 (http://www.washingtonsblog.com/2015/01/death-american-dream-22-numbers.html).
21. Richard Fry and Rakesh Kochhar, America's wealth gab between middle income and upper income families is widest on record; Pew Research Center, December 17, 2014 (http://www.pewresearch.org/fact-tank/2014/12/17/wealth-gap-upper-middle-income/). http://www.salon.com/2016/04/28/robert_reich_wealth_inequality_is_even_more_devastating_than_inco
22. Ibid.
23. Robert Reich, Wealth inequality is even more devastating than income inequality, Salon, April 28, 2016.
24. Matt Bruenig, The top 10 percent of white families own almost everything, The American Prospect, September 8, 2014 (http://prospect.org/article/top-10-percent-white-families-own-almost-everything).
25. Antonio Moore, America's Financial Divide: The Racial Breakdown of US Wealth in Black and White, the Blog, June 28, 2016 (http://www.huffingtonpost.com/antonio-moore/americas-financial-divide_b_7013330.html).
26. Richard Fry and Rakesh Kochhar; America's wealth gap between middle-income and upper-income families is widest on record, Pew Research

Center; December 17, 2014 (http://www.pewresearch.org/fact-tank/2014/12/17/wealth-gap-upper-middle-income/).
27. Richard Fry and Rakesh Kochhar, America's wealth gap between middle-income and upper-income families is widest on record, the Pew Research Center; December 17, 2014 (http://www.pewresearch.org/fact-tank/2014/12/17/wealth-gap-upper-middle-income/).
28. Chris Matthews; Wealth inequality in America: It is worse than you think; Fortune, October 31, 2014 (http://fortune.com/2014/10/31/inequality-wealth-income-us/).
29. Joseph Lawler, Washington Examiner, June 6, 2015.
30. Larry Schwartz; 35 soul-crushing facts about American income inequality, AlterNet; July 13, 2015 (http://www.alternet.org/economy/35-mind-blowing-facts-about-inequality).
31. Ibid.
32. US Bureau of Labor Statistics; Characteristics of Minimum Wage Workers, 2014 (http://www.bls.gov/opub/reports/minimum-wage/archive/characteristics-of-minimum-wage-workers-2014.pdf).
33. Ibid.
34. US National debt clock http://www.usdebtclock.org/
35. Larry Schwartz; 35 soul-crushing facts about American income inequality, Salon, July 15, 2015 (http://www.salon.com/2015/o7/15-soul-cruching-facts-about-american-incom-inequality-partner/).
36. Sarah Anderson, Off the Deep End: The Wall Street Bonus Pool and Low-Wage Workers, Institute for Policy Studies, March 11, 2015.
37. Ibid.
38. Renae Merle, The five top-earning hedge fund managers each made over $1 billion in 2015, *the Washington Post*, May 12, 2016.
39. Krissah Thompson and Scott Clement, Majority of Americans think race relations are getting worse, The Washington Post, July 16, 2016.
40. Jeff Voudrie, Past 10 Years of US GDP Growth Reveal Disturbing Trend, Jeff Blog, March 2, 2015 (http://www.seeitmarket.com/past-10-years-us-gdp-growth-reveal-disturbing-trend-14156/).
41. United States GDP Annual Growth Rate1948–2016, Trading Economics (http://www.tradingeconomics.com/united-states/gdp-growth-annual).
42. American Dream; Investopedia (http://www.investopedia.com/terms/a/american-dream.asp).
43. Ibid.
44. Federal Reserve Bank President: The American Dream Has Moved Abroad.-WashingtonsBlog.com, April 11, 2016 (http://www.washingtonsblog.com/2016/04/new-york-fed-president-american-dream-moved-abroad.html).
45. Ibid.
46. Ibid.

47. Ibid.
48. Michael Snyder, The Death Of The American Dream In 22 Number; Freedom Outpost, February 3, 2015.
49. Ibid.
50. Larry Schwarz, 35 soul-crushing facts about income inequality, Sloan, July 15, 2015.
51. Chris Mathews, 4 things you didn't (but should) know about income inequality, Fortune, June 11, 2015 (http://fortune.com/2015/06/11/income-inequality/).
52. See, Mohamed Rabie, Saving Capitalism and Democracy, (Palgrave Macmillan, 2013) pp. 82–3.
53. Slavoj Zizek; Clinton, Trump and the triumph of global capitalism; In These Times, August 24, 2016 http://inthesetimes.com/article/19410/clinton-trump-and-the-triumph-of-ideology
54. Noam Chomsky, the greatest threat to world peace, In These Times, February 5, 2014. http://inthesetimes.com/article/16227/the_greatest_threat_to_world_peace_is_the_united_states
55. Ibid.
56. Carl Herman, 2014 Gallup International poll: US # 1 threat to world peace, Washingtonsblog.com March 21, 2014 (http://www.washingtonsblog.com/2014/03/2014-gallup-international-poll-us-1-threat-world-peace.html).

CHAPTER 6

Capitalism and Democracy

Capitalism is a system of economic production and management that served many nations well for more than 150 years. It helped economies grow and opened new opportunities for countless workers, as it raised labor productivity and improved the living standards of billions of people. However, capitalism was hijacked around the middle of the 1980s by the so-called "free market system," causing traditional capitalism to lose its dynamism and social mission. And under pressure from the United States, the International Monetary Fund (IMF) and the World Bank, most nations, particularly the underdeveloped ones, were forced to adopt the free market system. However, the prescribed "economic restructuring" programs devised by the IMF to fix the underperforming Third World economies have failed; and, as a consequence, they have caused life conditions in most countries to deteriorate, while causing the rich to get richer, the poor to get poorer and most countries to become dependent on foreign aid and loans to survive.

The Great Recession has exposed the limits of the free market system and its many shortcomings; it proved that the system was incapable of creating jobs for the unemployed or distributing the fruits of economic growth fairly among social classes and nations. In response to the Great Recession, all affected states used traditional economic tools to deal with the crisis. While some countries, such as the United States, used expansionist policies to revive their economies, others resorted to cutting spending and reducing budget deficits to restructure their economies and make them more competitive. However, as will be explained later, both policies have failed to

M. Rabie, *The Global Debt Crisis and Its Socioeconomic Implications*,
https://doi.org/10.1007/978-3-319-66215-2_6

achieve their objectives; instead, they have caused the debts of nations to skyrocket.

Owing to the positive role capitalism played in the life of Western societies for over a century, it became an integral part of the Western culture, particularly the American culture. And in order to keep the good name of capitalism, the promoters of free markets replaced the free market concept with "market capitalism," while emptying capitalism of its social and economic mission.

The capitalist system grew out of the institution of private property, which appeared with the development of agriculture some 10,000 years ago. As the agricultural age advanced and the state was created, trade expanded and economic and financial activities appeared, causing capital to play an important role in economic life. In the meantime, private property caused society to be divided into two social classes: landlords who owned most of the fertile land and were generally rich, and peasants and farm workers who owned little or no land and were generally poor. Land at the time was the major source of wealth and power, while poverty was the major cause of need and weakness. As a consequence, a socioeconomic gap slowly emerged in every agricultural society, separating the rich from the poor. Lacking wealth and power, the poor were forced to work for the rich in order to survive, while the rich were able to exploit and at times enslave the poor and keep them submissive. As the socioeconomic gap widened with the passing of time, the poor lost much of their freedom and social status, while the rich gained more freedom, power and social status at the expense of the poor; wealth enables its owners to gain more power, and power enables its owners to gain more wealth.

Since wealth usually translates into power, wealthy people are able to have more power and use it to influence change in their favor. In contrast, people who lack wealth have little or no power, and because of that they are less able to make a difference in their lives or the life of society. Therefore, wealth facilitates the acquisition of more power and power facilitates the acquisition of more wealth, making it very difficult for the poor to gain either wealth or power and climb the social ladder. On the other hand, people with power and wealth are usually able to have more freedom to do the things they like to do and engage in activities that enrich their lives; people with no wealth and power on the other hand usually have little freedom to do what they prefer to do, and are often forced to do whatever others ask them to do. Contrary to conventional wisdom, freedom in society is limited: when some have more freedom, others have less.

The inequalities that wealth and power usually create and perpetuate in society cause conflict to become a major characteristic of social relations, forcing the poor and weak to seek justice and struggle to gain freedom. Since tribal man lived his entire life in a classless society largely free of the imperatives of wealth and time, the concepts of freedom and justice had to wait for the agricultural age before they could be born and appreciated.

As agricultural tools, means of transportation and sea navigation technologies were developed during the last centuries of the agricultural age, trade expanded and capital began to play an active role in individual and societal life. Tools caused the productivity of land and labor to improve, and thus they enabled their owners to create and accumulate more wealth. During the industrial age, capital emerged as a major factor of production, enabling its owners to develop more efficient technologies, expand manufacturing, diversify economic activities and gain more wealth, power and freedom. However, as capitalists were gaining more power and freedom, the poor were losing whatever power and freedom they had in the past, causing their ability to create and accumulate wealth to be vastly curtailed. Nevertheless, the poor workers did not surrender to economic exploitation and suppression for long; they responded by organizing into labor unions, developing a consciousness of their own and revolting against the capitalist system and its masters; and this enabled them subsequently to reclaim most of their rights.

Tools, machines and production systems enable man to produce more of what he needs using the same amounts of whatever resources are required for production, or to produce the same amounts as before using less time and energy and fewer resources. In both cases, progress is made because man gets more of what he needs and likes to have; he gets more products or more time to engage in creative activities that enrich his life and the lives of others. Meanwhile, as man uses his tools, he learns how to make them more efficient, develops new ones and realizes the role of technology in societal life. This in turn causes technological knowledge to accumulate and enables man to produce more goods and services, change socially and culturally, and make more progress.

Evolution of Capitalism

The Industrial Revolution caused all industrial societies to experience wave after wave of socioeconomic and sociocultural change that led, within a century, to the transformation of all life conditions; the social, cultural and economic aspects of life, as well as the social, economic and political structures of society. In the meantime, new economic arrangements evolved slowly where capital was separated from labor, and fairly large economic organizations employing large numbers of workers emerged. These new production arrangements instituted new relationships between man and machines, capital and labor, worker and worker, urban and rural communities. The economic system that emerged from this process is what we call *capitalism*; a system characterized by dynamism and continuous transformation that "is unique in generating persistent and powerful tendencies to change."[1]

As manufacturing spread, the number of entrepreneurs, workers, suppliers, financiers, merchants, technicians, professionals, and consumers multiplied, causing the traditional state control over the economy to be weakened. As a consequence, the new capitalist class was able to gain more economic power and freedom of action at the expense of the state and the general public. But despite the loss of state control, the economy kept functioning, production kept increasing, and the efficiency of allocating natural and human resources and end products in society steadily improved.

Several factors contributed to making the capitalist system as efficient as it proved to be. The major ones are:

1. Competition among a large number of enterprises and suppliers of raw material;
2. A growing mass of consumers that caused the size of markets to expand;
3. A growing middle class tied to the production process of manufacturing;
4. Government regulation of financial products, exports and imports; and
5. Labor unions that convinced capitalists to pay workers fair wages and social benefits.

As the industrial age advanced, economic activities diversified and labor productivity increased, the capitalists slowly realized that they could not continue to expand production and accumulate more wealth unless markets continued to expand; and that requires the expansion of export markets and sharing some of the profits with their fortunate workers. As a result, capitalists, encouraged and supported by the new industrial state, spearheaded the inhumane colonialist enterprise and accepted some of the demands of their working people. Therefore, capitalists felt obliged by self-interest to pay their workers more money in order to become active consumers of whatever they produced, and enthusiastic supporters of colonialism.

In the meantime, the desire to industrialize faster and gain more wealth and power led the industrial European states to compete for markets and sources of raw materials. Competition fostered colonialism, which is an exploitative economic enterprise and a repressive political system in which all active members of the colonialist power participated, making capitalists, politicians, workers and most members of the industrial society partners in the colonialist enterprise. In the meantime, colonialism helped capitalism to become more efficient in allocating resources, diversifying activities, raising productivity, creating national wealth and distributing the fruits of its actions in ways that benefited most members of society. However, capitalism made both recession and inflation an integral part of the economic system; thus causing capitalist states to experience recurring recessions, inflation and financial crises that led to widening the socioeconomic gap between rich and poor.

As the poor became aware of their social status, they began to organize and demand change, asking for a larger share of the economic pie. But no matter how much the poor get, they always feel worse off when they compare themselves with their rich neighbors. Awareness of the nature and extent of the socioeconomic and sociopolitical gaps separating them from the rich always leads them to feel deprived, which often causes conflict to arise in society. While this awareness grew slowly and incrementally during the last century, it grew faster and became more pronounced with the development of the infomedia process in the 1990s and beyond. Infomedia has made it possible for all people on all sides of the wealth and power divides to know how the rich and poor live on the other sides.

In the wake of the Great Depression of the 1930s, and the emergence of Marxism as a competing political and economic system in the Soviet Union, Western capitalist states felt threatened from the inside and outside. While their economic system was causing income and wealth inequalities to rise and poverty to spread, and financial and economic crises to occur frequently, communism's premise of class conflict and promise of classless society convinced them to take action to face both challenges. As a consequence, states enacted new laws and regulations to limit the freedom of corporations and strengthen state oversight of banks and financial markets, and raised taxes on the rich. States also created welfare systems to provide the necessary services to their citizens, such as comprehensive health care and free education in most European countries, help for the poor and needy in America, and programs managed by the state and corporations to guarantee secured retirement for the elderly.

These actions were instrumental in transforming capitalism from an exploitative system to an institution serving the interests of society, which led capitalism to become an engine building the national wealth of the capitalist state. By the end of the 1970s, however, the system began to fracture under the influence of the free market philosophy and the economic and financial policies of the Reagan administration. As a consequence, the constructive societal role which capitalism played during the previous two generations came to an end, causing income mobility to retreat. "One thing that is clearly not maximized by free markets is equality."[2]

Panitch and Gindin argue that "US grand strategy during the Cold War required not only containing communism but also taking active measures to open up the world politically, culturally, and, above all, economically."[3] While this is largely true, the communist challenge had made such action an imperative. The opening up of world markets had two objectives: to spread American hegemony over as many regions of the world as possible, and to demonstrate to other people the economic, scientific and military achievements of capitalism.

As Western capitalist states were making more economic, technological, scientific and cultural progress in the second half of the twentieth century, and becoming militarily more powerful, most other nations were falling behind economically, scientifically and militarily. Communism and its socialist system, which was born in Europe in reaction to the exploitative nature of capitalism, could not match the capitalistic states' achievements; and as a result, communism could not survive for long. At the end of the 1980s it collapsed and the Soviet Union disintegrated, signaling the failure of socialism as a system to allocate available resources efficiently and distribute economic benefits fairly.

Adam Smith was the first philosopher to understand the dynamics of an industrial economy and its social implications, and also the first to observe that economic progress brings with it income inequality. But this consequence was defended at the time because wealth in the absence of inequality would lose its meaning, and the incentive for hard work would disappear. If the wealth of a nation were to be evenly divided among its members, hardly anyone would be tempted to work for another, and contentment rather than unfulfilled expectations would govern cultural attitudes. In other words, total equality hinders sociocultural transformation and retards economic progress. In contrast, wide income and wealth disparities lead to socioeconomic divisions, sociocultural segmentation and economic marginalization, all of which divide society into conflicting groups and cause economies to slow down.

Evolution of Democracy

Democracy is commonly defined as "a form of government in which the supreme power is vested in the people or in their elected agents under a free electoral system."[4] In 1863, US President Abraham Lincoln defined democracy as "government of the people, by the people, for the people."[5] This means that democracy is a system of governance that regulates the relationship between the state and the public in ways that enable the governed to elect their governors and participate in making the decisions that affect their lives, while empowering them to hold their representatives and state officials accountable for their actions.

However, democracy is not a stable state of political affairs; it is rather an evolving political process that affects the dominant cultural values and attitudes and worldviews of people, and is affected by people's actions and the general social and economic conditions of society. Since cultures are products of people living together in one place for generations under changing life conditions, the institutions of democracy are shaped by the historical experiences of nations and the movement of societies from one civilization to another. And because different nations have had different experiences and live under different economic and environmental conditions, democracy expresses itself in varied forms and in different arrangements.

The origins of democracy and its basic principles of equality, justice and accountability may be attributed to organized religion. Since its inception in ancient times, religion has declared that every person must answer to a higher authority or a god. The three monotheistic religions of Judaism, Christianity and Islam state that no one is exempt from the commandments of God; and all people are equal in his presence. These principles led initially to an amelioration of the status of slaves and undermined the rationale for absolutism of temporal authority. However, religion was unable to stop absolutism or prevent exploitation or slavery; it even allowed its teachings to legitimize the tyrannical rule of dictators who violated people's rights with impunity. To legitimize absolutism, many kings and emperors in older times embraced religion and claimed to be gods, or related to the gods, or gods' representatives on earth authorized to rule in their names. By so doing, they were often able to use religion to unify people, consolidate power and establish dynasties that survived, in certain instances, for centuries.

As nation-states began to emerge in Europe in the sixteenth century, the new rulers discovered that they did not have enough power to challenge Church authority and consolidate their political positions without the active support of the merchant class and city dwellers. While the rulers needed the financial support of merchants, city dwellers were more interested in protecting their social and political freedoms, for which most of them had paid a heavy price under the feudal system. But as rulers, merchants and city dwellers were cooperating to achieve shared goals, new ideas, technologies and economic activities emerged to pose a challenge to both the theocratic state and the nation state. "This challenge was first felt most poignantly by the Church, to the benefit of the nascent nation-states. But it would not be long before the despotic monarchies that had replaced the earlier communes would also lose their power, beset and overthrown by the new image of man, and not God, as residing at the center of things."[6]

The Renaissance in Europe was an era of fundamental change; it paved the way for the transition of societies from the agricultural age to the industrial age. It was an era of trade expansion, economic diversity, geographical discoveries, religious reform, political restructuring, and scientific developments and innovations. Kings and princes during this era were interested in consolidating their political powers, while traders and city dwellers were interested in protecting their freedoms and economic interests. As a result, representatives of both forces joined hands to fight and defeat the Church and its political authority and economic doctrine. Since the new state could no longer claim or wish to claim a religious mandate, it had to have the implicit, if not the explicit, consent of its citizens to gain legitimacy and rule.

Therefore, the interest of the merchant class in maintaining economic freedom, the interest of city dwellers in gaining religious and social freedom, and the interest of rulers in building national armies combined to lay the foundations for the development of both capitalism and democracy. Describing the dynamics of change at the time, Paul Kennedy says, "There exists a dynamic for change, driven chiefly by economic and technological developments which then impact upon social structures, political systems, military power and the position of individual states and empires."[7]

Within a century of the dawn of the Industrial Revolution, a new society with a new culture and a new economy emerged in all industrialized countries. The new society had three social classes, each one being based more on interests and less on values and religious beliefs: an industrial working class, a middle class and a capitalist class. Although relationships between all classes were antagonistic and uncooperative, the middle and capitalist classes shared interests in expanding political and economic liberty. To protect this liberty, all classes accepted political plurality and participated in the development of democracy. Economic liberty, therefore, served as a catalyst for the development of both capitalism and democracy, which grew together and eventually became mutually reinforcing.

The intellectual origins of modern democracy are to be found in the political philosophy of the seventeenth and eighteenth centuries in the West. The leading political thinkers of the time emphasized the responsibility of governments to protect individual rights from both capital and religion. The separation of religion and state in the middle of the seventeenth century led to the recognition that individuals have legitimate rights that no power should violate. The idea then was how to limit state and religion intervention in people's lives, particularly in their pursuit of material gain and happiness, which meant freedom and wealth. The state was also happy to see people concentrate on material gain rather than on religion, which still represented a threat to the secular state. But when the state attempted later to reclaim Church powers and curtail people's freedoms, it was faced with popular uprisings that forced it to retreat. Democracy, supported by a vibrant middle class and a productive capitalist system, continued to make progress and gain legitimacy well into the twentieth century.

Yet, despite the convergence of these factors, the emergence of a conscious middle class in the nineteenth century was probably the most significant development as far as capitalism and democracy were concerned. The middle class soon became a major force contributing to industrial diversification, economic expansion, the development of national cultures and advancing democracy. While capitalism provided the middle class with the economic opportunity to grow, democracy provided it with an effective tool to protect its freedom and economic interests under the supervision of the state.

The development and control of a national economy were meant to provide the state with the resources to build and maintain a national army, finance its activities and programs, promote a national culture, and please and appease citizens. But the capitalist system proved to be beyond state control, because capitalism is driven by self-interest, not national interest, and is guided by powerful market forces that seem to be elusive and protective of their independence. "Capitalism is a process of creative destruction, as it builds, it destroys, causing conditions on the ground to experience one wave of change after another."[8]

Democracy's Relationship to Capitalism

As capitalism was growing and trade expanding, corporations needed state protection to expand abroad and invest in industries such as oil exploration, mining and infrastructural projects. In the meantime, the state was interested in expanding its influence to other realms, and the Church was interested in "civilizing the uncivilized" peoples of the world. As a result, the politics of nationalism, religion and capitalism worked together to give birth to the colonialist enterprise and enable it to commit heinous crimes in many parts of the world. It was capitalism, with its quest to control natural resources and markets that made colonialism and imperialism global phenomena. For example, the British and American oil companies would not have been able to control the oil resources of Iran, Kuwait, Iraq and Saudi Arabia without US government support.

But despite the fact that "capitalism and national states grew up together, and presumably depended on each other in some way, yet capitalists and centers of capital accumulation often offered concerted resistance to the expansion of state power."[9] Therefore, as corporations got stronger and wealthier, they moved swiftly to control the political process. It did not take long before capitalists and corporations were able to achieve societal pre-eminence, using deeds rather than words, and employing money and lobbying and the mass media to reach their goals.

Money, without which neither the state nor politics could function and meet desired goals, was used by the rich to manipulate politics and buy politicians, making elections, particularly in the United States, an unequal contest between those who have money and others who do not. Senator Richard Durbin admitted in 2010 that the barons of the banking sector "frankly own" the US Congress.[10] The triumph of economics over politics in the twentieth century represents a setback for democracy and its principles of liberty and equality, as well as for capitalism and its social role in fostering the national economy and the middle class. As a result, the political process lost its independence and ability to function freely, allowing money to determine what is fair and what is not, and what is in the national interest and what is not.

While politics was losing its independence and objectivity owing to the influence of money, the state was losing its capacity to care for its citizens. In the meantime, the public was losing its sovereignty and ability to influence change in its favor; it could no longer resist the temptations of the new luxuries of life and avoid debt and manipulation by the media. Moreover, capitalism, supported by a conservative political movement in the 1980s, began to destroy labor unions, causing the middle class to shrink and lose much of its economic power and political influence. "It was unions that made the American economy work for the middle class, and it was their later decline that turned the economy upside-down and made it into a playground for the business and financial classes."[11] And with the decline of labor unions, democracy was weakened and its promises of fairness and equal opportunity were shattered.

During the first decades of the twentieth century, which witnessed the Bolshevik Revolution of 1917, the socialist system instigated by Marxist ideas posed a serious threat to capitalism and its rationale, compelling Western states in general to enact progressive tax laws, design and implement new social programs to expand public education, empower workers and create a welfare state to help the poor, the sick, the unemployed and the elderly. Both the upper and middle classes at the time provided, quite willingly, the money needed to finance the welfare state because they feared socialism and the sociopolitical order it envisioned. Decades later, however, neither the middle class nor the upper class was willing to finance welfare programs, because the financial price of such programs was increasing year after year, and communism was failing and no longer feared. In order to accomplish their objectives of lower taxes and limited social programs, the upper and, to some extent, the middle classes began to call for smaller governments, less state intervention in public life, fewer financial regulations and more restrictions on immigration. Money and the media were used to manipulate public opinion, distort facts and pressure the executive and legislative branches of government to accommodate the desires of the rich.

These were changes that paved the way for a new culture based on individualism, where individuals and corporations have rights but few social responsibilities. In 2010, the US Supreme Court ruled in "Citizens United vs. Federal Election Commission" and again in 2014 that individuals and corporations have the right to spend on election campaigns; thus giving wealthy individuals and corporations the right to give as much money as they wished to finance campaigns. But by easing campaign restrictions, the court's ruling helped open the floodgates to massive corporate spending in the presidential election campaign of 2012, the congressional election campaign of 2014 and the presidential election campaign of 2016.

Commenting on the Supreme Court rulings, Senator Charles Schumer said, "This in itself is a small step, but another step on the road to ruination; it could lead to interpretations of the law that would result in the end of any fairness in the political system as we know it."[12] Fred Wertheimer, president of Democracy 21 said, "The Supreme Court majority continued on its march to destroy the nation's campaign finance laws, which were enacted to prevent corruption and protect the integrity of our democracy. The court re-created the system of legalized bribery that existed during the Watergate days."[13] Senator John McCain said, "I am concerned that today's ruling may represent the latest step by a majority of the court to dismantle entirely the longstanding structure of campaign finance law erected to limit the undue influence of special interests on American politics."[14]

The 1980s witnessed the triumph of conservative economic thinking and social ideas promoted by the upper and middle classes under US President Ronald Reagan, British Prime Minister Margaret Thatcher and German Chancellor Helmut Kohl. A "culture of contentment" soon emerged to tie the wealthy capitalists, the media barons and most public personalities, members of the upper and middle class, and the comfortable among the retired elderly, and empower them to dominate the political scene. John Kenneth Galbraith described this alliance as "a new, loosely connected group of unequal individuals sharing an interest in preserving the status quo and ignoring the poor, the common good, and the future for the sake of the present."[15] As a consequence, the old capitalist system was replaced by a free market system designed to serve the interests of the rich at the expense of everyone else.

Under the influence of the free market system, and because of the pressure applied by special interest groups, the Western welfare state began to retreat, and social responsibility toward the poor, the elderly and even the nation began to lose its appeal. "The fortunate and the favored, it is more than evident, do not contemplate and respond to their own longer-run well being. Rather, they respond, and powerfully, to immediate comfort and contentment. This is the controlling mood."[16] Because of this mood, poverty and all of the social ills associated with it, such as crime, homelessness, drug addiction, violence and disrespect for human life, spread slowly, and gradually became endemic in America and other parts of the world.

In the 1950s, leaders of the capitalist system fought fiercely with the political establishment to gain more freedom, urging governments to give special attention to the economic elite's desires. One of capitalism's stern advocates at the time, banker J.P. Morgan, said before a Senate subcommittee that "If you destroy the leisure class you destroy civilization." Morgan defined the leisure class as "all those who can afford to hire a maid."[17] But by equating the leisure class with civilization, he seems to have said that no one in society is civilized and thus counts other than the rich. By the end of the 1980s, the leisure class had triumphed, and the gap that separated it from the rest of society had become not only socioeconomic but sociocultural as well. A decade later, the leisure class had become the most dominant power in America, controlling three major societal processes: economic, political and infomedia.

In the wake of the dramatic ending of the Cold War in 1989, democracy and capitalism emerged as the most promising political and economic systems, if not the only acceptable ones. They appealed to the great majority of people everywhere, and particularly to those who had lived the longest and suffered the most under the authoritarian rule of communist regimes and Third World dictators. For decades before the collapse of communism, however, the Western media was busy exposing most people of the world to Western cultural values, lifestyles and standards of living. As a result, most people living under communism and dictatorships had become aware of the promise of democracy and the economic achievements of capitalism years before the end of the Cold War. As communism collapsed under the weight of its failure, the largest international wave of democracy followed; switching to capitalism was also a part of that wave. By the beginning of the twenty-first century, almost every state in the world had become a legitimate democracy, a democratizing state or a state claiming to have established democratic principles.

Nevertheless, the last two decades have witnessed a reversal of these trends. The reversal has come about because of several factors, noteworthy among them being:

1. A misguided US foreign policy particularly in the Middle East;
2. The failure of the economic restructuring programs imposed on many poor nations by the World Bank and the IMF;
3. Senseless US wars that caused the destruction of Iraq, Syria, Libya and Yemen, killed millions of people and transformed these four states into failed states;
4. Western appeasement of Third World dictators in the name of security;

5. The spread of radicalism and terrorism in many parts of the world; and
6. The revival of racism in the West in general.

The last two developments, it must be noted, have come as a result of the first four. While dictators, authoritarian rulers and hardcore ideologues have continued to resist democracy, accepting only cosmetic changes that lack substance, they welcomed the economic plans devised by the World Bank and the IMF. The acceptance of certain democratic changes was driven by a need to please the West so it continues to provide financial aid, and not by a belief in capitalism or freedom. Such rulers still hope that the economic restructuring programs will enable market capitalism to deliver on its promise before political reforms take root and institute effective democracy. But no economic restructuring plan can succeed without sociopolitical restructuring, and no genuine sociocultural transformation can take place without freedom. Freedom, equality, social justice and education are the essence of democracy, and the basic conditions for societal development and progress.[18]

Today, nations that are industrialized or industrializing are either democratic or in an advanced stage of being democratic; nations that are agricultural or living in pre-industrial times are either authoritarian or largely undemocratic. Societies that live in mature industrial and post-industrial ages are either nonideological or moving away from ideology; societies that live in the pre-industrial age are either ideological, experiencing a revival of ideology, or still attached to outdated ideological notions. Since all societies are being divided into subsocieties along sociocultural lines, each state has one group or more that lives in a different civilization and experiences ideological revival. The American South is a good example of a subsociety living in a largely different age and experiencing religious revival and racism.

The triumph of economics over politics in the 1980s has made the political process a mere tool in the service of the economic elite. Democracy, consequently, has lost its ability to do the things it was supposed to do; it has lost its vision as well as its mission. Decades ago, Walter Lippmann described American democracy by saying, "In the cold light of experience, he [the private citizen] knows that his sovereignty is a fiction. He reigns in theory, but in fact he does not reign. Contemplating himself and his actual accomplishments in public affairs, contrasting the influence he exerts with the influence he is supposed to exert according to democratic theory, he must say of his sovereignty what Bismarck said of Napoleon III, at distance it is something, but close to it, it is nothing at all."[19] Eric Alterman says, "When attempting to determine why the people's will is so frequently frustrated in our system, one must turn first and foremost to the power of money; the system is rigged, and it's rigged against us."[20]

The most serious challenge facing all democracies today is the gradual deterioration of the status of the middle class. What makes this issue very serious is the fact that governing is increasingly being monopolized by a small rich, self-centered and largely corrupt class. And because this class uses money and the media to manipulate people and stay in power, democracy continues to fail people and lose their support. As money began to control politics in the major capitalist societies, the middle class began to suffer one setback after another. And as workers were pressured to abandon labor unions, industrial jobs were shipped to other countries; as a result, incomes could not keep pace with rising costs of living and public trust in governments declined. A Gallup survey of public opinion conducted in 2015 indicated that public trust in the three branches of the US government had reached unprecedented lows. While trust in the presidency declined to 33%, confidence in Congress sunk to 8%; and in the Supreme Court to 32%. Trust In public schools, banks, newspapers and big business was 31, 28, 24 and 21%, respectively.[21]

An analysis of public trust in the US government conducted by Pew Research Center says, "Trust in government often, though not always, moves in parallel with satisfaction in the overall state of the nation. Over the course of the past half-century, the two measures have mapped very closely. Currently, just 19% say the government is run for the benefit of all—and an identical percentage says they can trust the federal government just about always or most of the time. The long-term erosion of public trust in the federal government has been mirrored by a steep decline in the belief that the government is run for the benefit of all Americans."[22]

The middle class in the democratic West in general and the United States in particular have become like a runner who runs on a fast-moving treadmill. He runs faster and faster just to stay in place and avoid falling off the track. But struggling to stay in place, while others keep marching forward accumulating more wealth and gaining more power, causes the middle class to become exhausted and disoriented. The unfortunate who are vulnerable because of old age, poor health, inadequate income, lack of decent education or minority status are falling off the treadmill and joining the growing ranks of the relatively poor, causing poverty, need and hunger to spread and deepen their roots.

In 2014, an estimated 48.4 million Americans (15.3 %) were living in poverty; 15.5 million, representing 21.1% of all children under the age of eighteen were living in poverty; and 4.6 million seniors aged sixty-five and older were in poverty. Even these relatively high numbers have been disputed by many economists and organizations as being understated, because the old poverty guidelines developed by the government do not reflect the actual cost of living.[23]

There is no doubt that there are millions of Americans who qualify today as members of a middle class based on their incomes. However, what makes a group of people a social class is not income only; people need to meet four conditions to form a class and to be able to act as such. They have to have a middle-class income, shared interests, similar values and outlooks, and, most importantly, a shared consciousness. People who are considered members of the US middle class today lack most of these requirements; they work for different and often competing branches of government, business enterprises and not-for-profit organizations. In addition, some of them are highly educated, sharing similar lifestyles and ambitions with the rich, and others are hardly educated but share similar conservative values with advocates of free markets and smaller governments. Moreover, many of the American middle class are members of the armed forces and retired army, security and intelligence officers who tend to pursue interests and have worldviews that differ, sometimes significantly, from those shared by most other members of the middle class.

Nevertheless, capitalism and democracy have produced many positive results that include countless scientific discoveries and technological innovations and cures for diseases, as well as unprecedented economic growth; they also produced high standards of living, tolerance and cultural diversity, social and political freedom, respect for human rights and environmental protection. However, almost all of these accomplishments have lately come under attack by the conservatives. Greed and lack of social responsibility that drive the rich to squeeze the poor and escape paying a fair share of taxes on the one hand, and the rapidly declining fortunes of the middle class, and apathy of the poor on the other, have made both systems of market capitalism and political democracy unable to serve the interests of the public.

All systems, regardless of their nature and objectives and achievements, have lives of their own that are destined to end one day. Such lives could be short or long, stagnant or dynamic, productive or unproductive, dull or interesting, but never perpetual. As they approach their limits, all systems come to be in need of reform. While significant modifications may be sufficient in the short run, fundamental restructuring or replacement is inevitable in the long run; no social system or idea or roadmap or organization can escape this fate. "Since the onset of the first industrial revolution, human institutions have typically had a lifespan of around 70 years. In the first generation, the elite build the institutional structures needed to meet the economic challenges of their time. The second generation maintains them as best as they can. And the third generation of the elite, which more often than not is corrupt to the bone, merely aims to live as well as it can off the existing system, which by now has become utterly ossified."[24]

Democracy in general and American democracy in particular has largely become a game played by the affluent for their own benefits and according to rules they developed to exclude others. "The rich and comfortable have influence and money. And they vote. The concerned and the poor have numbers, but many of the poor, alas, do not vote. There is democracy, but in no slight measure, it is a democracy of the fortunate."[25] The democracy that President Lincoln described as being "government of the people, by the people, for the people," has become "government of the rich, by the rich, for the rich;" and therefore the democracy people enjoyed years ago has become a "*monocracy.*"

Since the traditional middle class in the West is slowly but methodically being dismantled, and because the traditional political party has lost a significant portion of its role in society, the two major pillars of democracy are crumbling and cannot be saved without drastic change. Moreover, current trends of sociocultural, socioeconomic and sociopolitical changes seem to indicate that the transition to the age of knowledge is creating new situations that serve the interests of the media, economic monopolies, and the rich and powerful only; and that these changes are least conducive to the revival of the middle class or political plurality. What we have today and expect to have more of in the near future is sociocultural diversity, not sociopolitical plurality, a weaker not stronger middle class, a more biased not fairer media, and more discrimination and bigotry as opposed to less tolerance and understanding.

While the actual and perceived conflict between socioeconomic classes is largely interest-related, conflict between sociocultural groups is largely value-related. The first type of conflict lends itself to compromise solutions, while the second does not, which usually precipitates deeper animosities and conflicts. Democracy, the mechanism to manage and resolve conflict of interests, will have to be restructured to produce a new model capable of reconciling conflicts of values as well as conflicts of interests. Therefore, sociocultural plurality in the new democratic model will have to play a major role in politics beside traditional socioeconomic plurality, making power subject to sharing by all groups and classes. Otherwise, democracy will be left to the rich and powerful to monopolize, excluding everyone else.

Although the democratic system as a whole still enjoys legitimacy in the West, history teaches us that no state or system of governance could continue to govern and enjoy public support without meeting, at the very least, the basic needs and minimum expectations of citizens, which tend to grow and change continuously. Today, owing to the evolving needs and expectations of people, all democratic regimes are facing increasing challenges from the inside that disrupt political stability and affect national economies in negative ways. Greece, Spain, France and Italy give examples of democratic states under stress.

Two major factors are helping the US democratic system to maintain its legitimacy: first, lack of an alternative system of governance with a proven record of fairness; and second, the transformation of the democratic and market capitalism concepts into an ideology that has become an integral component of American popular culture. This transformation was engineered by the conservatives of the Republican Party, promoted by the mass media and financed by America's business elite. Politicians of all shades and colors who never stop talking about the greatness of America, the "American Dream" and "American exceptionalism" have led this transformation. Therefore, any attempt to restructure the American political or economic system has to take culture into consideration and the need to transform it.

Since the state came into existence thousands of years ago, men and women everywhere have continued to struggle to define and claim their rights. People have used religion, magic, philosophy, manipulation, science and appeal to power to gain some of what they thought to be theirs; at times they had to resort to violence to attain their legitimate rights. But despite the many sacrifices and great achievements in this endeavor, the struggle for freedom, liberty, social justice and respect for human rights is still incomplete; it may never be completed. Democracy was one of our notable achievements on the road to freedom and social justice and equal opportunity. And while it succeeded as a sociocultural value, its success as a political system leaves a lot to be desired. As a cultural value, democracy must be embraced and helped to deepen its roots in all societies and in all cultures.

As a political system, democracy needs to be restructured to regain relevance and be able to carry out its noble mission.

Notes

1. Robert Heilbroner: *21st Century Capitalism*, 1993, 27.
2. Weinberg: "Utopias," *The Atlantic Monthly*, June 2000, 108.
3. Leo Panitch and Sam Gindin; The Making of Global Capitalism, Verso, 2013, p. 11.
4. Webster's Encyclopedic Unabridged Dictionary of English Language, 1989, 384.
5. Abraham Lincoln; Abraham Lincoln on Line. http://www.abrahamlincolnonline.org/lincoln/speeches/gettysburg.htm
6. Charles Van Doren, A History on Knowledge, 158.
7. Paul Kennedy, The Rise and Fall of the Great Powers, 439.
8. Lester C. Thurow, "Building Wealth," *The Atlantic Monthly,* June 1999, 62.
9. Charles Tilly; Big structures, large processes, hug corporations; Russell Sage, 1984, p. 140.
10. Michael Kazin, *The Nation*, September 6, 2010, 17.
11. Kevin Drum, Plutocracy Now, *Mother Johns*, March/April 2011, 24.
12. Bill Mears and Tom Cohen, Supreme Court allows more private money in election campaigns, CNN, April 2, 2014 (http://www.cnn.com/2014/04/02/politics/scotus-political-donor-limits/).
13. Ibid.
14. Ibid.
15. See John Kenneth Galbraith, *The Culture of Contentment*, 1–13.
16. Ibid.
17. Quoted in Arthur M. Schlesinger, Jr., The Coming of the New Deal, 479.
18. See Mohamed Rabie, A Theory of Sustainable Sociocultural and Economic Development, Palgrave Macmillan, 2016.
19. Quoted in Richard Harwood, "The Messenger Shouldn't Bear all the Blame," *The Washington Post,* Feb. 15, 1996, A 21.
20. Eric Alterman, Kabuki Democracy, *The Nation,* September 2, 2010, 12.
21. Jeffry M. Jones, confidence in US institutions still below historical norms, Gallop; January 15, 2015 (http://www.gallup.com/poll/183593/confidence-institutions-below-historical-norms.aspx).
22. Beyond trust: how Americans view their government, November 23, 2015. http://www.people-press.org/2015/11/23/1-trust-in-government-1958-2015/

23. Hunger and Poverty Facts and Statistics, Feeding America. http://www.feedingamerica.org/hunger-in-america/impact-of-hunger/hunger-and-poverty/hunger-and-poverty-fact-sheet.html?gclid=COa36t6y5M4CFUxahgod9NsNiA?referrer=https://www.google.com/
24. Charles Gave; The collapse of the left, Gavekal; September 16, 2016. http://research.gavekal.com/search-result?search=&fr=&to=&au%5B%5D=7083&selectItemau%5B%5D=7083&at%5B50%5D=50&items_per_page=
25. John Kenneth Galbraith, the Good Society, 1997, p. 8.

CHAPTER 7

Market Capitalism and Materialism

In the second half of the eighteenth century a new way of organizing manufacturing and producing things began to emerge in England, giving birth to the Industrial Revolution, which ushered in a new wave of change that transformed all aspects of life in every industrial state. Industrial workers were no longer free to determine their work hours and how to perform their work; tasks were assigned, working hours were specified, regulations were imposed and hierarchical relationships within the workplace were enforced. For the first time in history, the worker could own neither the place of his work, nor the means of production, nor the end products he produced. His only source of income was his labor, and his labor and time were the only commodities he could trade. Industrial man was in fact transformed through manufacturing and production relations into a machine, causing work to become the focal point of his life. The economic system that emerged from this process is what we call capitalism.

Developments precipitated by the Industrial Revolution caused manufacturing to spread rapidly and the number of firms, suppliers, workers, financiers, entrepreneurs and consumers to multiply in decades. As a consequence, traditional state control over economic activities was vastly weakened. But despite the loss of state control, the economy kept functioning, production kept increasing, the efficiency of the allocation of resources and the distribution of goods and services in society steadily improved, and capitalists kept accumulating more wealth. Consequently, it was concluded that the market had an "invisible hand" that guided its

M. Rabie, *The Global Debt Crisis and Its Socioeconomic Implications*,
https://doi.org/10.1007/978-3-319-66215-2_7

operations, and that the logic of free markets might be superior to any other economic management system.

Nevertheless, until the late 1970s markets remained subject to state regulations that were meant to ensure the proper functioning of supply and demand forces and keep markets competitive, while protecting the rights of workers and consumers. In the late 1970s and early 1980s, most financial and economic regulations were either removed or relaxed, causing markets to become freer and easier for big corporations to manipulate and, therefore, less competitive. And while the proponents of deregulation claim that free markets maximize efficiency and wealth creation, Steven Weinberg says, "One thing that is clearly not maximized by free markets is equality," which seems to have worsened with the advancement of economic and cultural globalization.[1]

Capitalists, who own the means of production, hire people to work for them in factories and workshops in exchange for wages and other benefits determined by the capitalists themselves. Workers have no control over how products are made or how to price or distribute them. Since the forces of supply and demand in such an economy are supposed to determine the value of each good and service, capitalism is considered by its promoters the most efficient economic system to allocate natural and human resources among the many alternative uses and users. But for the forces of supply and demand to function efficiently, the numbers of producers, distributors and consumers have to be large; and information regarding the quality, availability and prices of raw materials and workers has to be accessible to all parties. Otherwise, neither potential consumers nor owners of raw materials nor workers will be able to make intelligent decisions concerning what to buy and where to buy it, or where to sell their assets and talents, and for how much.

Capitalism functions in four spheres of societal life: labor that makes the goods and services; firms that organize the production of all goods and services; financial institutions that handle money transactions for all parties; and information that makes educated decisions regarding investment and consumption possible. While labor makes the goods and services that capitalists offer for sale, goods and services are usually sold to the highest bidder to pay labor for their work and make money for capitalists. The financial institutions facilitate all transactions involving labor, suppliers of raw materials, consumers and taxes. Such institutions also facilitate the borrowing of money by investors and consumers to keep the system functioning, and enable capitalism to produce more, build personal and national wealth, and meet consumers' needs and desires. Information collected by specialized public agencies and private institutions allows them to make educated decisions regarding investment, consumption and credit.

In the wake of the disastrous Great Depression of the 1930s, Western governments in general were forced to intervene to regulate markets, spend more money helping the poor and the unemployed, and assume control of the process of collecting and disseminating information. As a result, an uneasy balance between the four spheres of economic activity was established; this endured for four decades. While corporations assumed control of production operations and the hiring and firing of workers, the state assumed control of collecting information and regulating financial transactions and markets. As a consequence, capitalism was transformed into an efficient economic system and a socially responsible institution, creating new jobs and national wealth, raising living standards and caring for workers and communities. In the 1980s, however, conservative forces on both sides of the Atlantic Ocean were able to control politics and redirect the economic policies of the United States, Britain and Germany toward the free market system or market capitalism; they called for markets to be granted the right to manage economic and financial and labor affairs without restrictions. Meanwhile, the information and communications revolutions enabled corporations to dominate the sphere of collecting and disseminating information. This caused the rules that governed the old balance between corporations, labor, financial institutions and information to be undermined.

As communism collapsed and the Soviet Union disintegrated in 1991, the proponents of the free market system declared victory and moved to convince or coerce most other nations to follow their lead. And this in turn gave rise to globalization. "This triumph has inaugurated—for the first time in the history of humankind—the reign of a single, acceptable way of viewing things in the area of economics, which is considered by its proponents as being universally valid, in both its premises and applications."[2] Harvey Cox sees the free market through the eyes of its promoters as a god: "The market is becoming the only true God, whose reign must now be universally accepted and who allows for no rivals."[3]

The collapse of the Soviet Union and the discrediting of socialism enabled market capitalism and democracy to become the dominant political and economic ideology. However, the Great Recession revealed that free markets were largely responsible for the crisis, as they manipulated banking and credit transactions and took unwarranted risks; they were also unable to foresee either the mortgage or the financial crisis, or manage their consequences.

Free Markets

A free market is a place and/or a space that gives the forces of supply and demand a free hand to determine the value of every good and service on the market. For markets to remain free, free market advocates oppose government regulations and reject the right of any third party to intervene in setting guidelines for competition or production relations or financial transactions. This means that supply and demand forces must dominate economic activity and determine the value of everything from labor to raw materials to money to information to life itself. But did free markets ever exist? The answer is no; markets have never been free, and cannot be free; and therefore the forces of supply and demand cannot determine the fair price of any commodity.

When markets are largely free, which rarely happens, supply and demand forces would be in a good position to communicate to owners of raw materials the degree of interest that manufacturers have in their products and at what prices; and communicate to producers the degree of consumers' interest to purchase the goods and services offered for sale and how much they are willing to pay for them. This facilitates the allocation of available resources and end products among the many alternative uses in ways that satisfy the desires of both sellers and buyers. While consumers get the goods they like most, producers get to produce what is in high demand and maximize profits; and that in turn causes the utilization of resources to be optimized. When the demand for a certain good or service exceeds the supply, the price goes up; when the supply exceeds demand, the price goes down. But for such a process to proceed smoothly, the number of sellers and buyers has to be substantial, transactions have to be numerous and transparent, and complete information regarding what is being offered for sale and at what price must be known to all parties concerned, which exists in theory but never in practice.

The promoters of market capitalism claim that the freer the markets are, the more prices reflect consumer habits and desires, making the information which prices convey to concerned parties more reliable. Though this argument is correct to a great extent, experience proves that markets have never been as free as claimed or as efficient as desired. Monopolies, oligopolies and manipulation of supply and demand have eliminated the possibility for free markets to exist; in addition, barriers to market entry, be they natural or engineered, have undermined the ability of markets to be competitive. Even exchange rates of currencies, which are thought to be determined by the forces of free market, were subjugated to manipulation by major European and American banks that colluded to fix interest rates and influence the values of currencies.[4] Markets have to be free of monopoly, oligopoly, manipulation and barriers to entry to be efficient; however, the promoters of market capitalism say that corporations should be free to form monopolies and oligopolies and cartels, which are called "business alliances".

The emergence of the free market philosophy came at a particularly unfortunate time for the world in general and the United States in particular. It came as the US economy was passing through a transitional period separating the industrial age from the knowledge age. Though this transition is still incomplete, most Western economies have shifted from reliance on the production of manufactured goods to the creation and marketing of services and information and financial products. Since these activities are able to create great personal wealth but little national wealth, they cannot create enough jobs for the unemployed. As a consequence, the Western economies have become less able to function efficiently, causing unemployment and underemployment to become structural in many parts of the world.

A market economy is able to function fairly efficiently only in free societies that appreciate the role of government in regulating certain aspects of economic life to ensure markets' honesty. States usually intervene to regulate oligopolies, prevent monopolies, provide equal opportunity, keep income and wealth gaps reasonable, protect the environment and discourage socially undesired economic activities while supporting the socially desirable ones. The US experience between the 1940s and 1980s proves that state regulations were necessary for the proper functioning of the markets and the protection of workers' rights and guaranteeing the quality and safety of end products. When economic and financial regulations were loosened in the 1980s, the American economy became more vulnerable to economic and financial crises, and the market forces were able to gradually dismantle labor unions, weaken the middle class, widen the income and wealth gaps between rich and poor, and undermine the democratic system. Markets without supervision are wild animals that serve the interests of the rich and powerful at the expense of the poor and powerless, and pay no attention to the common good. "So the consolidation of capitalism through the last decades of the twentieth century did not bring a new plateau of stability. Instead, this global financial volatility left the developing countries of Asia, Africa, and Latin America increasingly dependent on the crisis-management role of the US empire."[5]

Society and economy are tied to each other by a cause and effect relationship; each major action taken by either side, and each substantial change experienced by it destabilizes the relationship, forcing the other side to react to restore balance. But every reaction is in itself a new action that induces the first side to react in a similar fashion. Because of such dynamics, the relationship between economy and society continues to change and languish in a state of imbalance. This makes the market economy both an economic system to manage the economic problem and a powerful force of sociocultural transformation. Capitalism "has taken the form of waves of invention that have altered not only the productive capabilities of society but its social composition, even its relationship to nature itself."[6]

I believe that the socialist system articulated by Marxism during the Cold War era may have been the last attempt launched by politics to control economics. The disintegration of the Soviet Union put an end to socialism as an economic system controlled by the state. The demise of socialism was due to two major factors: its failure to live up to popular expectations and deliver on its promises; and its failure to undermine capitalism or empower the industrial working class to challenge big corporations and protect workers' interests. And with that failure, economics won its last battle against politics. Nevertheless, capital has not won its fight against the world's vanquished masses who continue to suffer from need, lack of health services, and educational and economic opportunities. Therefore, the struggle for freedom, social justice, equal opportunity and respect for human rights will continue and make the war between money and ethics, greed and fairness, power and need a never-ending human tragedy.

The triumph of Donald Trump in the 2016 presidential elections is expected to make the struggle between economics and politics, rich and poor more costly to the masses and their supporters, because money has gained the upper hand in America. The Trump cabinet choices are an indication that he is determined to empower capital to tighten its control over politics, and use its newly acquired powers to restructure the social order in America. While it is not easy to change everything, the Trump era promises to be a difficult one for the overwhelming majority of the American people; and by the time the vanquished and their supporters regain power, capital will be in a strong position to hinder change and cause ideological polarization to be deepened, and sociocultural fragmentation will become a fact of life in America. That in turn creates a need for a social revolution to restructure the democratic system and change the social order in ways that guarantee equality of opportunity and social justice.

In a capitalist economy, markets are largely regulated and competitive, and the system is geared toward the production of manufactured goods and the building of national wealth that benefits all citizens. In contrast, free market economies are largely unregulated and hardly competitive, and the system they represent is geared toward the production of information and financial products. The first system, owing to the nature of its activities, tends to create good manufacturing jobs and generate national, corporate and personal wealth that benefit most people and strengthen the middle class. In contrast, the second system creates more personal wealth than national capital, and works to weaken rather than strengthen the middle class; and the wealth it creates tends to be concentrated in the hand of a small business elite of managers of large banks, corporations, insurance companies, hedge funds and media conglomerates. And while the first system facilitates social mobility, the second limits social mobility and allows the socioeconomic, sociopolitical and sociocultural gaps in society to widen and deepen.

Materialism and Society

Every human being comes to life with a strong desire to own things, which leads him to invest a good portion of his time and energy in acquiring those things that are available and desirable. In older times, tribal man had very little to acquire because he was always on the move and could not produce things of value to own. But when man moved from the tribal age to the agricultural age, the institution of private property appeared and gained legitimacy; and that enabled private property to play an important role in shaping social relations and structures. In the meantime, hamlets and villages, which the agricultural man had built and settled in, enabled him to own and enjoy much more things than his predecessors. However, private property remained simple and limited to items that did not exceed, in most cases, farmland, primitive tools, some money, a small family house and sometimes claims of knowing the truth about life and the afterlife.

About two and a half centuries ago, owing to the Industrial Revolution, man moved from the agricultural age to the more advanced and complicated industrial age, leading him to become more materialistic and possessive. As a result, private property expanded to include industrial plants, capital, education, technological knowledge and many things that are used to enhance life comfort, facilitate travel and expand the range of recreational and entertainment choices. Today, owing to the Knowledge Revolution of the 1990s, man's desire to own more wealth and material things has increased, causing ownership of financial and material assets to become the ultimate source of individual satisfaction as well as power and prestige.

With every subsequent age in which man has lived, the wealth and income and power gaps between the haves and the have-nots have widened; socioeconomic gaps have deepened; and new sociocultural divides have appeared and persisted. Such divides are dividing societies not only into social classes on the basis of income and wealth, but also into competing and at times conflicting groups on the basis of cultural values and often contradictory convictions. These are groups that seek different ways of living which cause them to be estranged from one another. And as these groups multiply and divides between them deepen, traditions, values, convictions and relationships that tie members of each society together begin to fracture, leading each group to live a different life and entertain different dreams. For example, while the poor in most societies still worry about daily survival and find it difficult to dream of a brighter future, the rich worry more about how to manage their huge financial assets, gain more wealth and power, and outdo their neighbors and competitors.

The absence of the institution of private property in pre-agricultural times made the tribal society largely classless, and that helped the overwhelming majority of tribal people to be free and avoid the experience of exploitation and slavery. But when man began to farm the land and build permanent settlements, private ownership slowly emerged as an institution of great importance. This divided society into two major classes, a rich class of landlords and a poor class of peasants, farm workers and slaves. As a result, exploitation appeared, allowing the rich to exploit the poor and acquire more wealth and power at their expense. On the other hand, the industrial age, by expanding the range of economic activities and careers, caused the creation of a relatively large middle class that was neither rich nor poor. Owing to its position and economic weight, the middle class played a constructive role in industrial society, facilitating social mobility and limiting the power of capitalists to exploit the poor. However, it could not slow down the growth of the income and wealth gaps separating the three social classes; it also failed to understand the nature of the sociocultural divides fragmenting societies into competing groups.

With the discrediting of the Marxist system, Western states in general relaxed economic and financial regulations, giving the rich and powerful the freedom to pursue their ultimate material goals, which often seemed unlimited—this causing the poor to feel frustrated and denied their rights. In the meantime, the spread of democracy and respect for people empowered more groups in every society to form cultural ghettos, as it enabled many minorities and older cultures to be revived, causing societies to be fragmented into sociocultural groups. Such groups tend to be separated from each other, as well as from the larger societies in which they live. Meanwhile, the rich and powerful began to blame the poor for their poverty and miserable conditions, as if neglect and discrimination, and lack of adequate education and equal opportunity, do not matter.

This simply means that every subsequent society in history has been more materialistic than the previous one, and thus more inclined to exploit other people for the sake of money and power. In fact, at every turn in human history, wealthy individuals, groups and nations have used sheer power to suppress others and discriminate against them, employing political, economic, religious and military power to exploit the powerless and impoverish the poor, without much regard to fairness or morality. Therefore, every step toward more materialism and power is in itself a step away from the values of equality, social justice and respect for human rights; and therefore a step toward cultural fragmentation, social exclusion and conflict.

Greedy capitalists are usually very clever, but almost always unwise; they are largely driven by a blind desire to maximize their returns in the short run and ignore the long run, believing that they will be able to accumulate enough wealth and power to overcome future economic crises and political upheavals. But this actually means ignoring the needs of the poor and the rights of other people, as well as the need to protect shared interests such as the environment. In the age of knowledge, people on either side of the income and wealth divides have become aware of the life conditions and lifestyles of people living on the other side; and this will ultimately lead the poor to revolt against the systems and people responsible for keeping them poor and submissive. People blinded by materialism need to remember that almost all thieves and criminals are also clever but lack wisdom; while they know how to steal and commit heinous crimes without being easily caught, they almost always end up in dark prison cells or die a violent death.

Development is a function of several factors that include knowledge, innovations, capital accumulation, education, freedom and sociocultural change. This means that development must be understood as a comprehensive and continuous process of sociocultural, sociopolitical and socioeconomic transformation. Though material and cultural products are the major sources of personal and national wealth and individual satisfaction, they cannot be enjoyed unless shared with people who cannot afford them. However, for people to work hard and acquire wealth and get the satisfaction they aspire for, they need to feel that they are entitled to keep most of the money they earn. So the absence of the material incentive undermines individual drive for excellence, weakens innovation and creativity, and retards development. Nevertheless, no society is able to fully enjoy social peace without respecting the rights of the poor and tending to the needs of those who are unable to earn enough money to live a decent life.

The record of human progress over time suggests that private property, both material and intellectual, has contributed substantially to everything man has invented, produced and enjoyed in life. Therefore, private property and the income and wealth gaps it creates are expected to stay with us for as long as human life continues. Nevertheless, private property and personal wealth, and the power they generate and bestow on their owners, must be regulated by the state and directed toward enriching the life of society as a whole. Otherwise money and power will become tools to gain more of the same and exploit more individuals and groups and nations, thus denying them their legitimate economic, political, social and cultural rights, as well as the opportunity to develop their capabilities and free themselves from need.

The concentration of wealth and power in the hands of a small political, economic and media elite in America has enabled the rich and powerful to confiscate many of the rights of the rest of the people, in violation of democratic principles and human rights. As the number of the super rich increases, envy among the rich and super rich deepens and competition intensifies leading most of them to ignore the ethics of fairness and equality. "The special attention accorded to labor-capital inequality should come as no surprise. The mere fact that a share of productive income goes to capital might seem to contradict basic principles of justice and immediately raise the question of redistribution: why should a person who inherits ownership of capital receive income denied to those who inherit only their labor power?"[7]

On the other hand, need and jealousy, and a strong desire to imitate the rich's lifestyles encourage the poor to ignore honesty and at times dignity as well. Consequently, the rich driven by greed and envy, and the poor driven by need and jealousy, have emerged as major forces motivating people to work hard, invest, compete, cheat and sometimes steal to get ahead. By the time the knowledge age arrived in the mid-1990s, interests rather than values had become the major organizing principles of individual and societal life and the foundations of social and economic relations in industrial societies, causing all societies, particularly the ones that depend on knowledge and free markets, to become more individualistic and materialistic.

Today, almost all societies are experiencing a dramatic decline in the influence of traditional values and business ethics that have guided life for many generations. Although many forces could be blamed for instigating this development, the overall human movement toward individualism and materialism on the one hand, and the abandonment of spiritualism and community on the other are largely to blame for the retreat of traditional values and business ethics. While rich individuals and societies try hard to acquire as much material things and power as possible, poor individuals and societies try harder to imitate the rich but do little to reclaim their legitimate rights. As a consequence, more emphasis is being placed on consumption and the appearance of wealth and less on education, had work, ethics and the essence of living a meaningful life.

Economist Joseph Schumpeter argued more than sixty years ago that the most damaging consequences of capitalism are the negative effects it has on the values that support the social order in society.[8] But what Schumpeter seems to have failed to notice is that cultures have a great capacity to transform themselves and adapt to change, and that cultural values, traditions and production relations are able to change and accommodate economic and technological change. Values that prevailed during the 1950s did not disintegrate, and the social order that tied people together at the time did not collapse; new values emerged slowly and a new social order formed gradually, creating new social, economic, cultural and political relationships compatible with the new economy. In the meantime, the excesses of materialism, consumerism and power associated with the advancement of industrial capitalism forced society to intervene and enact new laws to make the system less exploitative and more socially responsible. On the other hand, the need of capitalists to interact with their workers and often bargain with them in good faith had facilitated the emergence of a more equitable social order that underpinned the formation of a healthy and confident middle class.

In the fast advancing knowledge age, the socioeconomic gaps and sociocultural divides that separate classes and religious and ideological groups from one another are growing wider and deeper every day, while the state is getting weaker and less able to play its traditional role in ensuring fairness and equal opportunity. At the same time, a rich and powerful class determined to influence politics and corrupt politicians has prevented the traditional powers from intervening to facilitate the building of a new social order compatible with the imperatives of the new age. As a result, the need for a new social order capable of balancing the relationships between the rich and powerful on the one hand and the poor and powerless on the other remains unmet in all societies. While budgets of social and educational programs are being cut, taxes on the rich are being reduced and the poor are being neglected. Failure to rebalance class interests with values and traditions will ultimately lead to social unrest and possibly violence.

The rich under the old capitalist system concentrated on expanding manufacturing that drove economic growth and created millions of jobs; the super rich of today are devoting their energies to creating financial products that hardly contribute to economic growth or job creation. Because the first class had to interact with millions of workers on a daily basis, it became aware of the need to ensure the welfare of its employees and the development of communities hosting its operations. The new class, however, has no need to interact with workers or even with ordinary people, because it derives most of its wealth from dealing in virtual products within virtual communities away from the eyes of the public. And owing to their particular lifestyles, interests and educational backgrounds, the super rich have developed a unique global culture with its own values, traditions, ethics and even special vocabulary that most people have difficulty understanding. And because each member of this class has a house everywhere and no home anywhere, they have become aliens with no loyalty to place, nation, religion or ideology; the only god they know and worship day and night is money. And to remain faithful and close to their god, they are willing to manipulate, cheat, exploit and conspire against everyone and every cause. Having gained a lot of wealth and power, the super rich seem determined to do whatever it takes to ensure the continuation of the prevailing unjust and unsustainable social order.

As a consequence of these developments, the rich and super rich have shown little regard for community life, and almost no interest in the tragic conditions of the poor of the world. Nevertheless, the poor and powerless, despite their miserable life conditions, are not expected to revolt soon to reclaim their confiscated rights and force the creation of a new social order. During transitional periods that take societies from one civilization to another, ordinary people usually get confused, lose their general sense of direction and become more conservative and inward looking; and this in turn leads them to seek hope and comfort in religious teachings and traditional values that resist change, dampen expectations and encourage contentment. As a result, most people of the world are entering an era of diminishing expectations, where they expect less in the future and are resigned to accept this.

If we consider the global debt crisis as an example, we discover that the perpetuation of this crisis by managing it serves the interests of the large financial institutions and the people who own and control the flow of money. Today, American and European banks are able to borrow from central banks at near zero interest rates, lend the same money to needy developed and developing countries at much higher interest rates, and make substantial profits without taking meaningful risk. And since over fifty countries, including the United States and almost all European Union (EU) member states, can never repay their debt under prevailing economic and financial conditions; the global debt keeps rising, annual interest payments keep increasing and banks' profits keep rising, year after year. As a result, no financial institution is interested in thinking outside the box to try to find a solution to a crisis that threatens the financial system itself. In the meantime, the highly indebted countries keep seeing their public debt rise year after year, and the poor keep on feeling that their standards of living are declining day after day.

Every system based on materialism and interests only, regardless of its nature and objectives, is unjust; and every unjust system is inefficient because it does not provide for equal opportunity. And in the absence of equal opportunity, the majority of people lose many of their rights, especially the right to get good education, discover their talents, develop their capabilities and improve the quality of their lives. Unjust systems tend to concentrate wealth and power in fewer hands, strip the middle class of the resources it needs to maintain its social position and sociopolitical role, and impoverish a large segment of society, leaving the poor in distress. On the other hand, every economic system that is inefficient is also unjust, because it tends to waste natural and human resources and distributes economic and social benefits unfairly among participants in the production process.

History seems to suggest that when an economic or political system or social order fails to be just and efficient, society intervenes sooner or later to reform the system and restructure or replace the social order. This means that for social and economic and political systems to survive and endure, they have to be economically efficient, socially just, politically fair and amenable to change. Cultural values of honesty, integrity, social responsibility, fairness and tolerance have the capacity to foster social peace, ensure fairness and equality of opportunity, and improve the chances of material and non-material progress. In contrast, systems that ignore such values and traditions are incapable of responding to people's needs and aspirations, and, therefore, are destined to fail and die either a natural or violent death.

Notes

1. Steven Weinberg: "Utopias," *The Atlantic Monthly*, June 2000, 108.
2. Sophie Bessie: From social Exclusion to Social Cohesion: A Policy Agenda, 1995, 13.
3. Harvey Cox: "The Market as God," *The Atlantic Monthly*, March 1999, 13.
4. See The Guardian, Libor-rigging scandal: three former Barclays found guilty, July 4, 2016. https://www.theguardian.com/business/2016/jul/04/libor-rigging-scandal-three-former-barclays-traders-found-guilty
5. Leo Panitch and Sam Gindin; The Making of Global Capitalism, p. 17.
6. Robert Heilbroner, 21st Century Capitalism, 35.
7. Thomas Piketty, The Economics of Inequality, p. 26.
8. Joseph Schumpeter, Capitalism, socialism and Democracy, 1950.

CHAPTER 8

Debt, Inequality and Economic Growth

In the early 1980s, a $1.2 trillion Third World debt was considered a threat to the stability of the international monetary system and the world economy, leading the United States, in coordination with the World Bank and the International Monetary Fund (IMF) to intervene and compel the indebted nations to implement economic reform measures based on austerity, which included the adoption of the free market system. But instead of reforming the economies of the indebted states, the austerity programs caused several nations to lose a decade or more of economic growth and political stability. Now that several Western states, including the United States and Japan have borrowed nearly $54 trillion, no serious warning shots have been fired by the United States, the World Bank or the IMF.

If the 1980s were a lost decade for several African, Asian and particularly Latin American nations primarily because they borrowed approximately $1.2 trillion, the decade that started in 2007 has already proved to be disastrous for many developed and developing countries. Because of borrowing too much money, Japan has lost more than two decades of growth, starting in the 1990s; the United States and Italy have lost the first decade of the twenty-first century; while Greece, Spain, Portugal, Ireland, Lebanon, Jordan, Egypt and a few other states are likely to lose more than a decade. The experience of the indebted Latin American nations of the 1980s suggests that a nation that loses a decade of growth owing to economic restructuring programs is unlikely to fully recover and resume normal growth by the end of that lost decade.

M. Rabie, *The Global Debt Crisis and Its Socioeconomic Implications*,
https://doi.org/10.1007/978-3-319-66215-2_8

A View of the Inequality Problem

Reports indicate that income and wealth distribution in the world has increasingly become more unequal than ever before. "A study by the World Institute for Development Economics Research at the United Nations reports that the richest 1% of adults owned 40% of global assets in the year 2000, and that the richest 10% of adults accounted for 85% of the world total assets. The bottom half of the world adult population owned just 1% of global wealth, and another study found that the richest 2% of the world population owned more than half of global assets as of the year 2000."[1] However, a study done by UNICEF in 2011, says, "As of 2007, the wealthiest 20 percent of mankind enjoyed nearly 83 percent of total global income compared to the poorest 20 percent, which had exactly a single percentage point. Perhaps more shocking, the poorest 40 percent of the global population increased its share of total income by less than one percent between 1990 and 2007."[2] The study concludes, "Not only does inequality slow economic growth, but it results in health and social problems and generates political instability. Inequality is dysfunctional, and there is a grave need to place equity at the center of the development agenda."[3]

In 2012, Annie Lowrey reported that the gap between the very rich and everyone else in America was extremely wide: "Income inequality has soared to the highest levels since the Great Depression, and the recession has done little to reverse the trend, with the top 1 percent of earners taking 93 percent of the income gains in the first full year of the recovery."[4] However, according to Bernie Sanders, "the latest information that we have shows that in recent years, over 99 percent of all new income generated in the economy has gone to the top 1 percent." In reaching this conclusion, Sanders and other economists have used pre-tax, pre-transfer income growth during the economic recovery from 2009 to 2013.[5] As a result, 99% of all Americans are getting no increase in their incomes. It is true that millions of poor Americans receive social security, tax credits, food stamps and other forms of government benefits, but the rest are not getting such help, causing their standards of living to decline.

Estimates of total wealth in the world vary substantially from one source to another. For example, Allianz, a financial service giant, estimated global wealth in 2014 at $153.2 trillion, while Credit Suisse estimated the same wealth in the same year at $263 trillion. According to Allianz, 43% of this wealth is owned by the richest 1% of the world's population. Allianz estimated the US share of the global wealth to be 41.6%, more than any other nation in the world. Yet America, according to Allianz "has the largest wealth inequality gap of 55 countries studied."[6] The following are the wealthiest ten nations in the world, ranked according to their wealth share.

1. United States	41.6%
2. China	10.5%
3. Japan	8.9%
4. Britain	5.6%
5. Germany	3.9%
6. France	3.5%
7. Canada	3.0%
8. Italy	2.9%
9. Australia	2.0%
10. South Korea	0.6%

In addition to calculating wealth distribution among major nations in the world, Allianz calculated the distribution of wealth in each country using the Gini coefficient. This is a technical measure of inequality in which 0 is perfect equality, and 100 is total inequality, which means one person owning all the wealth.[7] Allianz "found that the United States had the most wealth inequality, with a score of 80.56," which means that wealth is concentrated in the hands of a small segment of American society. The following is a list of the countries with the highest wealth inequality:

1. United States	80.56
2. Sweden	79.90
3. Britain	75.72
4. Indonesia	73.61
5. Austria	73.59
6. Germany	73.34
7. Colombia	73.18
8. Chile	73.17
9. Brazil	72.86
10. Mexico	70.00

As mentioned earlier, Credit Suisse estimated global wealth in 2014 at $263 trillion; however, owing to the appreciation of the US dollar, the estimate for 2015 was reduced to $259.9 trillion. The 2015 report says that "Our estimates suggest that the lower half of the global population collectively own less than 1% of global wealth, while the richest 10% of adults own 88% of all wealth and the top 1% account for half of all assets in the world."[8]

And though Allianz says that the US share of global wealth was $41.6 trillion in 2014, Credit Suisse estimated US share in 2015 at 37% only, despite an increase of $4.6 trillion between 2014 and 2015.[9] As for other nations, Credit Suisse said Europe, which has about 12% of the world's population, owns 30% of the global wealth; China, which has about 21% of the population, owns 9% of the wealth; and Latin America, which has about 8% of the population, owns 3% of the wealth.

The *Guardian* newspaper said in January 2016, "The vast and growing gap between rich and poor has been laid bare in a new Oxfam report showing that the 62 richest billionaires in the world own as much wealth as the poorer half of the world's population ... a trend showing that 1 percent of people own more wealth than the other 99% combined. Oxfam said that the wealth of the poorest 50 percent dropped by 41 percent between 2010 and 2015, despite an increase in the global population of 400 million; in the same period, the wealth of the richest 62 people increased by $500 billion to $1.76 trillion."[10] Oxfam also reported that in 2010 the 388 richest people owned the same wealth as the poorest 50% of the world's population. However, this number dropped to eighty people in 2014 before falling again to sixty-two in 2015, six of them being women.[11]

Duncan Exley, the director of the Equality Trust of Britain, said: "Inequality, both globally but also in the UK, is now at staggering levels. We know that such a vast gap between the richest and the rest of us is bad for our economy and society. We now need our politicians to wake up and address this dangerous concentration of wealth and power in the hands of so few."[12] This statement came in reaction to the report issued by Equality Trust of Britain which said that "Britain's 100 richest families had increased their wealth by at least £57 billion since 2010, a period in which average incomes declined."[13] All of these reports indicate that the rich are getting richer and the poor are getting poorer in good and bad times. As a consequence, growth rates are slowing and are expected to remain slow for years to come, unless current economic, financial and social policies are changed.

Credit Suisse said in its 2014 report, "Our estimates for mid-2014 indicate that once debts have been subtracted, a person needs only USD 3,650 to be among the wealthiest half of world citizens. However, more than USD 77,000 is required to be a member of the top 10 percent of global wealth holders, and USD 798,000 to belong to the top 1 percent. Taken together, the bottom half of the global population own less than 1 percent of total wealth."[14] Though the wealth needed to belong to the richest 1% seems large, many Americans own homes worth more than $1 million, yet they are unable to live decent lives because they do not have incomes to support themselves, pay property taxes and maintain their homes. In fact, millions of Americans can hardly afford to continue living in homes they bought twenty and thirty years ago.

The Credit Suisse report says, "Wealth is one of the key components of the economic system; it is valued as a source of finance for future consumption, especially in retirement, and for reducing vulnerability to shocks such as unemployment, ill health or natural disasters. These functions are less important in countries that have generous state pensions, adequate social safety nets, good public healthcare, high quality public education ... Conversely, the need to acquire personal assets is particularly compelling and urgent in countries that have rudimentary social insurance schemes and reduced options for business finance, as is the case in much of the developing world."[15] The reference to the situation in the developing countries and their need for attention is important: most Third World states do not have adequate social safety nets, good healthcare or good education. In fact, as people live longer in those countries, traditional family ties weaken, making the future of most poor people in those states rather bleak; as collective family obligations are the major social safety net in most poor countries.

Causes and Impact of Inequality

Western states in general and the American state in particular claim to give a lot of money to the poor nations; and they do. But estimates of money going from the poor states to the rich ones each year are said to be many times what the rich give to the poor. On January 14, 2017, the *Guardian* published an article written by Jason Hickel explaining this issue: information in the article is based on a report issued by the US-based Global Financial Integrity (GFI) and the Centre for Applied Research at the Norwegian School of Economics. The following is a summary.

The financial resources that get transferred between rich and poor countries include aid, foreign investment and non-financial transfers such as debt cancellation, workers' remittances and unrecorded capital flight. "What they discovered is that the flow of money from rich countries to poor countries pales in comparison to the flow that runs in the other direction. In 2012, the last year of recorded data, developing countries received a total of $1.3 trillion, including all aid, investment, and income from abroad. But that same year some $3.3 trillion flowed out of them. In other words, developing countries sent $2 trillion more to the rest of the world than they received. If we look at all years since 1980, these net outflows add up to an eye-popping total of $16.3 trillion—that's how much money has been drained out of the global south over the past few decades. What this means is that the usual development narrative has it backwards. Aid is effectively flowing in reverse. Rich countries aren't developing poor countries; poor countries are developing rich ones."[16]

The report says that these large outflows consist of payments on debt, estimated at over $4.2 trillion in interest payments alone since 1980: "a direct cash transfer to big banks in New York and London, on a scale that dwarfs the aid that they received during the same period. Another big contributor is the income that foreigners make on their investments in developing countries and then repatriate back home. But by far the biggest chunk of outflows has to do with unrecorded capital flight. GFI calculates that developing countries have lost a total of $13.4 trillion through unrecorded capital flight since 1980. Multinational companies also steal money from developing countries through "same-invoice faking", shifting profits illegally between their own subsidiaries;"[17] If theft through trade in goods is added to theft through trade in services, it brings the total net resource outflows to about $3 trillion per year. "That's 24 times more than the aid budget. In other words, for every $1 of aid that developing countries receive, they lose $24 in net outflows. The GFI report finds that large net outflows have caused economic growth rates in developing countries to decline, and are directly responsible for falling living standards."[18]

This report makes it clear that the aid narrative told by the rich states hides the true story: it is meant to provide a cover for the magnitude of the misdistribution of resources around the world as well as the role of the rich countries in keeping the poor ones underdeveloped and in need of aid. "It makes the takers seem like givers, granting them a kind of moral high ground while preventing those of us who care about global poverty from understanding how the system really works. Poor countries don't need charity. They need justice. And justice is not difficult to deliver. We could write off the excess debts of poor countries, freeing them up to spend their money on development instead of interest payments on old loans."[19] And this should explain, at least partially, why the overwhelming majority of people in poor countries continue to be poor and languish in political instability.

In fact, the economic restructuring programs imposed on many poor nations by America, the World Bank and the IMF included the privatization of public enterprises, most of which are now owned by foreign corporations that function as parasites sucking the blood of their hosts without giving them anything in return. As income and wealth inequalities persist, they reduce economic growth rates and make reducing world poverty a largely unattainable goal. Poor counties of the world, in addition to the wide wealth and income inequalities, suffer from gender and minority inequality as well as inequalities in access to healthcare, good education, land ownership, jobs, loans and other vital social and economic services.

Jonathan D. Ostry of the IMF, who researched the impact of inequality on economic growth, says that his research suggests that the widening disparity since the 1980s might limit US economic expansion by as much as a third. "Growth becomes more fragile" in countries with high levels of inequality like the United States.[20] Annie Lowrey says, "The concentration of income in the hands of the rich might not just mean a more unequal society; it might mean less stable economic expansions and sluggish growth."[21] The concentration of wealth and income in fewer hands also means a weaker middle class, more poverty, more frustration and, at times, more alcoholism, violence and crime. In fact, prolonged economic crises usually transform themselves into social crises that encourage people to revolt in order to change the unjust social order by force.

Countless reports have said that inequality has reduced the real incomes of the middle classes and the poor in most parts of the world; as a result, their ability to borrow and spend has shrunk substantially. And though the rich's incomes continue to increase, their being only 10% of any country's population makes any increase in their spending not nearly enough to compensate for the loss of spending by the other 90%. Meanwhile, the ability of members of the middle and poor classes to borrow seems to have reached its limit. US credit reports suggest that the American people owed about $1 trillion on their credit cards in 2016,[22] equal to the peak of 2008, the year of the Great Recession. As a consequence, economic growth rates have remained low in most countries and declined in countries that have had healthy growth rates in the past decade.

As for China, UBS Group AG estimates that "Total debt equals almost 260% of annual economic output, up from less than 160% in 2007. While the official ratio of nonperforming loans in China's banks remained low at 1.6%, analysts and economists said the pace is picking up and many debts are hidden in the books of nonbank lenders while banks roll over many loans. Increasingly, new lending is being used to service debt rather than fund new ventures and energy-saving technologies."[23] According to research firm

Gavekal Dragonomics, "households and companies now spend the equivalent of 20 percent of GDP on interest payments, more than the US, Japan or the UK, and equal to Korea, citing figures from the Bank for International Settlements."[24] And as China's economy slows and the yuan weakens, the Chinese are moving their money out of the country, causing potential consumption and investment to shrink. As a result, says Mark Magnier, "Beijing finds itself in a dilemma: if the government cuts interest rates, more capital flees' if it raises interest rates, more debt-plagued companies risk going bust, fueling joblessness."[25]

There is evidence that when workers get less money and fewer social benefits, the managers and shareholders of corporations get more, causing inequality to widen and thus reduce the capacity of the economy to grow. Meanwhile, declining wages and benefits cause participation in the labor force and labor productivity to decline. Susan Jones wrote, "The labor force participation rate [in the United States] reached its lowest point in 38 years."[26] For example, American participation in the labor force in September 2015 was 62.4% as compared to 66% for 2007. Joseph E. Stiglitz, a Nobel laureate in economics said, "What worries me is the idea that we're in a vicious cycle ... Increasing inequality means a weaker economy, which means increasing inequality, which means a weaker economy. That economic inequality feeds into political economy, so the ability to stabilize the economy gets weaker,"[27] causing the possibility of social instability and violence to rise.

Michael Snyder says, "Corporate defaults [in the United States] are currently at the highest level that we have seen since 2009. In fact, the average credit rating for U.S. corporations is now lower than it was at any point during the last recession. This is yet another sign that we are in the early chapters of a major league economic crisis ... 23.2 percent of all Americans in their prime working years do not have a job right now. Big corporate giants all over America are in deep, deep financial trouble, and this is going to result in a tremendous wave of layoffs in the coming months."[28] As corporate defaults and bankruptcies rise, manufacturing jobs and factory orders and corporate profits decline. As a consequence, "major retailers are shutting down hundreds of stores, causing corporate layoffs to increase ... If the government was actually using honest numbers, people wouldn't be talking about the potential start of a new recession. Instead, they would be talking about the deepening of a recession that never ended."[29]

As for the United States public debt, "The US government debt continues to spiral out of control ... but when Barack Obama first entered the

White House it was only 10.6 trillion dollars. That means that our government has been stealing an average of more than 100 million dollars an hour from future generations of Americans every single hour of every single day since Barack Obama was inaugurated."[30] The public debt has continued to rise day after day: it reached $20.17 trillion in September 2017.

The World Bank says in its "Global Economic Prospects 2016" report, "Emerging market economies have been an engine of global growth during the 2000s, especially after the 2007–08 global financial crisis. However, times are changing. Growth rates in several emerging market economies have been declining since 2010."[31] Based on the World Bank's evaluation of the state of the American, European, Japanese and Chinese economies, it is easy to conclude that we are likely to witness another great recession soon, unless we move to change course before it is too late. The longer we wait to liberate all nations from the public debt burden, the more complicated the situation will become, causing the badly needed socioeconomic adjustments to be a more painful restructuring process.

Most financial experts tend to see the rising of stock prices on Wall Street as indicating that the American economy is on its way to full recovery; but this is a claim that cannot be substantiated. Since the economic boom of decades ago, investors in the stock market have begun to view buying and selling shares as a means to play the market, not to invest in the market. Today, most buyers and sellers of shares are no longer investors in the traditional sense: they do not consider expected dividends at the end of the year to make their decisions to buy, hold and sell; instead, they make decisions on the basis of the actual and projected prices of shares. Trading in the US stock market has become a new form of gambling in a highly dynamic and vastly unpredictable casino. But unlike Las Vegas's glamorous casinos, this one is subject to manipulation by major players. This means that the seemingly healthy American stock market should be seen as a part of a financial bubble that is clouding our view of reality.

In concluding this section on debt, inequality and economic growth, it is timely to quote the following paragraph from the World Economic Forum's outlook report of 2015: "The inherent dangers of neglecting inequality are obvious. People, especially young people, excluded from the mainstream end up feeling disenfranchised and become easy fodder of conflict. This, in turn, reduces the sustainability of economic growth, weakens social cohesion and security, encourages inequitable access to and use of global commons, undermines our democracies, and cripples our hopes for sustainable development and peaceful societies."[32]

In fact, as public debt increases, annual interest payments increase and cause budget deficits to increase as well. This in turn reduces governments' abilities to finance the many social and economic programs that help the poor, the needy and the young, and maintain public services. As a result, economies weaken; income and wealth inequalities widen, and demand for most goods and services fails to expand sufficiently to sustain previous growth rates. And this, in turn, causes inequalities to widen further and raises the possibility of spreading political instability, radicalism and violence. The global rates of economic growth over the last three years prove the negative impact of the public debt on the world economy: while the growth rate was 3.4% in 2014, it declined to 3.1% in 2015 and 2.7% in 2016. On the other hand, violence in the Middle East, terrorism in several African and Asian countries, turmoil in Brazil, demonstrations in several European countries and the unprecedented waves of political and economic migrants in Europe and the United States are sings of the deteriorating economic and noneconomic life conditions.

Nevertheless, people in charge of world financial and economic affairs seem unwilling to acknowledge one important fact related to economic policy: this is the fact that globalization of the world's major capital, investment and trade markets has caused deep structural changes that have weakened the effectiveness of the traditional monetary and fiscal tools that have dealt with previous economic and financial crises. While stimulus packages and near zero interest rates have failed to revive most economies, austerity measures such as those forced on Greece and Spain were only able to make a bad situation worse. While stimulus programs have failed to invigorate the French and Japanese economies and enable them to regain their vitality, austerity programs such as the one implemented in Britain tend to hurt the people who need help most, such as students, the poor, the unemployed and the elderly; they also weaken states' capacities to invest in vital social programs and the future.

Diminishing Expectations

When people feel that the future does not look good enough to believe in and trust, as most Americans, Europeans, Arabs and Latin Americans seem to feel today, they enter a psychological phase characterized by "diminishing expectations." This is defined as "a historical era characterized by a general human presentiment that the future does not promise as much as the past did, and a resigned acceptance of the less that is expected to come."[33] As a result, people in general become less optimistic yet more content with their lot, leading many of them to lose the incentive to work hard. People experiencing diminishing expectations tend to feel that nothing can change their lot in life, no matter how hard they may try. As a consequence, believing in faith and fate becomes a mindset that governs such people's attitudes as well as their views of themselves and others.

In times of social and political stress and economic uncertainty, most people tend to lose their sense of direction and self-confidence, and to doubt the utility of the values and lifestyles that got them into trouble in the first place. And this causes those people to modify their attitudes according to a new mental model characterized by diminishing expectations, which leads them to become inward looking and socially and politically more conservative. A general feeling of economic decline leads people to expect less in the future and to be content with the less that is expected to come; and as many people stop working, labor productivity and participation in the workforce decline. Such a phase causes economic recovery to be slow and painful and less inclusive; meanwhile, lack of inclusivity causes wealth and income inequalities to widen.

Nevertheless, eras of diminishing expectations do not just present serious problems; they present valuable opportunities as well. However, problems in an era of diminishing expectations are usually easy to recognize and feel, while opportunities are hard to see and appreciate. This leads most people to concentrate on solving problems and overlooking opportunities. As a result, drastic measures, such as those related to austerity, are usually viewed as necessary to address urgent problems and pressing vulnerabilities, while opportunities are often ignored as risky endeavors.

In contrast, during eras of "rising expectations" most people tend to feel rather good and concentrate on opportunities, ignoring any vulnerabilities that emerge. Voices calling for attention to be paid to vulnerabilities are usually met with stiff resistance, because people tend to view them as unwarranted anxieties that dampen optimism. This leads to constraining the ability of committed intellectuals, strategic thinkers, foresighted economists and concerned scientists and officials to express their views freely and warn the public of the probable implications of inaction. In the meantime, the rich are allowed to exploit opportunities and gain more economic and political power, while the poor are left to languish in poverty and negligence. And owing to the fear of dampening optimism, decision-makers usually avoid making the necessary corrections, leaving problems to fester until they reach the crisis point and become hard to manage. This is where most Western and developing nations are today.

History seems to suggest that prolonged economic crises transform themselves slowly into social crises; and prolonged social crises lead eventually to social unrest and sometimes revolutions. Such revolutions usually seek to change the economic, political and social structures of society, and replace the existing social order with a new one characterized by fairness and sustainability. For example, only 20% of the Egyptian people who went out onto the streets during the Arab Spring in 2011 did so for political reasons; the other 80% of demonstrators were interested in jobs and economic opportunities to free themselves from need and poverty.

Can America repay its debt any time soon? Under current economic, financial and tax policies it can neither repay its debt nor reduce it by one dollar; nor can it stop the debt to GDP ratio from rising. For America to reduce this ratio, the annual increase in the GDP must exceed the annual interest payments on the debt. To start repaying its debt, the government needs to have a budget large enough to cover regular programs and a surplus to pay the annual interest on the public debt. According to the National Debt Clock.org, the US public debt was $19.72 trillion on November 8, 2016; and the GDP was estimated at $18.06 trillion, while the annual debt service was estimated at $494 billion.[34] Based on this information, the interest rate on the debt would be 2.5% annually.

Since the growth rate for 2016 was 1.9%, the US GDP should have grown in 2016 by $343 billion, and the debt interest should have been $493 billion, $150 billion more than the growth of GDP. Since the government does not have the money to pay this interest, the public debt to GDP ratio has risen slightly. This simply means that America cannot stop borrowing to service its skyrocketing debt, causing the public debt to increase year after year. The Federal Reserve policy that reduced interest rates to near zero has not and could not change this fact; it could only reduce debt servicing payments, but this hurt all savers, not just in America but also in most other parts of the world. However, the Federal Reserve has begun to raise rates, causing interest rates in general and the cost of servicing the debt to increase as well. High debt to GDP ratios, as previously explained, cause wealth and income inequalities to widen, poverty to increase, participation in the labor force to shrink and apparently labor productivity to decline as well. Inequality, in turn, causes the economy to slow down.

Notes

1. Distribution of Wealth and Income," *Boundless Sociology*, Boundless, 21 Jul, 2015) (https://www.boundless.com/sociology/textbooks/boundless-sociology-textbook/global-stratification-and-inequality-8/a-comparative-analysis-of-global-stratification-in-mexico-71/distribution-of-wealth-and-income-416-10395/).
2. Global Inequality: Beyond the Bottom Billion – A Rapid Review of Income Distribution in 141 Countries, United Nations Children's Fund, UNICEF, p 11. http://www.unicef.org/socialpolicy/files/Global_Inequality.pdf
3. Ibid.
4. Annie Lowrey, Income Inequality May Take Toll on Growth, *the New York Times*, October 16, 2012 (http://www.nytimes.com/2012/10/17/business/economy/income-inequality-may-take-toll-on-growth.html?_r=0).
5. Katie Sanders, Bernie Sanders says 99 percent of 'New' income is going to top 1 percent, April 19, 2015 (http://www.politifact.com/truth-o-meter/statements/2015/apr/19/bernie-s/bernie-sanders-says-99-percent-new-income-going-to/).
6. Eric Sherman; America is the riches, and most unequal, country, Fortune, September 30, 2015.
7. Ibid.
8. Global Wealth Report 2015, Credit Suisse, October 2015, p. 13.
9. Ibid., p. 8.
10. Larry Elliott, Richest 62 people as wealthy as half of world's population, The Guardian, January 18, 2016.
11. Ibid.
12. Ibid.
13. Ibid. (https://www.theguardian.com/business/2016/jan/18/richest-62-billionaires-wealthy-half-world-population-combined).
14. Credit Suisse, Global Wealth Report, October, 2014, p. 11.
15. Ibid., pp. 12–13.
16. Jason Hickel; Aid in reverse: how poor countries develop rich countries; The Guardian, January 14, 2007. https://www.theguardian.com/global-development-professionals-network/2017/jan/14/aid-in-reverse-how-poor-countries-develop-rich-countries
17. Ibid.
18. Ibid.
19. Ibid.
20. Annie Lowrey, Income Inequality May Take Toll on Growth, *the New York Times*, October 16, 2012.
21. Ibid.
22. US Debt Clock (http://www.usdebtclock.org/).

23. Mark Magnier; China's economic growth in 2015 slowest in 25 years, the Wall Street Journal, January, 19, 2016.
24. Ibid.
25. Ibid.
26. Susan Jones, Labor Force Participation Remains at 38 Year Low, CNSNews.com, October 2, 2015.
27. Annie Lowrey, Income Inequality May Take Toll on Growth, *the New York Times*, October 16, 2012.
28. Michael Snyder, Corporate Debt Defaults Explode to Catastrophic Levels Not Seen since the Last Financial Crisis, Washingtonsblog, March 31, 2016.
29. Ibid.
30. Michael Snyder, 19 facts that prove things in America are worse than they were six months ago, Economic Collapse Blog, April 22, 2016 (http://www.washingtonsblog.com/2016/04/19-facts-prove-things-america-worse-six-months-ago.html).
31. Global Economic Prospects 2016, the World Bank, p. xv.
32. Deepening Income Inequality, Outlook on the Global Agenda 2015, World Economic Forum (http://reports.weforum.org/outlook-global-agenda-2015/top-10-trends-of-2015/1-deepening-income-inequality/).
33. Mohamed Rabie, *The New World Order 1992*, 18.
34. US debt clock: National debt of United States. http://www.nationaldebtclocks.org/debtclock/unitedstates

CHAPTER 9

Globalization and the Debt Crisis

Economic globalization is an evolving state of world economic and financial affairs that has its infrastructure, superstructure, institutions and rationale. Its infrastructure is the information and telecommunications networks, including the Internet and social media; its superstructure is international laws and treaties, particularly formal arrangements governing trade and the creation of economic communities and free trade zones; and its major institutions are the World Bank, the International Monetary Fund (IMF), the World Trade Organization (WTO) and the United Nations and its specialized agencies. As for the rationale of globalization, it claims that free trade benefits all people, and for the world economy to grow and improve the living standards of people everywhere, free movement of goods, services, ideas, investment capital and labor needs to be facilitated. Though this argument sounds logical, the experience of the last two decades refutes these claims. The global political and economic elite, driven by greed and unlimited power, have managed to manipulate states, markets and people, widen the income and wealth gaps between rich and poor within and between nations, and cause millions of people to lose satisfaction, job and income security, and social recognition; and feel worse off than before, even those whose living conditions have improved.

At the time of the debt crisis of the 1980s, economies were national and the nation state was largely in control of its own destiny; states that owed a lot of money were held accountable for their deeds and misdeeds. Since large American and European banks at the time had a lot of money to invest, some states were enticed to borrow, while others were coerced to borrow

M. Rabie, *The Global Debt Crisis and Its Socioeconomic Implications*,
https://doi.org/10.1007/978-3-319-66215-2_9

money they did not need. In reaction to the crisis, triggered by the failure of some states to service their debt, the US government, in coordination with the IMF and the World Bank, intervened and forced the highly indebted states to restructure their national economies. The restructuring programs were used to launch the free market philosophy, which helped globalization to expand and ultimately cover the entire globe. "The American state, in the very process of supporting the export of capital and the expansion of multinational corporations, increasingly took responsibility for creating the political and juridical conditions for the general expansion and reproduction of capitalism internationally."[1] As a consequence, the nation state lost control over its economy, causing its power to address the needs of its citizens to be undermined. And owing to the establishment of the WTO in 1995, the nation state lost much of its sovereignty as well, giving free markets and globalization the freedom to expand and dominate the global economic and cultural scene, causing poor people and states to lose their abilities to shape their future.

Dominique Strauss-Kahn, former managing director of the IMF, said in 2011, "Globalization has delivered a lot . . . but it also has a dark side: a large and growing chasm between the rich and the poor. Clearly we need a new form of globalization to prevent the 'invisible hand' of the loosely regulated markets from becoming 'an invisible fist.'"[2] Despite this criticism, the situation has continued to worsen. In support of Strauss-Kahn's argument, Joseph Stiglitz says that globalization must be managed to benefit all citizens. In contrast, the promoters of globalization and free markets argue that markets need to be free of regulations to benefit all peoples. For example, Robert Kaplan said, "The traditional social contract that binds all citizens to the common good is gradually becoming an impediment to participation in the emerging global economy."[3]

One of the major consequences of globalization as it continues to unfold is the unleashing of the human desire to own as many things as possible, causing many nations and billions of individuals to drown in debt. Today, no one is able to stop globalization or reverse its course, and no state has enough courage to abandon the free market system. Since we are unable to stop either market capitalism or globalization, we need to understand the dynamics of both forces to regulate them and manage their consequences. We therefore need to develop new tools to distribute the gains and losses of globalization and market capitalism fairly among social classes in each society and among nations of the world.

Globalization and Free Trade Zones

President Obama's interest in expanding American exports overseas and creating more jobs at home was one of the reasons that motivated him to negotiate the Trans-Pacific Partnership (TPP) trade agreement. In contrast, enriching the rich seems to have been the driving force that motivated most members of Congress to support the creation of free trade zones. However, many Democratic members of Congress and US labor unions are opposed to forming new free trade zones, because their experience with the North American Free Trade Agreement (NAFTA) has been bad. While NAFTA has failed to increase American exports as promised, it has encouraged many US manufacturers to relocate production operations to Mexico, causing an estimated 1 million American workers to lose their jobs; NAFTA has also contributed to the freezing of wages for industrial workers owing to competition from cheap Mexican labor. Because of these facts, the newly negotiated TPP became one of the hottest topics of the 2016 presidential elections campaign. However, the TPP's primary objective is not to expand trade as claimed, but to encircle China and limit the space open to it. This means that TPP was designed to serve a geostrategic objective rather than an economic one. Nevertheless, President Trump fulfilled his campaign promise and cancelled America's participation in TPP.

According to the Economic Policy Institute (EPI), "The North American Free Trade Agreement was the door through which American workers were shoved into the neoliberal global labor market. By establishing the principle that U.S. corporations could relocate production elsewhere and still sell back into the United States, NAFTA undercut the bargaining power of American workers, which had driven the expansion of the middle class since the end of World War II. The result has been 20 years of stagnant wages and the upward redistribution of income, wealth and political power."[4] According to the EPI, NAFTA affected US workers in four principal ways:

First, NAFTA caused the loss of some 700,000 jobs as production moved from the United States to Mexico. Most of these losses came in US states where manufacturing is concentrated. The vast majority of workers who lost their jobs suffered a permanent loss of income. Second, NAFTA strengthened the ability of US corporations to force American workers to accept lower wages and social benefits. As soon as NAFTA became law, corporate managers began telling their workers that their companies intended to move to Mexico unless they lowered the cost of their labor. Third, the destruction of many Mexican agricultural communities and small business sectors caused the dislocation of several million Mexican workers and their families, and that was a major cause in the dramatic increase in illegal workers flowing into the US labor market. This put further downward pressure on US wages, especially in the already low-paying market for less skilled workers. Fourth, and most important, NAFTA was the template for the rules of the emerging global economy, in which the benefits would flow to capital and the costs to labor.[5]

Jeff Faux of the EPI says, "The American governing class—in alliance with the financial elites of its trading partners—applied NAFTA's principles to the World Trade Organization and to the policies of the World Bank and IMF. These principles constitute a deal under which employers of China's huge supply of low-wage workers were allowed access to US markets in exchange for allowing American multinational corporations the right to invest there."[6] This means that the Chinese government's agreement to allow US multinational corporations to invest in China has come at the expense of US workers, particularly the industrial and less skilled workers; and this in turn has caused the US trade deficit with China to increase year on year. For example, the US trade deficit with China, which was $34 billion in 1995, increased to $84 billion in 2000 and reached $367 billion in 2015.[7]

NAFTA, according to the EPI, was a doctrine of socialism for capital and free markets for labor, which means giving capitalists the right to share profits while forcing workers to compete with each other in open global markets. "Despite the rhetoric, the central goal of NAFTA was … to free American corporations from US laws protecting workers and the environment and to pave the way for the neoliberal agenda in the US—the privatization of public services, the deregulation of finance, and the destruction of the independent trade union movement. The inevitable result was to undercut workers' living standards all across North America. Wages and benefits have fallen behind worker productivity in all three countries."[8]

In 2004, Public Citizen said, "The outcomes of NAFTA include a staggering $181 billion US trade deficit with NAFTA partners and the related loss of 1 million net US jobs, growing income inequality, displacement of more than one million Mexican farmers and a doubling of desperate immigration from Mexico. Rather than creating the promised hundreds of thousands of US jobs, NAFTA has contributed to an enormous new US trade deficit with Mexico and Canada, which had already equated to an estimated net loss of one million U.S. jobs by 2004."[9]

An expanding free market system, cheaper and more efficient transportation systems, much faster and more reliable communications systems, and an American strategy to impose market capitalism on the world have led national economies to link with one another and form a global economy. In the meantime, the internationalization of major trade, financial and investment markets, and the open skies created by infomedia and other networks have made economic and cultural globalization a dynamic, self-sustaining and ever expanding global process that recognizes no political borders and respects no ideologies, traditions or sovereignties. As a consequence, globalization has enabled regions within national borders to move in different directions at different speeds according to their particular abilities and historic connections to exploit available opportunities, causing income, knowledge and socioeconomic gaps within and between societies to widen. On the other hand, traditional incentives and corporate tendencies to cooperate for the sake of a national interest have almost vanished, and mergers and the formation of business cartels across international lines have become the new model for corporate cooperation, and tools for consumer exploitation.

Adam Smith remarked more than two centuries ago that the division of labor is limited by the extent of the market. Thus, globalization, which works to expand markets to include all states, has forced upon the world community an international division of labor that reflects the competitive advantages of its participants. Meanwhile, the Internet, computer technology and satellite communications have created a totally new global labor market for knowledge workers. Peter Drucker said almost twenty years ago, "E-Commerce is creating a new and distinct boom, rapidly changing the economy, society, and politics."[10] Today, large corporations are creating new corporate cultures that differ from the cultures of the countries in which they originate as well as from the cultures of countries in which they operate. As a consequence, the sociocultural fragmentation of societies has been accelerated, causing most traditional cultures to become a thing of the past. In fact, all cultures have been changed in ways that have strengthened some, weakened others and deformed many more.

As globalization and the information and communications revolutions help the major trade, financial and investment markets to link together and form a global economy, they empower people to form virtual communities and associations based on shared values, as well as shared interests. Organizations such as human rights advocacy groups and religious communities, and even terrorist groups, are being formed on the basis of shared values across political lines, while organizations such as the Davos Economic Forum and bankers' associations are being formed on the basis of shared interests across cultural lines. Meanwhile, the free movement of capital, technology, knowledge, ideas and highly educated and talented individuals enables the few to reap most of the benefits of globalization; and this causes most people to feel the frustration and pressure of change without tangible benefits. As this process continues, the wealth and income gaps keep widening at national and global levels, which causes the middle class to shrink and the global economy to slow down. This also causes nation states to lose control of their economies and, with that, their abilities to meet domestic challenges and serve citizens.

The semi-skilled and unskilled workers of the world in particular are being forced by this change to compete with each other in a global market that forces wages to sink to the lowest levels possible for the sole benefit of the large corporations and their owners. This makes the claim that unregulated markets help the world's poor largely misleading, if not utterly false. Demonstrations organized by the world's poor and their supporters in many countries are desperate attempts to influence the direction of global change and improve their life conditions. However, because they are poor and largely undereducated, they lack the means to organize globally and effect change in their favor; but their ability to cause global change in their favor is weak and getting weaker, because the rich are gaining more economic and political power at their expense. In fact, some of the world's poor are scared of change, and, as a result, they tend to resist it and feel content with what they have.

Meanwhile, the world's rich individuals and corporations are cooperating to strengthen their control of the global economy and gain more political power. This power is being used to corrupt politicians and manipulate the media to further their economic and financial interests. And as economists on both sides of the ideological divide continue to argue over the benefits and drawbacks of globalization, the living conditions of the world's poor deteriorate further and calls for economic sustainability become louder; but hope of achieving sustainability or peace becomes dimmer. Globalization is expected to continue to expand and impact the lives and destinies of all peoples, because it is a historical development that has reached a speed where no one can stop or undo its consequences.

Interests, which have triumphed over values, and universal values that are about to triumph over narrow ideological ones, are linking the world's elites and young in many ways. Interests are linking business people and corporations and pushing them to close ranks to protect their entrenched interests against the state and the public. On the other hand, organizations dealing with human rights, environmental concerns and the deteriorating conditions of the world's poor are slowly linking conscious intellectuals and scientists, social activists and college students together and encouraging them to challenge corporations, and to work harder to make our world safer, livable and more humane.

Globalization has caused the economies, politics and security concerns of almost all nations to be linked to each other, causing major national issues such as poverty and epidemics to become international, and major international issues such as the financial crisis and terrorism to become national. Today, there is no major national issue anywhere that has no international dimension; and no international issue that does not have national roots. As a result, the ability of every state to deal with major challenges on its own has been vastly weakened. The debt crisis is one example that demonstrates the intricate and complex relationships that tie national and international financial and political institutions together, and cause even regional approaches to dealing with such issues to fail. This simply means that there is no national or regional solution to the issues of debt, poverty, income and wealth inequality, sustainability or the environment: all nations need to collaborate to find workable and humane ways to address these issues and the many challenges we face. No nation, therefore, can afford to close its eyes and pretend that it does not see or feel the pain of others.

Since change affects societies whenever and wherever it happens, a changing global economy affects every national economy and society. As it moves forward, globalization forces societies to experience sociocultural, socioeconomic and sociopolitical changes that bring with them benefits and losses, winners and losers. Some of the benefits are reflected in promoting human rights and social justice; in calling for the protection of the environment and the middle class; in international efforts to cancel Third World debt and eradicate poverty and disease; and in promoting the principles of democracy and equality. Global change has also caused an Arab awakening that, despite its utter failure, seems to have rewritten the traditional rules of popular revolutions, as well as the way in which to organize demonstrations against injustice and the excesses of market capitalism and institutions that ignore the world's poor and the disadvantaged.

Globalization based on the philosophy of free markets cannot continue and be appreciated unless the gains and pains it generates are shared by all participants. As corporations move from one country to another, they move with them production operations, financial services, management systems, new cultures, and research and development institutes, causing centers of economic and financial power and technological innovations to be scattered. In the process, they create winners and losers of individuals, groups, regions and states everywhere. Therefore, to ensure that globalization helps the poor as it empowers the rich, states need to intervene to enact laws and regulations to guarantee fairness and strengthen business ethics and social responsibility. State action is also needed to prevent national centers of economic and financial power from acquiring excessive political power.

In addition, the public needs to become more aware of the advantages and disadvantages of globalization and how to make globalization work in its favor. Despite the financial crisis of 2008, globalization continues to cause wide capital, production and human dislocations around the globe, and to create fear and apprehension as well as wealth and poverty everywhere. In the meantime, lack of global cooperation to enact adequate financial regulations has encouraged powerful states to ignore the rules, while preventing smaller ones from doing the same. Most poor and weak nations are unable to ignore the rules because they cannot free themselves from the chains of economic restructuring imposed on them by the IMF and the World Bank, or repay their public debt. As a result, states that have pretended to abide by the rules but continue to ignore them, such as China, have emerged as the biggest winners of free trade and globalization; and states that could not ignore the rules have emerged as the biggest losers. In addition, most wealthy individuals are able to ignore the rules and manipulate the law because they are able to buy justice in most countries.

In the age of agriculture, particularly towards its end, state influence helped commerce expand, causing farm products and tools and farming techniques to be regionalized. In the industrial age, which followed the agricultural age, economic growth and diversification, financial services and colonialism caused manufactured goods and capital to be internationalized. As a result, capital was able to seek investment opportunities wherever they existed; and this, in turn, has strengthened the trend that regionalized agricultural products centuries earlier, empowering it to expand internationally. Today, the fast-emerging knowledge age is not only reinforcing older trends; it is causing ideas, services, knowledge, technology, information, human talent and cultures to go beyond all borders. This means that the answer to the inequalities and the unsettling consequences of globalization is not in rejecting globalization but in managing its many aspects.

Commenting on the economic success of the Asian nations in an age of growing globalization, Joseph Stiglitz said, "It was their ability to take advantage of globalization, without being taken advantage of by globalization that accounts for much of their success."[11]

Notes

1. Leo Panitch and Sam Gindin; p. 6.
2. Howard Schneider, IMF chief sees recovery as a work in progress, *The Washington Post*, April, 12, 2011, A13.
3. Robert D. Kaplan, "The Return of Ancient Times," *The Atlantic Monthly*, June 2000, 16.
4. Jeff Faux, NAFT's Impact on US Workers, Economic Policy Institute December 9, 2013. http://www.epi.org/blog/naftas-impact-workers/
5. Jeff Faux, NAFTA's Impact on US Workers; Economic Policy Institute, December 9, 2013. http://www.epi.org/blog/naftas-impact-workers/
6. Ibid.
7. Trade in goods with China, Foreign Trade, US Census bureau, US Department of Commerce. https://www.census.gov/foreign-trade/balance/c5700.html
8. Jeff Faux, NAFT's Impact on US Workers, Economic Policy Institute, December 9, 2013.
9. NAFTA's 20-Year Legacy and the Fate of the Trans-Pacific Partnership, Public Citizen February, 2014.
10. Peter Drucker: "Beyond the Information Revolution," *The Atlantic Monthly*, October 1999, 50.
11. Joseph Stiglitz: Making Globalization Work, 2006, 31.

CHAPTER 10

The Debt Crisis and the US Economy

In this chapter, the 2008 financial crisis will be reviewed, with emphasis on its causes and manifestations, and the policies adopted by the US government to deal with it and stimulate the American economy. At the end, I shall try to evaluate the results of these policies in view of the goals they sought to accomplish.

The Financial Crisis

In response to the financial crisis of 2008, the US government intervened to prevent a meltdown of the financial sector; it put together a $700 billion bailout package. This package, officially called the Emergency Economic Stabilization Act of 2008, sought to save the banking system, restore confidence in the US economy and calm the global financial markets. The mandate of this Act was to authorize the US Treasury to purchase bad debts, which included mortgages, auto loans, college loans and other bills. $250 billion of this money was deposited in banks to give them the cash needed to restore public confidence, and to resume normal operations and lending to the public. Since the US economy depends heavily on lending to finance many business and consumer activities, it was natural to give priority to rescuing the faltering banks and save the system from collapse. The *Guardian* called the crisis a heart attack: "It was the year the neo-liberal orthodoxy that ran the world for 30 years suffered a heart attack of epic proportions."[1]

M. Rabie, *The Global Debt Crisis and Its Socioeconomic Implications*,
https://doi.org/10.1007/978-3-319-66215-2_10

However, Mike Collins writing in *Forbes* seven years later said: "Most people think that the big bank bailout was the $700 billion that the treasury department used to save the banks during the financial crash in September of 2008. But this is a long way from the truth because the bailout is still ongoing. The Special Inspector General for TARP (Troubled Asset Relief Program) summary of the bailout says that the total commitment of government is $16.8 trillion with $4.6 trillion already paid out. But it isn't just the government bailout money that tells the story of the bailout. This is a story about lies, cheating, and a multi-faceted corruption which was often criminal."[2] In fact, the US government lied to Congress and the American people in outlining the commitment it made; and in an attempt to justify its lies, it said that the bailout was needed to restore American and international confidence in the banking system and the US economy.

"During the housing bubble Wall Street was considered the heart and soul of free market capitalism, but when they were in danger of total collapse they fell on their knees as socialists, begging the government and tax payers to bail them out."[3] This means that by taking money from the government banks defamed market capitalism and proved that it had failed to be responsible and efficient. This is probably why major banks claimed that they were financially sound and did not need the bailout money, but the government ordered them to take it in order to calm the markets. This sounds as if bankers, by taking government money, were doing the US government and the American people a great favor. Despite these claims, some banks went back to the government and asked for more bailout money because they were in bad financial shape. "In fact, $7.7 trillion of the secret emergency lending was only disclosed to the public after Congress forced a one-time audit of the Federal Reserve in November of 2011. After the audit the public found out the bailout was in trillions not billions; and that there were no requirements attached to the bailout money—the banks could use it for any purpose."[4]

Allan Sloan wrote an article in *Fortune* in 2012 in which he talks about what he calls "the 5 myths of the great financial crisis." He said, "I've been writing about the financial meltdown and its aftermath almost continually since I joined *Fortune* the month after the symptoms surfaced. Now, five years into the problem, I find myself getting increasingly angry and frustrated watching myth supplant reality about what happened, and seeing fantasy displace common sense when it comes to fixing the problems that got us in this mess."[5] In explaining the myths, Sloan starts by refuting the suggestion raised by conservative economists and politicians that governments should have left the markets to correct their own mistakes. And by refuting this argument, he implicitly affirms the need for government intervention when economic or financial crises occur.

"When giant institutions like Washington Mutual and Wachovia and Leman Brothers failed, and the likes of Citigroup, Bank of America, GE Capital, Merrill Lynch, Morgan Stanley, Goldman Sachs, and huge European banks were near collapse, letting all go under would have brought on the financial apocalypse. We would have ended up with a down turn worse than the Great Depression. The federal government (including the Fed) had to front trillions of dollars and guarantee trillions of obligations—a total I calculated last year at more than $14 trillion—to stop the panic."[6] Sloan says that the government did the right thing by bailing GM and Chrysler, but it was wrong to bail out creditors at financial companies. As for the causes of the financial crisis, Sloan blames the markets and banks.

"It was the private market—not government programs—that made, packaged, and sold most of these wretched loans without regard to their quality. The packaging, combined with credit default swaps and other esoteric derivatives, spread the contagion throughout the world. That's why what initially seemed to be a large but containable U.S. mortgage problem touched off a worldwide financial crisis."[7] And since neither TARP nor the new regulations imposed enough restrictions on the size of banks and executive compensation, Sloan doubts that the new financial regulations enacted by Congress in 2010 are strong enough to correct the problem; he therefore does not rule out another financial crisis in the near future.

Matt Taibbi, writing for *Rolling Stone* in 2013, tried to analyze the crisis, its root causes and aftermath. He said: "the most appalling part of the story has been the lying," and he claimed that everyone who was involved in fixing the crisis had lied, including the banks and regulators. "The public has been lied to so shamelessly and so often in the course of the past four years that the failure to tell the truth to the general populace has become a kind of baked-in, official feature of the financial rescue. Money wasn't the only thing the government gave Wall Street—it also conferred the right to hide the truth from the rest of us. And it was all done in the name of helping regular people and creating jobs."[8]

The information that became public later indicated that banks needed the bailout money because many of them were on the verge of collapse; yet banks did not use the cash to extend loans to small businesses or help homeowners unable to make mortgage payments. Instead, they deposited bailout money in the Fed. "In August 2008, before the bailout began, there were just $2 billion in excess reserves at the Fed. But by October, the number had ballooned to $267 billion—and by January 2009, it had grown to $843 billion. That means there was suddenly more money sitting uselessly in Fed accounts than Congress had approved for either the TARP bailout or the much-loathed Obama stimulus. Instead of lending their new cash to struggling homeowners and small businesses, the banks were literally sitting on it."[9] By July, 2013, reserves at the Fed reached $1.4 trillion, $200 billion more than the entire gross domestic product (GDP) of Russia.

In February 2009, Congress approved a $787 billion stimulus package to revive the economy which was at the time contracting. The plan was called the American Recovery and Reinvestment Act (ARRA); its purpose was to end the recession by stimulating consumer spending and saving between 900,000 and 2.3 million jobs. The plan was also meant to restore consumer confidence and encourage spending, increase domestic demand and help the economy to grow. "It also aimed to restore trust in the finance industry by limiting bonuses for senior executives in companies that received TARP funds."[10] And though the plan was a ten-year package, $720 billion, or 91.5%, was budgeted for the first three fiscal years. It allocated $185 billion in FY 2009, $400 billion in FY 2010 and $135 billion in FY 2011.[11]

The provision requiring that bonuses for senior executives be limited was totally ignored; neither banks nor mortgage companies respected it, nor did regulators insist on enforcing it. The reason for this unacceptable behavior is simple: the Federal Reserve was created and is owned by the banks themselves, and the people who have been running the US Treasury Department were and still are former employees of large banks and investment firms. This has made the US Federal Reserve system "a system of the banks, by the banks, for the banks". For example, Fannie Mae and Freddie Mac needed nearly $400 billion in assistance to avoid bankruptcy in 2008; yet they gave their employees about $100 million in bonuses between 2008 and 2010. "According to the New York comptroller's office, Wall Street bonuses totaled $22.5 billion in 2009,"[12] the year in which the US economy contracted. However, in 2008, bonuses totaled $17.6 billion. And in 2010, the *Economist* reported that bonuses were $20.8 billion.[13]

This means that between 2008 and 2010, the worst years of the Great Recession, bonuses given to Wall Street executives totaled $60.9 billion, almost twice the money given by the government to homeowners who were badly hurt by the housing bubble. "According to the latest report of the Special Inspector General for TARP, the government has only expended

$19 billion on TARP housing programs as of the end of last year (2015). There's another $18.5 billion available to be spent."[14] Even if this money eventually gets spent to help homeowners, the total would be 37.5 billion.

The objectives of the Obama economic recovery plan were:

1. To preserve and create jobs and promote economic recovery;
2. To assist those most impacted by the recession;
3. To provide investments to increase economic efficiency by spurring technological advances in science and health;
4. To invest in transportation, environmental protection and other infrastructure that will provide long-term economic benefits;
5. To stabilize state and local government budgets, in order to minimize and avoid reductions in essential services and counterproductive state and local tax increases.[15]

In 2010, President Obama signed a new stimulus package worth $858 billion. This package, however, was more of a tax cuts deal than new spending; it extended the Bush tax cuts through 2012, and extended the unemployment benefits through 2011. It also gave $55 billion in tax cuts for industry, cut social security taxes by 2%, which added about $120 million to workers' spendable income, and extended college tuition credit. And though the plan is essentially a tax cut plan, it nevertheless gave people more money to spend but reduced contribution to the social security fund and reduced the US government income from taxes. As a consequence, the plan added billions of dollars to the 2011 budget deficit and thus to the US public debt.

Matt Taibbi said: "In the end, there was no lending requirement attached to any aspect of the bailout. Banks used their hundreds of billions for almost every purpose under the sun, but lending to the homeowners and small businesses and cities they had destroyed. And one of the most disgusting uses they found for all their billions in free government money was to help them earn even more free government money. The bailouts didn't result in much new business lending. If anything, the bailouts actually hindered lending, as banks became more like house pets that grow fat and lazy on two guaranteed meals a day than wild animals that have to go out into the jungle and hunt for opportunities in order to eat."[16] The bailout money enabled banks to buy other companies and finance mergers; which caused the sizes of the already big banks to become bigger and thus less manageable and more risky.

Banks have two ways open to them to make money without taking risk. First, they are able to borrow from the Federal Reserve at near zero interest rates, and then lend this money to the government at higher interest rates by buying bonds issued by the US Treasury to finance the government's humongous budget deficits. Second, banks are able to deposit whatever money they have in the Federal Reserve and earn interest on it, also risk free. As a consequence, banks have lost most incentives they had in the past to lend money to consumers and small businesses where risk is involved. Banks, as a result, have become like parasites; they live and prosper on sucking the blood of their victims without giving them anything in return; and in the process they expose their victims to all kinds of diseases.

Now that the US public debt has exceeded $20 trillion, the equivalent of 107% of American GDP, we need to ask two basic questions. First, how did the debt get so large so fast? Second, how do we deal with a seemingly unstoppable debt before we face another serious economic and financial crisis? There are three major forces that have caused and continue to cause the debt to grow: first, the Great Recession and its aftermath; second, a failed economic policy that lowered taxes without being able to increase revenues; and third a slowing economy that continues to lose manufacturing jobs and causes income and wealth inequalities to widen. Even before the 2008 crisis, the debt grew by 50% between 2000 and 2007, increasing from $6 to $9 trillion; this increase came primarily from the Bush administration's war ventures in Afghanistan and Iraq, and the tax cuts enacted by Congress in 2000. And owing to the $700 billion bailout, the debt grew from $9 trillion to $10.5 trillion in a few months. In addition, "the economic stimulus package and other stimulus spending added another $3 trillion in two years. Military spending boosted spending, while revenues from taxes declined after the recession."[17] In fact, the current US economic and social policies, the slow growing global economy and lower tax rates have placed the national debt on an escalator that moves up and does not move down.

US Public Debt

The size of the US economy and the many ways in which America influences economic, financial, political and security developments in the world makes any discussion of the global debt crisis incomplete without analyzing the US debt problem, and evaluating its impact on the world economies and peoples.

Since 2000, the United States has been borrowing a lot of money to balance its budgets and compensate for tax cuts favoring the rich; Money is also needed to finance conspicuous consumption and wage war on many fronts. Since these policies have continued, the United States cannot stop borrowing and accumulating debt year after year. Following the 2008 crisis, interest rates were reduced to near zero in order to save big banks from bankruptcies. But tax reductions and near zero interest rates caused the wealth and income inequality gaps to widen further, which in turn caused rates of economic growth to slow down. In June 2017, the US public debt exceeded $19.94 trillion. In an attempt to show how serious this is, the National Debt Clock.org says, "If you lay $1 bills on top of each other they would make a pile **2,166,210 km**, or **1,346,020 miles** high. That's equivalent to **5.64** trips to the Moon."[18]

According to the Congressional Budget Office (CBO), the US budget as of August 2016 was as follows: outlays of $3.9 trillion, revenues of $3.3 trillion, and deficit of $590 trillion.[19] Trading Economics, which gets its numbers from the US Bureau of the Public Debt, says that the ratio of the US public debt to the GDP was 95.2% in 2010; 99.4% in 2011; 101% in 2012; 102% in 2013; 103% in 2014; and 104.2% in 2015; as for 2016, it is expected to reach 106.4%.[20] This means that the United States has not only failed to control its borrowing appetite; it has also failed to stabilize the debt ratio to GDP.

If current economic growth and budget deficits trends continue as projected by the CBO, US debt will increase year after year without interruption. For example, the 2016 budget deficit reached $587 billion, about $150 billion more than 2015. "A slowdown in the growth of federal revenues, as well as rising government spending, pushed the US deficit up in the 2016 fiscal year for the first time since 2011, reversing the trend of falling deficits as the economy recovered in recent years."[21] The CBO also says that "If current laws generally remained unchanged, the deficit would increase from 2.9 percent to 4.9 percent of GDP over the next decade, which means that the deficit will increase by 3.6 percent annually."[22] As a result, the US government would be spending about 4.5% of its GDP annually just to service the public debt; in addition to spending 5–6% on the military and other security agencies. Since the government collects about 21% of GDP in taxes, it would be spending nearly half of all revenues on two items: servicing the public debt and covering security expenditures. As a consequence, the US government would not be able to meet its other domestic and foreign obligations without borrowing more money or raising tax rates substantially to generate enough revenues to cover its many expenses, which no Congress would approve.

The CBO estimates the cumulative budget deficit between 2017 and 2027 to be $9.4 trillion, causing the debt to reach $29 trillion by 2027. Assuming that the US economy will grow over the next decade at the average rate of the last 7 years of 2.1%, the GDP will be about $23 trillion in 2027. As a result, the debt ratio to the GDP will be about 124%. Furthermore, assuming that the average interest rate over the same 10-year period is 3%, interest on the debt in 2027 will be about $870 billion. Nevertheless, it is unlikely that the United States would be able to stay the course for ten more years without a major recession that would force it to change course.

In light of these numbers, can the US government repay its debt at any time in the foreseeable future? Can it even service its debt without going deeper into debt year after year? The answer to both questions is no. The United States, along with many other nations, has long passed the point where it could service its debt without borrowing, let alone repay it.

Can the United States do something to ameliorate the debt problem in the short run? Yes, it can do a lot to reduce the severity of this problem and limit its negative social, political and economic consequences. But to do so, the US administration and members of Congress need to acknowledge the severity of the debt problem and its negative impact on wealth and income equality, as well as on the performance of the American economy. "High public debt has been shown to slow down economic growth and to exert upward pressure on interest rates. Slow economic growth reduces employment and business prospects for American families, and it has a negative effect on family incomes and wealth."[23] Second, they need to realize that the traditional fiscal and monetary tools of financial management have become largely dysfunctional, which is a hard pill for most economists to swallow in the age of market capitalism. And third, they need to close tax loopholes and raise taxes on the super rich. However, no action can liberate the United States or any other indebted nation from the debt burden and revive the global economy except paying the debt of all nations now—and the only plan that can accomplish this objective is the Ramo Plan that I outlined in Chap. 3.

If the US administration and Congress continue to follow the mostly outdated economic and financial policies and give priority to political infighting and special interests, America's problems will only get worse. Senator Tom Coburn, commenting on the political infighting and the severity of the budget deficit and the debt crisis, wrote on April 5, 2011, "of my Republican friends I would ask: what good is a Republican Party without a republic? And of my Democratic friends: what good is your commitment to the poor without an economy to sustain your commitments?"[24] In fact, for members of Congress, politics comes before policy, special interests before the national interest and rigid ideology before rational thinking.

The 2016 presidential elections campaign has demonstrated that ideology does not only divide Republicans from Democrats, but also divides each party into two competing camps. Each party seems to be going through an agonizing process of internal transformation that includes thoughts, views and attitudes. While the transformation within the Republican Party has pushed it more towards the right, the transformation within the Democratic Party has pushed it more towards the left, causing the ideological divide between the two camps to widen and deepen. As a consequence, it is unlikely that the parties will reach consensus on any important issue, except perhaps giving more money to the military to wage yet more senseless wars.

It seems that smart economists and politicians have realized that neither the United States nor any highly indebted European state will be able to repay its debt at any time in the future. As a consequence, the debate over budget deficits and public debts on both sides of the Atlantic Ocean has shifted from talking about how to repay the debt to how to manage the debt and stabilize its size in relation to each state's GDP. But debt management, to be explained in the next two chapters, has made the situation in both Greece and Spain worse than before.

At the time of writing, September 2017, the size of the US public debt had exceeded the size of the American GDP by five percentage points. For the United States to gradually reduce its debt as a percentage of its GDP, the annual increase in the American GDP has to exceed the annual debt servicing. If interest payments exceed the annual increase in the GDP, the debt will grow in size as well as a percentage of GDP. On the other hand, for the United States to repay its debt over the long run, it has to start having budget surpluses that exceed the annual debt servicing payments. According to the Congressional Budget Office, the last time the US government had a surplus was in 2001. From 2001 to 2009, budget spending increased by 6.5% of GDP (from 18.2% to 24.7%) while revenues declined by 4.7% of GDP (from 19.5% to 14.8%), causing deficits and the public debt to increase substantially. However, spending has declined as a percentage of GDP to 20.7% in 2015, and revenues have increased as a percentage of

GDP to 18.1%; this has caused the size of the budget deficit to shrink substantially. As for 2016, economic growth has been less than expected, and so have the revenues, causing the deficit to increase from the projected $517–$587 billion.

It must be noted, however, that numbers change continuously owing to projected and actual revenues and expenditures. Nevertheless, all projected and actual revenues and expenditures and growth rates suggest that the annual increase in GDP will be less than the annual interest on the public debt for as far as the eye can see. As a result, the debt is expected to increase in size as well as in percentage of GDP, unless the government changes its economic, financial and tax policies. Nevertheless, some economists and politicians think or hope that the economy will resume normal growth soon, which will enable America to cope with its many financial and social problems; unfortunately such people are mistaken. The times of high growth rates are over for the reasons already mentioned and also others, which I will discuss in the last chapter.

America's Debt Options

What are the US options for dealing with its mounting debt problem? Under current economic and tax policies, there are only a few, none of which is pleasant. The first is to default, which is no option for the world's largest economy and dominant superpower; the second to increase the current tax rates by 30% or more, which is neither possible nor desirable; the third is to go deeper into debt and larger budget deficits, which risks causing the economic growth rate to decline further and complicate the many social and financial challenges facing America; and the fourth is to rely on borrowing from the American people and cause its economy to enter a permanent state of lower growth rates and loss of dynamism, like Japan.

However, can the United States live with a continuously rising debt to GDP ratio and tiny economic growth rates like Japan? (Japan's public debt is estimated at 232% of GDP.) I do not believe it can. The American socioeconomic conditions and cultural values are different from those of Japan, and therefore what works for Japan is unlikely to work for the United States. On the other hand, Japanese high savings rates have enabled the state to borrow from its citizens and recycle their money on their behalf. In contrast, the US government, owing to low savings rates and a culture of consumerism, owes about half of its debt to foreigners. Despite these differences, using domestic savings to finance deficits seems to have caused

Japan's economy to stagnate and lose dynamism. But since its population is largely stagnant and its standards of living are high, Japan does not have to create millions of jobs year after year. In contrast, the United States, owing to continued population growth, has to create over a million jobs annually, and spend billions of dollars to help the needy due to widespread poverty.

Nations usually borrow to close temporary budget deficits, or to invest in projects designed to increase the production capacity of their economies, which usually causes state revenues to rise and eventually closes deficits gaps. The United States has been borrowing to finance wars and conspicuous consumption, both of which have hurt rather that helped the US economy and the American people. Though economists have suggested different "sustainable" debt to GDP ratios, experts seem to say that when debt reaches 90% of GDP it causes potential growth to decline by 1% annually. America has passed this threshold by fifteen points.

Nevertheless, no debt to GDP ratio is sustainable or unsustainable without qualifications. Sustainability is a function of three factors: the annual growth rate, the size of the budget deficit and expected interest rates. Any state can borrow until markets say no more, just as happened with Greece. At such a point, markets would have lost confidence in the economy and the state's ability to manage its financial affairs. Since almost all Western states have failed to manage their financial affairs, the statement has become not "too big to fail" but rather "too tall to fall." However, unless they take drastic measures, all highly indebted states will eventually fall under the heavy weight of the debt they are carrying on their backs and the backs of their citizens.

Since all options seem to be bad and risky, the only way to deal with the debt problem is to find a creative formula to repay the entire debt now, which the Ramo Plan is designed to do. This, as explained earlier, has the capacity to liberate not only America from its debt, but all other rich and poor nations, restructure the international monetary system, revitalize the world economy and help poor nations to develop their economies, transform their cultures and join the industrialized world; and thus make global sustainable development achievable.

If the United States were to repay its debt now as the Ramo Plan suggests, its budget deficit would be reduced by more than 50% immediately. Such an action would restore consumer and business confidence in the US economy, reassure the international financial markets and give the US government an opportunity to grow its economy while restructuring spending and tax policies gradually. And if the United States were to climb back within the coming ten years to where its finances were in 2001, when revenues were 19.5% of GDP and the budget was 18.2% of GDP, it would be in a position to contain its debt and start reducing its size.

The last time the United States had a surplus was in 2001. However, the Afghani and Iraqi wars launched in 2001 and 2003, respectively, have increased expenses and created an ever expanding budget deficit. Meanwhile, tax cuts enacted by the Bush administration and chronic tax loopholes have caused revenues to decline and thus enlarge the size of the budget deficits. If these tax cuts and loopholes were to be eliminated, revenues would increase substantially, but not enough to close the chronic budget deficit. However, if the tax cuts and loopholes were to be closed and the public debt were to be repaid in its entirety, the US budget deficit would more likely be eliminated, and no group or industry would lose anything. And if the United States stops its senseless wars and repays its debt now, it will restore its global credibility and enter a new era of economic prosperity and peace.

While the per capita debt today exceeds $61,000, up from $49,000 in 2012, it is expected to reach $80,000 in ten years as the total debt reaches $29 trillion. On the other hand, if the US government continues to finance budget deficits by borrowing and printing money, it would not take the financial markets long to lose confidence in the US economy and the dollar. To avoid being in such a situation, in 2009 the Federal Reserve articulated a creative plan to manage the debt and deficit problems: the Federal Reserve creates money, lends it to US banks at near zero interest rates, and banks, in turn, use this money to buy bonds issued by the US Treasury to finance budget deficits. But by inventing this scheme, the Federal Reserve has caused the wealth and income gaps to widen and social mobility to decline substantially; and in the process, the scheme has caused the middle class to shrink and the economy to slow down. Only the big banks, other financial institutions and hedge funds managers have benefited from this scheme, which has come at the expense of most Americans and savers throughout the world.

Helicopter Money

Believing that a new recession is coming soon, the *Economist* said on February 20, 2016, "Policymakers in rich economies need to consider some radical approaches to tackling the next downturn." In considering alternative approaches, the article goes on to say that "there is a deeper concern that, if or when that recession comes, policymakers will have very few options for dealing with it."[25] It is clear that the *Economist* sees no point in repeating what has been done before; implying that neither stimulus programs nor austerity measures are able to deal with the expected recession. As a consequence, the *Economist* suggests, though reluctantly, using what economist Milton Friedman called "helicopter money," which means printing as much money as needed to repay the entire public debt. Since the US government can take such an action, neither central banks nor Congress nor financial markets have a role to play in such a scenario.

However, only a few states can use helicopter money to repay their debt; they are the United States, members of the Eurozone acting collectively, Britain, Switzerland, Japan and probably China. While the United States and, to some extent, Britain and Japan are able to take an action like this on their own, it is very hard for members of the Eurozone to agree to it. Germany is unlikely to accept it, because its conservative ruling party feels that Germany is financially strong and able to handle the debt issue without having to resort to such a scheme. The German ruling elite, in fact, does not believe that states such as Greece, Spain and Italy deserve to be liberated from debt without paying a price for financial mismanagement.

There is no doubt that America can print as much money as needed to repay its debt and more, as the US Federal Reserve has in fact been printing money since 2008 without interruption; but printing over $20 trillion in weeks or months cannot be done without serious consequences. An increase in the money supply of this magnitude is more likely to cause inflation, devalue the US dollar and invite other nations, particularly the Eurozone nations, China, Britain and Japan, to devalue their currencies in order to maintain the competiveness of their exports. Since most other currencies are pegged, in one way or another to the dollar, attempts to devalue the dollar in order to restore economic competitiveness become rather meaningless. However, such an action would undermine world confidence in America's wisdom and leadership; and this, in turn, would diminish the attractiveness of the US dollar as the world's premier reserve currency.

Is it fair and morally acceptable that America prints as many dollars as it needs to repay its debt and leave billions of people languish in debt and poverty? Is it fair and morally acceptable that the United States liberates itself from its debt burden when most of the money poor nations borrowed was stolen by dictators, corrupt politicians and foreign corporations and invested in America and Europe or deposited in their banks? The only acceptable way to repay the debt is to liberate all nations from the debt burden at once. Such an action would create a new sense of fraternity among all nations, revitalize the world economy and reduce poverty and need; it would also encourage most people to be optimistic and willing to contribute to making our world a better and more humane place for all of us to live in and enjoy. In fact, liberation from need and financial chains is the first and best cure for chronic social and cultural ills, as well as for the problems of alienation, ideological extremism and radicalism, all of which often lead to hatred and sometimes to terrorism and war.

The so-called helicopter money scheme and the Ramo Plan may appear similar, but they differ from each other in several ways:

1. Helicopter money is a scheme to enable one state or a few states to print money freely and repay their debt. Since this option is limited to some states, other nations will not be able to liberate themselves from debt using the same scheme. As a result, the poor nations will continue to suffer, and the global demand for goods and services will not expand enough to invigorate the global economy and cause growth rates to rise everywhere. Moreover, since some of the Eurozone states are highly indebted while others are not, it would be very difficult for all states to agree to such a plan.
2. By freeing the rich states of their debt while leaving the poor ones to pay interest on their debt to the rich states, the impoverished peoples of the world would be reduced to mere slaves working to enrich the rich, in exchange for getting insulted and humiliated and poorer day by day. This is more likely to cause mutual hatred, spread radicalism and increase terrorism. As a consequence, the world would be divided into rich masters and poor slaves, causing every party involved in this sick relationship to lose a good deal of its humanity.
3. Using the helicopter option to liberate the industrialized nations only from debt is likely to help the rich countries' economies to grow modestly for a few years, because the limited financial resources of the world's poor will prevent them from becoming active consumers. Meanwhile, an exclusive helicopter option would cause international interest rates to rise and cause poor nations' debt servicing to increase and their ability to grow their economies to decline substantially, in addition to keeping global demand weak.
4. An exclusive helicopter plan for the rich nations would hinder rather than facilitate the establishment of the funds proposed in the Ramo

Plan; the educational, humanitarian, environmental and sustainable development funds. And without such funds, the old economic, sociocultural and political problems would intensify, causing poverty to increase, resentment in poor states to deepen, and radicalism and terrorism to become endemic. In addition, civil and regional wars would be likely to spread, and the flood of economic and war refugees would rise, leading to more internal strife, racism and fear in Europe as well as in America.

5. Printing trillions of dollars to repay the richest nations' debt is more likely to disrupt the international monetary system and cause confusion and uncertainty. Poor nations that cannot do what the rich ones can would oppose such a plan, because accepting it means accepting outrageous debt servicing obligations and slavery, and possibly higher rates of inflation. Moreover, such a plan would poison the international atmosphere and create bitterness and hatred.. This in turn would lead to the formation of new international alliances that would seek to undermine the power and interests of the rich nations.

Therefore, if the United States were to free itself from the debt burden while leaving the poor nations to languish in poverty and sink deeper in debt, its action would be viewed as unfair and largely imperialistic. In fact, no nation should be entitled to indulge in conspicuous consumption for decades and then print money freely to pay for its bad behavior and financial and economic mismanagement. On the other hand, since taking such an actions would be unprecedented, it might have serious consequences no one is able to foresee. One of the more likely of these is a collective action by the poor nations to default on their foreign debt and stop paying interest to the rich nations and their banks, causing many Western banks to collapse; this would cause a global depression. Wholesale banking bankruptcy would be impossible for governments to deal with. A collective default by the poor nations would be fully justified and would be encouraged by the world's intellectuals, human rights organizations and many economists across the globe; and the feeling of bitterness towards America and the other rich nations would last for generations.

An examination of the achievements of the stimulus plan of the Obama administration and the Federal Reserve would reveal that it has rescued the American economy from a deeper recession, but it has not enabled the economy to regain its vitality or competitiveness. Even the lowering of the unemployment rate from 9% to 4.4% (official rate) has not come as a result of a robust economy but largely through lower labor participation in the workforce. If the number of workers who left the workforce since 2008 were to be added to the number of the officially unemployed, the total would bring the unemployment rate to 9.2%. In addition, the US economy has lost millions of high-paying manufacturing and mining jobs that cannot be recovered; and the millions of jobs it has created since 2009 have been in services that pay lower wages and little or no social and health benefits.

Moreover, the stimulus plan has caused the public debt to increase by 90% during the last eight years. While the debt was $10.6 trillion on January 20, 2009,[26] it exceeded $20 trillion in September 2017, which means that it has increased by more than $1.2 trillion every year since Barack Obama became president. And because of rising public debt and slow economic growth and near zero interest rates, social mobility has declined, the size of the middle class has shrunk, and wealth and income inequalities have risen sharply, causing the economy to lose its major driving force of growth. Since American exports are lagging behind imports, and because the economy continues to shift from manufacturing to services, it is not possible for the United States to recover the jobs it has lost since 2008 or the potential growth it once had, unless current economic and social policies are changed drastically.

Nevertheless, President Donald Trump declared that he will stimulate the economy, as if the economy has not been receiving one dose of stimulus after another for years. Trump would like to do his share of this by spending a trillion dollars rebuilding the crumbling infrastructure, cutting tax rates and bringing manufacturing jobs back home. Trump might be able to pressure some US companies and bring back a good number of jobs, but no matter how successful this may be, industrial jobs are declining, and industrial workers will not get the salaries and social benefits they once had. In addition, manufacturing jobs are vanishing everywhere; all industrial states, including Japan, China, Germany, Britain, Italy, South Korea and even India, are losing them to robots. Therefore, Trump will not be able to prevent US manufacturing jobs from declining.

Moreover, spending a trillion dollar on infrastructural projects will increase government spending substantially, while cutting tax rates will reduce government revenues; these are both causes of increasing budget deficits and national debt. Using tax reduction to stimulate the economy and create jobs is no longer a policy that works; yes, it worked during the Reagan administration in the 1980s, but times have changed and policies therefore must change. What worked in the industrial age four decades ago cannot work in the knowledge age, particularly since we are passing through the transitional period separating the two ages where old tools for managing economic and financial affairs are crumbling and no new ones are being developed in time to replace them. Instead of tax cuts, America needs to close all tax loopholes and raise tax rates on the wealthy, not reduce them. New times require new ideas, and global challenges require global solutions.

The *Economist*, based on an interview with President Trump, wrote on May 13, 2017 that "Mr. Trump's agenda comes with two dangers. The economic assumptions implicit in it are internally inconsistent. And they are based on a picture of America's economy that is decades out of date." The magazine adds that Trump's obsession with the effect of trade on manufacturing jobs "blinds Trumponomics to today's biggest economic worry: the turbulence being created by new technologies. And economic nationalism will speed automation: firms unable to outsource jobs to Mexico will stay competitive by investing in machines at home. Productivity and profits may rise, but this may not help the less-skilled factory workers who Mr. Trump claims are his priority." As a consequence, the *Economist* says that "Trumponomics is a poor recipe for long-term prosperity ... [It] offers no lasting remedy for America's economic ills. It may yet pave the way for something worse."[27]

Notes

1. Nick Mathiason, Banking Collapse of 2008: Three weeks that changed the world, the Guardian, December 27, 2008. https://www.theguardian.com/business/2008/dec/28/markets-credit-crunch-banking-2008
2. Mike Collins, the big bank bailout, Forbes, July 14, 2015. http://www.forbes.com/sites/mikecollins/2015/07/14/the-big-bank-bailout/#5c6d3a403723
3. Ibid.
4. Ibid.
5. Allan Sloan, the 5 myths of the great financial crisis, Fortune, July 13, 2012.
6. Ibid.
7. Ibid.
8. Matt Taibbi, Secrets and Lies of the Bailout, Rolling Stone, January 13, 2013.
9. Ibid.
10. Kimberly Amadeo, 2008 Financial Crisis: Causes, Costs and Could It Reoccur?, The Balance, October 19, 2016.
11. Ibid.

12. Stephen Gandel, Wall Street bonuses to top 2009, Forbes, August 28, 2013.
13. Wall Street Bonuses, The Economist, February, 24, 2011. http://www.economist.com/printedition/2011-02-26
14. David Dayen, Banks get bailed out, Homeowners get sold out, and the Feds make a killing, The Fiscal Times, March 11, 2016.
15. American Recovery and Investment Act of 2009, the Wikipedia. https://en.wikipedia.org/wiki/American_Recovery_and_Reinvestment_Act_of_2009
16. Matt Taibbi, Secrets and Lies of the Bailout, Rolling Stone, January 13, 2013.
17. Kimberly Amadeo, 2008 Financial Crisis: Causes, Costs and Could It Reoccur?, The Balance, October 19, 2016.
18. The national debt clock (http://www.nationaldebtclocks.org/debtclock/unitedstates).
19. Congressional Budget Office; https://www.cbo.gov/about/products/budget_economic_data
20. United States Government Debt'; US Day of Reckoning, Trading Economics (http://www.tradingeconomics.com/united-states/government-debt).
21. Anna Louie Sussman; US Budget Deficit Rose in Fiscal Year 2016, First Time in Five Years; The Wall Street Journal, October 14, 2016. https://www.wsj.com/articles/u-s-budget-deficit-rose-in-fiscal-year-2016-first-time-in-five-years-1,476,475,245
22. Updated Budget Projections: 2016 to 2026, Congressional Budget Office.
23. Mollie McNeill, U.S. Taxpayers don't realize they're paying billions to service the national debt, The National Interest, September 22, 2016. http://nationalinterest.org/blog/the-buzz/us-taxpayers-dont-realize-theyre-paying-billions-service-the-17796
24. Tom Coburn: "While Washington Slept," *the Washington Post*, April 5, 2011, A21.
25. Fighting the next recession: unfamiliar ways forward, the Economist, February 20, 2016.
26. Philip Bump, The story behind Obama and the national debt, The Washington Post, January 7, 2015 https://www.washingtonpost.com/news/the-fix/wp/2015/01/07/the-story-behind-obama-and-the-national-debt-in-7-charts/?utm_term=.c5b8cedbfd2d
27. Why Trumponomics won't make America great again; the Economist, May 13, 2017. http://www.economist.com/news/leaders/21721904-impulsiveness-and-shallowness-americas-president-threaten-economy-well-rule?cid1=cust/ednew/n/bl/n/20170511n/owned/n/n/nwl/n/n/na/29835/n

CHAPTER 11

The Spanish Austerity

Lee Tunstall, adjunct professor at University of Calgary remind us of Spain's golden age. She says: "It is worth remembering that Spain was once a global empire, and that during the 16th and 17th centuries, 'Golden Age' Spain had access to dazzling amounts of New World gold and silver. That this wealth came at the expense of two major New World empires, the Aztec and the Inca, is what we would perhaps refer to today as collateral damage. The 1990s and early 2000s were another Golden Age of renewal in Spain, with major infrastructure projects initiated and paid for by virtue of their entrance into the European Union in 1986. A real estate boom brought the 'wealth effect' to ordinary citizens, with more than 80 percent of Spanish citizens owning their homes. After the credit bubble burst in 2008, the country has spent the past four years trying to deal with its sovereign debt crisis and fend off bankruptcy."[1] Yes, the legacy of the past has many lessons we can learn from; but the past is gone and will never come back again. The present is the challenge we cannot avoid facing, and the future is the dream we must construct in order to have a better, safer and sustainable life.

Spain's unemployment rate now is about 20%, down from 27% in 2013, and its economy grew by 3.2% in 2015; however, millions of workers have been jobless since 2010, and "more than half of its young people have been out of work for years. There is talk of a lost generation in Spain and Greece. Like Greece, Spain's investment bubble burst when the [2008] financial crisis hit and it had to seek a bailout to prevent its domestic banks from collapsing. Spain's economy also shrank during the crisis and its debt to GDP [gross domestic product] ratio has shot up dramatically."[2] After six

M. Rabie, *The Global Debt Crisis and Its Socioeconomic Implications*,
https://doi.org/10.1007/978-3-319-66215-2_11

years of deep recession and four years of stiff austerity, the Spanish economy resumed growth in the second half of 2013. As a consequence, the economic school that believes in austerity claimed victory, saying that Spain proves that austerity works.

Leonid Bershidsky of Bloomberg said: "Spain and Ireland now have the euro zone's most dynamic economies: The International Monetary Fund expects Spain to expand by 3.1 percent this year (2015) and Ireland, by 4 percent—realistic expectations, in light of their progress in the first six months. Given this performance, one has to wonder how long any economists can continue to condemn austerity as deadly poison based on the example of Greece."[3] Spain's rate of economic growth in 2016 was 3.2% of GDP, and is projected to expand by 2.7% in 2017.

Yet economists Jorge Uxó and Ignacio Álvarez argue that austerity is a deadly poison: "Spain still has a real GDP 5 percent lower than in 2008, and has recovered only 30 percent of the jobs lost during the crisis."[4] Based on this information and growth projections, the International Monetary Fund (IMF) expects Spain to recover the growth it has lost since 2008 by the end of 2018. This means that Spain, under the austerity regime imposed by the so-called "troika" of the IMF, the European Commission and the European Central Bank (ECB), has lost a decade of economic growth. In addition, Spain experienced an overall unemployment rate of 27% and over 50% youth unemployment. Although the overall unemployment rate declined to 20% in the middle of 2017, youth unemployment remains unreasonably high at 45%. This means that the resumption of economic growth cannot be called economic recovery, because it failed to bring unemployment down to the pre-crisis level. And with high unemployment come poverty, social exclusion, hopelessness, lower standards of living, widening income and wealth gaps, and the undermining of the sociocultural fabric of society.

Background

When the global financial crisis struck in 2008, Spain was doing well and enjoying prosperity; it had a budget surplus, a housing boom, a flourishing tourist industry and a fairly diversified economy. In 2007, Spain's debt was 36% of GDP, about half the debt burden of the United States, Britain, France and Germany, and much less than half of Italy's and Greece's. However, Spain's economic growth model, built around construction in general and housing in particular, was profitable but not viable; as a consequence, the country could not wither the housing bubble. House building had been Spain's major growth sector for decades, but the pace accelerated in the 1990s, primarily because of the introduction of the euro, a booming tourist industry, growing immigrant population and the availability of easy credit. But as the bubble burst the Spanish growth model collapsed, causing the economy to collapse as well. "In a few years it had gone from budget surpluses, a growing middle class, and generous social supports to wrenching austerity and collapsing wages, triggered by the massive failure of Spanish banks."[5]

During Spain's housing boom, Spanish banks and several European banks rushed to extend loans to home owners; but when the bubble burst all such banks and many home owners were badly affected. "Doubtless, then, much of the recent history of the Spanish economy is driven by construction—and by the expansion and implosion of a large real estate bubble. According to the IMF, inflation adjusted house prices doubled in just seven years before losing 40 percent of their peak value."[6] The 2008 financial crisis exposed the fragility of the banking system in European states as well as in the United States, causing the housing bubble in America and Spain to burst and precipitate a global debt crisis, which continues to undermine the growth potential of the global economy and threaten the future of many nations.

When Spain joined the Eurozone in 2002, it gave up its right to have its own currency and create money as before. As a result, it could no longer adjust the euro value. And since the ECB controlled the issuance of the euro and interest rates, Spain, just like Greece, Ireland, Italy, Portugal and other Eurozone states, could not raise or lower interest rates to cool a heated economy or stimulate a stagnating one. In the meantime, lower interest rates, rising home prices, relatively high inflation rates and generous social benefits caused the Spanish economy to lose its competitiveness. In light of the Eurozone monetary restrictions, Spain could not devalue the euro, except through a process of internal devaluation. But internal devaluation requires that wages be reduced, social benefits be cut and budgets be slashed; and this causes any economic recovery that internal devaluation might trigger to be slow and not inclusive. As a result, the economic recovery, which started in 2013, is not expected to reduce unemployment substantially, alleviate poverty or restore the old living standards for years.

"The inability to set interest rates in line with the economic conditions meant that in the early 2000s, Spain and Greece couldn't raise interest rates to cool their over-heating economies. The over-heating was largely caused by the frenzied (and ultimately reckless) lending in both countries by

German and other core European banks. The European Central Bank set interest rates in line with economic conditions in Germany and France that proved too low for Spain and Greece."[7] In addition, giving up its right to print money meant that Spain, just like Greece and Portugal, had to borrow from its European partners to meet its needs and avoid default. Since budget regulations adopted by the Eurozone require strict adherence to GDP deficit ratios, no member state could exceed the prescribed ratios. And though some members have cheated, the ability of every member to adjust the deficit ratio is vastly constrained. As a consequence, Spain was forced to implement austerity measures between 2010 and 2013, causing unemployment rates to skyrocket and the public debt to treble in four years.

Owing to booming housing construction and tourism, Spain attracted millions of immigrants, many of whom worked for the construction industry: this employed some 20% of the total work force. "In less than three decades Spain rose from being a poor, backward country run by a dictator to a modern, wealthy, technologically-advanced European social democracy. In the 1990s, the Spanish bull economy grew at nearly 4 percent a year, much faster than most of Europe or the United States. Job creation soared and by the mid-2000s the unemployment rate was in single digits for the first time in modern history. Once again, houses were the heart of it: in 2007 the levels of private home ownership topped off at 87 percent, one of the highest rates in the world."[8] But the 2008 financial crisis caused the housing industry and the Spanish economy to collapse.

"The problem was that, along with this huge investment in infrastructure, came a massive increase in construction: 15 million new buildings and 4.2 million new homes appeared between 2002 and 2011—representing a 20 percent increase. With that came a significant rise in house prices and household debt, as banks offered mortgages of up to 50 years for 100 percent of the market price. By 2006, the ECB's base interest rate was close to 5.4 percent, having been around 2.6 percent just three years previously. As some 94 percent of mortgages in Spain are based on variable interest rates, monthly payments quickly became much higher at a time when employment figures nosedived."[9] This sequence of events is almost identical to what the United States experienced prior to the 2008 financial crisis. In Spain, public debt rose between 2006 and 2013 from 36% of GDP to 84%, the US public debt rose during the same period from 64% of GDP to over 100%. Today, Spain's debt is 117% of GDP and the US debt is 105% of GDP; the numbers for both countries are $1.3 trillion for Spain and $20.17 trillion for the United States.[10]

Austerity Program

Facing a probable economic collapse, the Spanish government initiated a massive stimulus package in order to revive its economy and pull it out of recession; but the stimulus, despite its huge size, failed to stabilize the economy and restore consumer confidence. There are several factors that contributed to this failure. The major ones are:

1. Loss of consumer confidence in Spain's banking system;
2. Bank failures and rising interest rates owing to the downgrading of Spain's bonds;
3. Declining income from tourism owing to the impact of the 2008 crisis on the American and European economies, as well as on the economies of most other countries;
4. Declining disposable incomes of consumers owing to rising unemployment; and
5. General public fear of seeing the Greek tragedy repeated in their country.

In the meantime, Spain's surplus of earlier years turned into growing deficits that caused the debt to double and treble and unemployment to rise further. "So with a high level of public debt, rising unemployment and a worrying number of foreclosures; what did the government do? Concentrate on its debt. To do this, it announced austerity measures in May 2010 worth 1.5 percent of GDP and further measures of the next six months worth an estimated 5 percent of GDP in total."[11] But as the economic situation deteriorated and tourism suffered, Spain's prime minister announced on July 11, 2012 a new 65 billion euros of austerity that included cuts in wages and benefits and a VAT increase from 18% to 21%.[12]

A report issued by People, Place and Policy, an independent forum for academic debate on the challenges faced by contemporary society, describes the situation in Europe as follows: "The recession that turned into a fully-fledged global financial and economic crisis in September 2008 has had and continues to have far-reaching consequences on the welfare and livelihoods of millions of Europeans. The initial 'credit crunch' and its subsequent effects on key economic variables such as per capita GDP and unemployment rates quickly translated into diminished living conditions and growing levels of inequality and deprivation that still persist."[13]

Tourism in particular is a very important industry to the Spanish economy and the welfare of the people. The tourist industry employs about 12% of the Spanish workforce; and the "total value of foreign and domestic tourism came to nearly 11 percent of the country's GDP and provided employment for about 2 million people."[14] Because of these facts, when Spanish tourism declined by 13% during the crisis, it caused unemployment to rise substantially; and when tourism returned to pre-crisis levels in 2014, it caused unemployment to decline. In fact, tourism seems to have been the driving force behind the recovery of the Spanish economy in 2013.

In response to the crisis and economic contraction, the Spanish government responded initially by increasing spending, but changed course owing to high interest rates, rising deficits and outside pressure to adopt a policy based on austerity. And because of Spain's membership of the Eurozone, the Spanish government was forced to cut spending and raise taxes, which caused the economic recession to worsen and the public debt to rise further. Zachary Woolfe of the *New York Times* wrote in 2013 that "The housing bubble that began with the introduction of the euro and burst in Spain in 2008 was not unlike the one that helped cause a recession in the United States. But the rigid austerity response-focused to Spain's crisis and the strictures of the nation's membership in the euro zone have prevented any similar recovery from taking hold."[15]

As millions of Spaniards were losing their jobs and incomes, defaults on housing loans skyrocketed, the number of foreclosures increased substantially, and many banks and major companies failed. Since several German, French and British banks had invested heavily in the Spanish construction industry, Spain's European partners rushed to rescue the country; however, their major concern was not the fate of the Spanish economy but the fate of their own banks and the euro. German banks' exposure in Spain at the time of the bubble was estimated at $149 billion. Central banks in the United States, Britain and Europe were and still are more interested in saving banks and large corporations than saving the poor and the unemployed. Central banks are convinced that if banks stop functioning economies will stop functioning as well; and this means the rescue of banks must come first.

When the Spanish government failed to rescue its banks, it requested a loan of 100 billion euros from the European Stability Mechanism. On June 9, 2012, the Eurozone finance ministers approved Spain's request, and the troika assumed responsibility for the negotiations with Spain. The conditions for the rescue package consisted of restructuring the banking sector, structural reforms and fiscal consolidation. As a result, taxes in Spain were raised, wages were cut, pension payments were frozen and spending on health, education and social services was reduced: "Between 2009 and 2013, the amount devoted to education and health care has been reduced by 18 billion euros and public investment by 33 billion euros."[16]

However, the turning point in the Spanish unfolding drama occurred on July 26, 2012, when ECB President Mario Draghi said that the ECB was "ready to do whatever it takes to preserve the euro." This announcement alone was able to restore confidence in the Eurozone financial system, discourage speculation on Spain's debt and lower interest rates. In July 2012, "Spanish banks borrowed a record €376 billion from the ECB".[17] Following this announcement, the ECB began buying Spain's and other states' government bonds, causing interest rates to decline and lighten the burden of debt servicing for Spain, Greece, Ireland, Portugal, Italy and other Eurozone members. Nevertheless, the housing bubble and austerity measures eliminated millions of jobs in Spain and caused the economy to sink into a deep recession that, at its peak, reached depression levels.

Wages declined, job security in the private sector almost vanished, poverty spread and the number of those living in poverty and at the edge of poverty increased by 3 million from 10.4 million in 2007 to 13.4 million in 2014. Economic stagnation and recession lasted almost six years before the economy began to show signs of recovery. In September 2013, the government announced that the economy grew for the first time in three years and exports were up 8%; nevertheless, unemployment continued to lag behind the economy, preventing social conditions and living standards from improving. In 2016, after three consecutive years of economic growth, the overall unemployment rate was reduced to 20% and youth unemployment declined to 43.9%.

Steven Hill of the *Atlantic* says: "Still, recovery has moved the country away from over-dependency on real estate and construction toward a more German-style economy driven by exports of everything from automobiles to hot tubs, pharmaceuticals, textiles, machinery and software. About 60,000 firms are now exporters, 9 percent more than last year (2015). Most observers seem to agree that exports have been aided by the reduction in wages that has been wrung from workers, with Spain's labor costs narrowing the gap with Germany by 5.5 percent."[18] But wage cuts have also lowered the living standards of all affected workers and caused an internal devaluation, which came at the expense of labor in general and the welfare of people who needed assistance most in particular.

Economic Recovery

According to a report issued by the Center for Economic and Policy Research and authored by David Rosnick and Mark Weisbort, the austerity plan pursued by Spain, starting in 2011, is based on "internal currency devaluation, labor market reform, fiscal consolidation, and structural and deregulatory reform,"[19] all of which were intended to boost growth through increased labor efficiency. However, when the recovery was confirmed at the end of 2014, the overall rate of unemployment was 21.6%, down from 26.3% in 2013, and youth unemployment was 47.7%, down from 56% a year earlier. On the other hand, "the number of people classified as at risk of poverty and social exclusion has risen with the unemployment rate, from 10.4 million people in 2007 to 13.4 million in 2014."[20] This means that most of the benefits of the recovery have gone to a few industries and groups, and the overwhelming majority of the unemployed and the youth have not received tangible benefits from the recovery. In addition, the increase in the number of poor shows that the recovery has caused the income and wealth gaps between rich and poor to widen.

The inability of Spain to devalue the euro may have been the major factor causing the failure of the initial stimulus package, which thus made the recession as long and painful as it has been. Factors responsible for Spain's economic recovery have mostly been external rather than internal; the only contribution of the austerity program to recovery has been the internal devaluation forced on people, which caused wages to decline and labor to be devalued. In fact, the recovery of the Spanish economy came as a result of a combination of factors that changed the dynamics of the Spanish economy and pulled it out of its prolonged recession. Although these factors were highly unlikely to happen at the same time, they did happen and helped Spain to avoid a Greek-style recession. Such factors include the following:

1. The decision taken by the ECB to reduce interest rates through quantitative easing, which made money available to banks to borrow at much cheaper rates;
2. The buying of government bonds by the ECB, which reduced interest rates and helped credit to recover in Spain and other Eurozone states; both of these measures are usually used to stimulate economies rather than as austerity measures;

3. Lower interest rates, which caused debt servicing to decline substantially and budget deficits to be less than they would otherwise be, leaving the Spanish government with more money to spend;
4. The depreciation of the euro against the US dollar, which made Spanish products and services, especially tourism, more competitive;
5. Falling oil prices, which encouraged consumers to increase spending while lowering the cost of producing many goods and services as well as government spending on energy;
6. Government easing of austerity owing to lower interest rates, which caused the potential size of the budget deficit to decline without reducing spending or increasing taxes; and
7. A new boom in tourism owing to political instability in Greece and the tourist states of Egypt, Lebanon, Tunisia, Turkey and Syria; terrorist attacks on France and Belgium have also convinced many tourists to go to Spain.

Paul Krugman says, "Since the global turn to austerity in 2010, every country that introduced significant austerity has seen its economy suffer, with the depth of the suffering closely related to the harshness of the austerity."[21] While economists advocating austerity disagree with this assertion, the IMF made a striking admission in its World Economic Outlook in late 2012: "The IMF's chief economist, Olivier Blanchard, explained that recent efforts among wealthy countries to shrink their deficits—through tax hikes and spending cuts—have been causing far more economic damage than experts had assumed."[22] Krugman says further: "It's true that you can't run big budget deficits forever, because at some point interest payments start to swallow too large a share of the budget. But it's foolish and destructive to worry about deficits when borrowing is very cheap and the funds you borrow would otherwise go to waste."[23]

Making an argument against austerity, Tim Worstall said in *Forbes*: "The actual, real world, economic outcome is appalling and the pain has been entirely inflicted by the euro and the lack of a possibility to devalue within it. It's not even true that Spain was being particularly badly run before the crash. Yes, they had a massive property boom as a result of being in the euro and thus having interest rates way too low for the state of the local economy. But government was trying to cool aggregate demand, running a budget surplus, raising capital requirements on banks and so on. The interest rate mismatch was obviously too large but again, that's a problem with the existence of the euro. Without the ability to devalue the only other option is that internal devaluation."[24] Internal devaluation is usually sought through reducing government spending, raising taxes and cutting wages that cause some workers to lose income, and others to lose their jobs and incomes. People who claim that austerity is responsible for Spain's recovery can be proved wrong by considering Greece; though Greece was forced to implement harsher austerity measures, for a longer time than Spain, the country's economy has so far failed to recover.

Widespread unemployment, poverty and social exclusion caused by the financial crisis and austerity measures have facilitated the creation of an anti-austerity movement in Greece, Ireland, Italy, Portugal and Spain; and as a consequence, trust in the major institutions of the European union (EU) has been undermined. In fact, the movement has become a threat to European efforts to solidify economic integration and strengthen European unity. In addition, declining trust in EU bureaucracy has empowered the right-wing parties in Europe to challenge the status quo and enabled them to gain more popularity and legitimacy. And with the rise of these parties comes discrimination against foreigners, racism and cultural closed-mindedness. Furthermore, the refugee crises, which started in the Middle East and moved to Europe via Turkey and Greece, have caused the social and moral fabric of European society to be weakened.

Commenting on the austerity and its negative results, Conn Hallinan said: "For the first time since Margaret Thatcher and Ronald Reagan rolled out a variety of neoliberal capitalism that captured much of the world in the 1980s, that model is under siege. The economic strategy of regressive taxes, widespread privatization, and deregulation has generated enormous wealth for the few, but growing impoverishment for the many. The top 1 percent now owns more than 50 percent of the world's wealth. The British election may have focused on immigration and the fear of 'the other' but this xenophobia stems from the anger and despair of people who have been marginalized or left behind by the globalization of the labor force that has systematically hollowed out small communities and destroyed decent paying jobs and benefits."[25] This comment does not only identify the forces causing the rise of the right in Europe; it also explains the revolt of the marginalized in the United States that enabled Donald Trump to win the 2016 American presidential elections.

The argument for austerity and against stimulus is not a rational one; it is an ideological argument meant to reduce the size of government. But by reducing the size of government, the ability of any state to deal with sudden economic problems and social issues is weakened. In Britain and the United States, the right has used scare tactics to magnify the potential threat of budget deficits and rising debts, while minimizing the hardships people usually suffer through losing their jobs and social benefits. Asking the masses to make the sacrifices required to revitalize an economy in recession by cutting taxes on the rich and reducing services to the general public causes the overwhelming majority of the people to be the losers, while enabling the rich and large corporations to be the winners. Reducing the size of government "has been transparently obvious in the United States, where many supposed deficit-reduction plans just happen to include sharp cuts in tax rates on corporations and the wealthy even as they take away healthcare and nutritional aid from the poor. But it's also a fairly obvious motivation in the UK, if not so crudely expressed."[26]

Austerity measures may be able to restructure an industrial economy in trouble because of a loss of competitiveness, and enable such an economy to regain competitiveness in a few years; but such measures are unlikely to succeed in developing countries, because almost all such countries have never been competitive. A plan that causes an economy to lose a decade of growth is a plan that vastly undermines the capacity of the economy to resume growth and become competitive in a decade or two. The experience of several Latin American and Middle Eastern counties proves that making great sacrifices to restructure an economy by cutting already low wages and reducing government spending and privatizing public enterprises has been largely disastrous. As such countries make sacrifices to restructure traditional economies in the hope of making them competitive, advanced economies would be raising labor and machine productivity, and thus making it much more difficult for the poor economies to catch up. In addition, no economic restructuring plan in a developing country can succeed without a similar sociocultural plan. Development is a comprehensive societal process: just like a bird, it needs two wings to fly and stay healthy—these wings being economic restructuring and sociocultural transformation.[27]

Austerity widens the income and wealth gaps in society, depresses wages, squeezes the middle class, increases poverty and creates classes of white, brown, yellow and black slaves; it also causes debt to increase in relation to GDP. In contrast, deficit spending causes the economy to expand as it encourages people with money to spend and invest their savings, because economic expansion gives savers an opportunity to participate in the economies of their countries and strengthen their loyalty to the corporations they work for or invest in. And although stimulus plans do increase the public debt, the size of the debt and its ratio to GDP are less than those caused by austerity, as the Spanish and Greek cases have demonstrated.

A report issued by the Organization for Economic Cooperation and Development (OECD) in May 2015 showed that Spain's high unemployment rates since the start of the 2008 crisis were responsible for widening the divide between rich and poor. According to the report, "the economic crisis hit low-income Spaniards the hardest, with the poorest 10 percent of the population losing 13 percent of their real incomes each year between 2007 and 2011. The top 10 percent, in comparison, lost 1.4 percent. Still, the wealth in Spain seemed to be less highly concentrated compared to the rest of the OECD countries. The top 10 percent of the Spanish population owned 43 percent of all household wealth; lower than the OECD average of 50 percent, while the bottom 60 percent owned 20 percent of all household wealth—well above the OECD average of 13 percent. Though poverty rates started to show some improvement since 2011, the portion of the population below the poverty line in Spain was 18 percent—almost double what it was before the economic crisis."[28]

Rosnick and Weisbort, as mentioned earlier, argued that "Spain's current economic recovery is unlikely to resolve the problem of mass unemployment in the foreseeable future. Indeed, the IMF estimates that Spain will have an unemployment rate of about 16.5 percent when it reaches potential output; that will be its full employment level unless there are structural changes in the economy that significantly increase potential output. However, there is little evidence that the kind of structural changes being proposed, such as making it easier for employers to fire workers, will greatly increase potential output."[29] While making it easier for employers to fire workers may improve labor productivity, it will cause most workers to feel insecure and lower public expectations; and this, in turn, will harm the economy's long-term prospects.

"Even Prime Minister Rajoy—who, as a politician, is required to be optimistic—is proceeding on the assumption that five more years of economic growth will be necessary for 20 million Spaniards to have a job, as was the case before the crisis."[30] On the other hand, Nadal, the conservative presidential advisor, reminds everyone of the high political and economic costs of the reforms that has so far been implemented. He says: "When they devalued their currency before, the companies immediately became competitive again. When you devalue within the euro zone, it takes a long time and is painful for everyone."[31]

The inability of the euro member states to devalue the euro partially explains the failure of the economies of Spain, Greece, Portugal and Ireland to recover sooner from the recession. There are two options to deal with such a situation: to leave the currency union and issue a new currency you can control, or adopt austerity measures to internally devalue the currency. Since the process of leaving the Eurozone is very complicated and may be costlier in the long run than staying in the union, all highly indebted states have chosen to stay in Eurozone.

The Ramo Plan, by creating a global central bank with the power to issue a new currency, and issue and sell and buy bonds, loosens the grip of national and regional central banks on interest rates. As a result, the global bank is able to lend money directly to states in distress. In fact, the Ramo Plan ends the debt crisis as well as the tug-of-war between those who favor austerity and others who favor stimulus for many decades to come, if not forever; it enables all nations to get rid of their debts in practically one day at no cost to any state, bank, investor or taxpayer. And in a new era free of debt and crippling loan conditions, the current economic thinking and the management of the international monetary system will be transformed. A new way of looking at the world from a humanistic view will emerge slowly and make our life less stressful and more productive. The experience of Spain, Greece and other nations affected by the 2008 crisis proves that no national strategy is able by itself to deal with such a crisis. Times have changed in the last three decades more than they did in the previous three centuries; and the pace of change is accelerating with no end in sight. Classical economic thinkers who are still attached to notions of reality in times long gone are being left behind history. Believing in the inevitability of recurring booms and busts is more like believing in an evil we created to control our lives. We therefore need to free ourselves from all evil to become humane and civilized.

Now that the Spanish economy has recovered, we must ask if the price was worth it; and if the crisis could have been handled differently. There is no doubt that the price has been very costly, and the crisis could indeed have been handled differently. Austerity has caused the following:

1. Raising unemployment from less than 10% in 2007 to almost 30% in 2013; and though the rate has declined to 20%, it is expected, as the IMF predicts, to stabilize at 16.5% when the economy reaches its potential output;

2. Increasing youth unemployment from 17% in 2007 to 55% in 2013; even if youth unemployment declines substantially, it should, according to the IMF, stabilize at about 30% by the time the economy reaches its output potential;
3. Forcing the poorest 10% of the population to lose 13% of their real incomes each year between 2007 and 2011 means that the austerity plan has lowered the poor's standard of living by 50% in five years;
4. Increasing the numbers of the poor by 3 million, from 10.4 million in 2007 to 13.4 million in 2013, is a crime in the age of plenty;
5. Raising the debt GDP ratio from 36% in 2007 to 117% in 2017, which means increasing the debt from about $470 to $1460 billion during ten years; and
6. Causing the Spanish economy to lose a full decade of growth and be burdened by a debt it can never repay.

As for the alternative, I believe that the problem caused by the housing bubble and the 2008 financial crisis could have been fixed by adopting a stimulus package similar to the American one. Adopting a stimulus package costing $250–$300 billion could have been enough to save Spain from a crippling recession lasting seven years, and about $990 billion in extra debt; it also would have helped Spain to maintain its welfare system, help rather than hurt the unemployed and the poor, and recover probably within two to three years. We also need to understand that, in light of the state of the global economy, there is no guarantee that Spain's recovery will continue. In fact, if interest rates were to increase by only 1%, Spain's debt service would increase by $14 billion annually; a three point increase would probably cause Spain and the rest of the world to face a new debt crisis of unforeseen proportions. Yet keeping interest rates as low as they are hurts retired people and others who save for the education of their children.

Notes

1. Lee Tunstall, Spain's Current Economic Pain Nothing New, the Huffingtonpost, March 12, 2013.
2. Lisa Tripp, Greece the only villain in euro crisis? Don't believe it, CNN, March 24, 2015.
3. Bershidsky, Two Points for Austerity: Spain and Ireland, Bloomberg, July 31, 2015.

4. Uxó and Álvarez, Is the end of fiscal austerity feasible in Spain?, Research Gate, February, 2016.
5. Steven Hill, To Hell and Back: Spain's Grotesque Recession and Its Surprising New Economy, The Atlantic, October, 2013.
6. David Rosnick and Mark Weisbort, Has austerity worked in Spain?, Center for Economic and Policy Research, December 19, 2015.
7. Ibid., Lisa Tripp.
8. Ibid., Steven Hill.
9. Paul Gambles, Spain: the bell is tolling on austerity bus is anyone listening? Linkedin.com, August 28, 2015.
10. See: United States Government Debt to GDP, Trading Economics, http://www.tradingeconomics.com/united-states/government-debt-to-gdp and Spain's Public Debt Reaches 100.9% Of GDP, The Spain Report, August 17, 2016. https://www.thespainreport.com/articles/847-160817122440-spain-s-public-debt-reaches-100-9-of-gdp
11. Ibid., Gambles.
12. Sergio Tirado Herrero and Luis Jimenez Meneses, Energy poverty, crisis and austerity in Spain, People, Place and Policy, (2016): 10/1, p. 42, April 20, 2016.
13. Ibid., Herrero and Meneses Energy poverty, crisis and austerity in Spain, People, Place and Policy.
14. Wikipedia, Economy of Spain.
15. Zachary Woolfe, Now onstage in Spain: Austerity, the New York Times, February 15, 2015.
16. Uxo and Alvarez, Is the end of fiscal austerity feasible in Spain? P. 7.
17. Wikipedia, 2008–16 Spanish financial crisis.
18. Ibid., Steven Hill.
19. Rosnick and Weisbort, Has austerity worked in Spain?, Center for Economic and Policy Research, December 19, 2015.
20. Ibid.
21. Paul Krugman, the austerity delusion, the Guardian, April 29, 2015.
22. Brad Plumer, IMF: Austerity is much worse for the economy than we thought, Wonkblog, the Washington Post, October 12, 2012.
23. Ibid., Krugman.
24. Tim Worstall, Krugman's right: Spain's austerity proves that it's the euro that is the problem, Forbes, September 14, 2015.
25. Conn Hallinan, From Brexit in the UK to Austerity in Spain, Europe is on the Edge, Foreign Policy in Focus, July 7, 2016.
26. Ibid., Krugman https://www.theguardian.com/business/ng-interactive/2015/apr/29/the-austerity-delusion
27. See, Mohamed Rabie, A Theory of Sustainable Sociocultural and Economic Development, Chapters 2 and 3, Palgrave Macmillan, 2016.

28. Gap widens between Spain's rich and poor, the Local, May 21, 2015.
29. Ibid., Rosnick and Weisbort.
30. Christoph Pauly, Spain emerges as model for Europe, Spiegel Online, March 25, 2015.
31. Ibid., www.spiegel.de/international/europe/how-spain-recovered-from-the-economic-crisis-a-1025327.html

CHAPTER 12

The Greek Debt Saga

In my analysis of the American debt problem, I explained why the United States, under current economic and tax policies, would not be able to repay its debt any time in the future. So, if the United States cannot repay its debt, how can Greece repay its debt? Greece has more debt to gross domestic product (GDP) than the United States does, and therefore is unable to repay its debt, not now and not ever. Today, the US debt to GDP is 105%; the Greek debt is over 180% of GDP. The European Commission, the European Central Bank (ECB) and the International Monetary Fund (IMF) seem to have accepted the fact that Greece will not be able to repay its debt any time in the future; yet they continue to deal with the crisis as if it is a passing cloud that cannot do much harm to Greece or to any other highly indebted state. Because of this attitude, the so-called "troika" has been engaged in a game of wasting time, money and energy on an issue that needs a totally different approach. This is why the handling of the Greek debt crisis by the troika has become a management scheme.

In October 2009, a year after the collapse of the Lehman Brothers financial house, Greece's prime minister admitted that his country had been understating Greece's budget deficits for years, and that the deficit would exceed 12% of GDP, nearly double the original estimate. As a result, credit rating agencies downgraded Greece's public debt to junk status, causing the cost of borrowing to skyrocket. Eurozone leaders and IMF officials were terrified, because Greece was about to default on its debts. Such a default, they reasoned, would impose huge losses on banks and investors and could easily cause another global financial crisis. Forcing

M. Rabie, *The Global Debt Crisis and Its Socioeconomic Implications*,
https://doi.org/10.1007/978-3-319-66215-2_12

Greece and banks to take such losses "would have had immediate and devastating implications for the Greek banking system, not to mention the broader spillover effects,"[1] said John Lipsky, first deputy managing director of the IMF at the time.

To avoid the possibility of default, leaders of the IMF, EU and Greece's creditors agreed on May 2, 2010 to provide Greece with 110 billion euros in loans over three years. The EU agreed to provide 80 billion euros, of which Germany's share was about 22 billion, and the rest was provided by the IMF and other creditors. But all that money was not enough to calm the fears of the financial markets, because other heavily indebted countries such as Portugal and Ireland were in similar positions. As a result, creditors, including the major Eurozone states, the ECB and the IMF, provided Greece with more money in exchange for a Greek commitment to implement austerity measures that included 30 billion euros in spending cuts and tax increases.

In an attempt to boost market confidence and prevent the debt crisis from spreading throughout Europe, the ECB launched on May 10, 2010 an unprecedented program to purchase government bonds of struggling states such as Greece and Spain, and the Eurozone finance ministers agreed to provide 750 billion euros to rescue struggling Eurozone economies. On February 21, 2012, the EU finance ministers approved a second bailout for Greece worth 130 billion euros in exchange for a Greek commitment to reduce its debt to GDP ratio from 160% down to 120.5% by 2020. This deal, which was the largest economic restructuring program in history, was concluded on March 9, 2012. On September 12, 2012, ECB President Mario Draghi announced an open-ended program to purchase bonds of struggling Eurozone states on the secondary market. Draghi's words and deeds were good enough to calm the financial markets and bring down the borrowing cost for Greece and other Eurozone states.[2]

On January 25, 2015, Syriza, the left-wing Greek party, won the general election based on its anti-austerity slogans. Following victory, the leader of Syriza, Prime Minister Alexis Tsipras, announced that he would renegotiate the bailout terms, call for debt cancellation and resume government spending. Five months later, on June 30, 2015, Greece missed a 1.6 billion euro payment to the IMF, making it the first time a Western state had defaulted to the IMF. In an attempt to prevent capital flight from Greece; Tsipras imposed capital controls, limiting bank withdrawals to 60 euros per day. However, under pressure from the EU and the IMF, Tsipras asked the Greek parliament on July 16, 2015 to approve new austerity measures.

A few days later, Greece and its European creditors agreed on a third bailout worth 86 billion euros, and the ECB resumed support for Greece's banks. But after receiving three bailouts in five years totaling approximately $265 billion and agreeing to implement specific austerity measures, Greece needed a new aid package in 2016 to make a debt payment and avoid default.

The terms of the 2015 bailout package included commitments to raise the retirement age, cut pensions, liberalize the energy market, expand property taxes and move forward with a privatization program. Though the Greek government had implemented most programs, Greece and its creditors found themselves in 2016 engaged in a new round of talks that lasted several months; Greece needed more money to make a debt payment that was due in July 2016. On May 25, 2016, the Eurozone finance ministers agreed on "a package of debt measures" that included freeing 10.3 billion euros so Greece could make the debt payment due in July, 2016. "However, the agreement excluded any reduction in the amount of money that Greece will ultimately have to repay to its creditors. Nonetheless, the new package included a waiver of an interest rate increase that was due in 2017. For 2018, the euro zone expects to implement a possible second set of measures following the successful implementation of the program,"[3] which means that Greece will have to fulfill the reform commitments it agreed to in 2015 that include cutting deficits and raising taxes, reforming the labor market and privatizing state assets.

The IMF described the terms of the 2016 bailout as "highly concessional;" but refused to contribute because it considers the Greek debt burden unsustainable; the IMF said that the Eurozone needs to go further in easing the repayment burden. Though the Eurozone can raise the money from the financial markets through its bailout agency, the European Stability Mechanism, the IMF seal of approval is politically important to the European governments that are under popular pressure, such as Germany, where there is resentment about the idea of rescuing Greece. Many people in Germany and other European countries see Greece's debt as a problem created by the Greeks, and therefore their responsibility to deal with. Germany has strongly opposed debt relief, because this has the potential to encourage other indebted Eurozone nations to abandon the austerity reforms.

IMF director for Europe, Poul Thomsen, welcomed the fact that the EU has recognized that the Greek debt is unsustainable and that debt relief is needed. However, Andrew Walker says that "Those words recall a cliché that has often been applied to agreements in the Greek story. There is certainly an element in this deal of 'kicking the can down the road.'"[4]

But despite Germany's reservations, finance ministers from other Eurozone countries have praised Greece for making "considerable efforts" to reform its economy and streamline state operations. French finance minister Michel Sapin said, "Greece needs room to breathe, it needs certainty. This deal is first and foremost a declaration of confidence in today's Greece." EU president Donald Tusk described the deal as "a strong message of stability for Greece, Europe and the global economy".[5] Greek finance minister Euclid Tsakalotos said the fresh bailout agreement delivered some ground for optimism that the country's vicious circle of recessions could be broken, paving the way for much-needed investment.[6]

Much of the aid given to Greece between 2010 and 2015 has revolved around banks. "Greece received 227 billion Euros ($270 billion) from other euro zone countries and the IMF. Of that, 48.2 billion Euros went to replenish the capital of Greek banks. More than 120 billion Euros went to pay debt and interest, and around 35 billion Euros went to commercial banks that had taken losses on Greek debt. Within Greece, the money was supposed to help replenish banks' capitals, to get them lending to revive the moribund economy. Instead, it sat in banks' coffers as bad debts piled up, and it bought time for Greeks and foreign investors to get their money out."[7] About 44 billion euros left Greece, despite capital controls imposed by the government; money was smuggled out of Greece and deposited in German and other European banks.

In addition to the bailout money, the ECB has provided more than 130 billion euros ($150 billion) in loans to Greek banks directly, including about 90 billion euros in the form of short-term emergency cash. The idea was that once banks were healthy and stable, they would resume lending to investors and consumers, and this, in turn, would help the economy to resume normal growth. But this has not materialized, because Greek banks did not heal enough to start pumping money in the economy. In fact, growth was never the primary consideration when Greece first started receiving bailouts; their main objective was to rescue Greek and other European banks, because if banks collapse, no measures would be able to stop another global financial crisis from happening. Nikos Vettas, the director general of IOBE, an economic research organization in Athens, said: "Whenever something happens with the banks, the whole economy stops, so money was given to the banks and the idea was that once they were stabilized, the economy would start running again. At least, that was the plan."[8]

Evaluating the Austerity Plan

Despite having received the biggest financial aid package in history, estimated at 326 billion euros, the fear is that Greece "is locked in an economic death spiral." This conclusion "was given further credence when Eurobank analysts announced [in August, 2016] that consumption and exports had fallen, by 6.4% and 7.2%, in the second quarter of the year; and the poorest 20% of Greece's 11 million people have suffered a 42% drop in disposable income since 2009."[9]

"This year [2017] was meant to be a year of recovery—instead, the uncertainty has prompted the [Greek] central bank to revise its growth projection downwards following the economy's contraction in the fourth quarter last year. Unemployment has increased from 23.2% to 23.5%. In a repeat of the chaos that beset the country's financial system at the height of the crisis in 2015, an estimated €2.5 billion of deposits left Greek banks in January and February. Consumption is also down."[10] Aliki Mouriki, a leading Greek sociologist, says that "The 37% of Greeks at risk of poverty and social exclusion really cannot make ends meet; they no longer have the means to meet basic needs, with consumption of milk and bread right down and payment of electricity bills at an all-time low."[11]

"Since Greece's debt crisis began in 2010, most international banks and foreign investors have sold their Greek bonds and other holdings, so they are no longer vulnerable to what may happen in Greece. In the meantime, the other crisis countries in the euro zone, like Portugal, Ireland and Spain, have taken steps to overhaul their economies and are considered less vulnerable to market contagion than they were a few years ago."[12] However, all the other crisis countries in the Eurozone have, despite receiving fresh loans and other assistance, seen unemployment rates rise, economic growth rates decline and debts skyrocket. For example, the rate of unemployment in Greece was estimated in 2015 at 25.6%, Spain 23.1%, Cyprus 16%, Portugal 13.5%, Italy 12.4%, France 10.5% and Ireland 9.9%. For the EU as a whole, the unemployment rate was 9.8%.[13]

The failure of all efforts to rescue Greece and revitalize its economy validates the argument that says austerity measures alone cannot rescue an economy from a serious crisis. Since 2010, Greece has been cutting budgets, raising taxes, recapitalizing banks and reducing monthly pension payments, but without success; it has failed to stabilize the situation or stop the economy from contracting. This simply means that neither the Greek people nor their economy benefited from the bailouts or the austerity programs; the only thing that Greece and its lenders were able to get in exchange for spending some $300 billion is more time and extra money to waste. Today, Greece's debt is the second highest in the world after Japan, estimated at 180% of GDP; Greek banks are still shaky; the economy is still contracting; and 23% of the labor force is still unemployed. Youth unemployment, which was about 20% in 2008, is now about 45%.

To ensure that bailout money is spent to restructure the Greek economy, save banks and meet debt obligations, the EC, ECB and the IMF imposed on Greece harsh conditions. Lenders asked Greece to cut its budget, raise taxes, end tax evasion, reduce pension payments, privatize the state's assets and overhaul the economy by streamlining government operations. Monthly pension payments, for example, have been cut twelve times since 2010. But despite all actions and bailout money, nothing worked. The debt burden increased from 262 billion euros in 2010 to 323 billion euros in 2015, bank deposits declined by almost 50%, and Greece's GDP was reduced from $299 billion in 2010 to $195 billion in 2016. That is 35% less than the $299 billion of 2010 and 45% less than the $355 billion of 2008.

As for the ratio of the public debt to the GDP, it was 177% in 2015, but rose to 180% in 2016. All reductions in the budget and cuts in wages and social programs has come at the expense of the poor, farmers, retired people and state employees who have not received a raise in five years. This means that the economic and social situation in Greece, despite three bailouts and more than $500 billion in financial aid and cheap loans from the ECB, has deteriorated, not improved. "These austerity policies were imposed with the stated goal of reducing Greece's debt. Yet they have in fact increased the debt relative to GDP, while Greek social fabric has been torn to shreds, and Greece has served as a funnel to transmit bailouts to French and German banks that made risky loans."[14]

Since the Greek debt has grown from 262 billion euros in 2010 to 323 billion euros in 2016, and the economy has shrunk by 35% during the same time, the debt management scheme administered by the troika has caused Greece to sink deeper in debt and waste about $400 billion. When the amount of money given to Greece in the form of debt reduction is added, the total bailout would exceed $500 billion. These figures raise three questions. First, was the decision to deal with the Greek debt piecemeal rational? Second, did the people and institutions that handled the debt issue understand the nature and magnitude of the problem they were facing? And, third, where did the more than $400 billion go?

As for the first question, the results of the Greek saga demonstrate that the way the West has dealt with the debt issue was irrational. Second, since the economic and financial situation in Greece today is worse than it was seven years ago, the people in charge of the debt problem must have lacked the knowledge to deal with the crisis. As for the third question, it is clear that most of the money given to Greece went to service the growing debt; and since lenders are states, banks and investment funds, the bailouts have served to save banks, enrich the rich fund managers and impoverish the poor, and, in the process, cause the wealth and income gaps in Greece to widen further. Moreover, the Greek debt saga has created global uncertainty that seems to have contributed to causing national and global economic growth rates to decline.

Paying Greece's debt back in 2010 in full would have saved lenders over 60 billion euros, saved the Greek people from poverty, high unemployment, depressed wages and standards of living and despair, and the loss of many opportunities. Paying the debt in full would have also saved the world the agony of worrying about the future, particularly in light of the continued declining global growth rates and the ever widening wealth and income gaps. But paying the entire Greek debt at once could not have been done without paying the debt of other nations; and this requires deep understanding of the intricate relationships that tie together the economic, political, security, social and cultural facets of life in every society, as well as the nature of the transformation the world is experiencing today.

As mentioned earlier, the IMF, the Eurozone states and the ECB seem to have concluded that Greece's debt is unsustainable, which means that Greece cannot repay its debt any time in the future. As a result, the European leadership and the IMF have been trying, they claim, to reduce the amount of debt to a "sustainable level." However, Greece's debt is over 180% of its GDP and is expected to rise to 187% by the end of 2017. I believe that any state with a debt load in excess of 60% of its GDP would not be able under current global growth rates ever to repay its debt, particularly if interest rates were to return to normal. Furthermore, declining global growth rates are making long-term economic prospects look bad for all developed and developing nations. To transform the global economic and financial environments and facilitate economic growth, we need to liberate all nations from the debt burden and create new conditions conducive to sustainable global development, which only the Ramo Plan has the capacity to do.

Notes

1. Jack Ewing and Liz Alderman, Bailout Money Goes to Greece, Only to Flow out Again, The New York Times, July 30, 2015.
2. Timeline, Greece debt crisis, Council on Foreign Relations. http://www.cfr.org/greece/timeline-greeces-debt-crisis/p36451, http://www.bbc.com/news/business-36376836
3. Andrew Walker, Will Greek debt deal really change anything? BBC World Service, May 25, 2016. http://www.bbc.com/news/business-36376836
4. Ibid.
5. Ibid.
6. New Greek Bailout Package 'Is A Breakthrough', Sky News, May 25, 2016. https://www.google.com/webhp?sourceid=chrome-instant&ion=1&espv=2&ie=UTF-8#q=Sky+News%2C+New+Greek+Bailout+Package%2C+May+25%2C+2016
7. Jack Ewing and Liz Alderman, Bailout Money Goes to Greece, Only to Flow Out Again, *The New York Times,* July 30, 2015.
8. Ibid.
9. Helena Smith; A year after the crisis was declared over, Greece is still spiraling down; The Guardian, August 13, 2016 https://www.theguardian.com/business/2016/aug/13/greek-economy-still-spiralling-down-year-after-crisis-declared-over#img-1
10. Helena Smith; Greek gloom as economy stalls amid latest bout of EU wrangling, The Guardian, April 8, 2017. https://www.theguardian.com/business/2017/apr/08/greece-last-protesters-diehards-rise-up-compromise-syriza-eurozone#img-2
11. Ibid.
12. Explaining Greece's debt crisis, *the New York Times*, June 17, 2016.
13. Ibid.
14. Noam Chomsky; Who Rules the World p. 3.

CHAPTER 13

The Nature of the Transition

The transition from the industrial age to the knowledge age has caused the four processes of societal transformation to be activated at once, which has enabled them to be more disruptive of all the systems that manage our lives and regulate our relationships. Today, the sociocultural process is causing social segmentation and ideological revival, chaos and radicalism, and thus less harmony and cohesiveness; the political process is causing more political fragmentation, conflict and fear, and less unity and peace; the economic process is causing the concentration of more wealth in fewer hands and less social mobility and less justice; and the infomedia process is working harder than ever to falsify the consciousness of the masses and ignore the need to inform them. The change instigated by these processes and the way they manage domestic and global affairs has created many reasons to provoke conflict and spread radicalism, and equally many reasons to contain conflict, fight radicalism and accommodate peaceful change.

Attempts to initiate drastic change and carry out social revolutions are unlikely to succeed in this age, because the interests of the many thousands of players participating in the national and global games cannot be reconciled. As a consequence, sociocultural and socioeconomic transformations can no longer be initiated by leaders, groups or even political parties alone, and the state is increasingly becoming less able to do so. This means that change and conflict, peace and war, fear and security, economic growth and stagnation have become global issues requiring creative ideas and wide cooperation at international level.

M. Rabie, *The Global Debt Crisis and Its Socioeconomic Implications*,
https://doi.org/10.1007/978-3-319-66215-2_13

Owing primarily to the information and telecommunications revolutions that include the Internet and social media, and economic and cultural globalization, change in the new age has become a multifaceted dynamic process of transformation that has no end in sight. Since the services of the information and telecommunications revolutions are needed everywhere, their impact on life stretches beyond all political borders and involves all cultures and peoples. And because the institutions through which these revolutions function are controlled by the rich and people with unusual talents, the ideas and actions of those people are impacting the lives of all individuals, groups and nations in ways previously unknown.

Though every society is changing and will change more in the future, no society is able to transform itself according to its wishes. In fact, the emerging knowledge age is creating a new society that seems destined to live in a state of perpetual change and transformation, causing the near future to look like a world that is in a permanent state of transition. But owing to the complexity and knowledge requirements of the new age, no state will see its entire society or culture or economy fully transformed; every nation will continue to need people to do certain jobs and be engaged in activities rooted in the industrial and agricultural civilizations. On the other hand, since neither values nor traditions nor belief systems accumulate over time, any change they may experience now and in the future could be reversed, at least partially. In contrast, scientific discoveries and innovations are being developed in response to growing needs, increasing life challenges and business expectations through a process that requires accumulation and specialization; consequently, once made, scientific knowledge and technological innovations cannot be reversed. As a further consequence, interactions between traditional values and belief systems on the one hand and new technologies and ideas on the other are causing conflict to arise and persist everywhere.

With every new age, life has become more complicated and knowledge more sophisticated and specialized, causing our ability to produce and use knowledge to become decisive in making further social, cultural, political and economic progress. Yet knowledge and the skills associated with it have always been unevenly divided both within and among societies. There is a knowledge gap between those who know and others who know less, and those who know less are less able to compete in an increasingly dynamic global economy. In the meantime, continued change is causing the knowledge gap to widen and deepen with every passing day, and transform itself into power and wealth gaps that reduce our ability to build just and peaceful societies.

As knowledge increases in society, it becomes more institutionalized, causing the influence of institutions to increase at the expense of individual and group players. And as institutions and social systems increase in number and complexity, change becomes multidimensional and largely uncontrollable and unpredictable, affecting all aspects of life, at all times, in all places. The people most involved with the production and application of knowledge tend to change faster, to benefit more and to achieve higher standards of living, causing socioeconomic gaps to widen and sociocultural divides to deepen within and between societies. In the meantime, national cultures are being divided into subcultures, national societies are disintegrating into subsocieties and the "national interest" is fast becoming a concept hard to define or relate to.

Since knowledge is an efficient tool to free people from need, knowledge workers have become less dependent on the state and their families and, as a consequence, they share few memories with others; and, because of this, they tend to be less committed to an ideology or a nation. Their primary interest is to succeed, make the best use of whatever knowledge they may have and get the most for it. In fact, knowledge workers have become modern nomads wandering from one place to another, from one organization to another and from one country to another in order to advance technically and succeed materially. They are driven by self-interest and a competitive global marketplace that leads most of them to become rootless, and often ruthless as well. Knowledge workers have difficulty accepting reality and therefore they are always on the move searching for new relationships to forge, new realities to shape and new opportunities to exploit. But while most knowledge workers seem less committed to national and ideological causes, some seem more interested in human causes and environmental concerns.

People in the emerging knowledge age have become more materialistic and less ethical and spiritual, and therefore less able to see human issues as worthy causes; the only thing they are able to see and worship is money. Materialism, which has gradually and quietly been acquiring the role claimed by religion in agricultural society, has become the major driving force in industrial society. In the knowledge society, money is gradually assuming the role of God. So people are rich and poor, not because God and religion have ordained it, but because economics and knowledge and culture have determined it. Man, consequently, is seen as the master of his fate, and neither God nor religion has anything to do with it. Because individualism has become a component of the philosophy of the knowledge age, both poverty and community are no longer seen as issues of particular concern to the elites that control society. Most people today seek to maximize pleasure, wealth and power, while minimizing worry, risk and pain.

People with knowledge, that is people with the right education and the right attitudes, have the capability to seize opportunities, make more money and move upward; they even have the capability to create new opportunities for themselves and for others to exploit. Moreover, people with money have the resources to acquire the right knowledge, gain access to the centers of power and expand the range of opportunities open to them. In contrast, people without wealth and good education are left behind, with nothing to enable them to compete in an increasingly complex world, where knowledge has become very important for making a decent living and gaining social recognition. "During this period of increasing income inequality, the value of a four-year college degree has dramatically increased. Those with one have continued to move ahead; those without one have fallen further behind."[1]

Since equality of opportunity is not enough by itself to facilitate social mobility, democracy cannot claim that it leads to equality and just society. "Gross inequality in wealth is itself a social evil, which poisons life for millions."[2] As inequality in wealth and income pushes poor people toward apathy and despair, it causes them to lose faith in democracy. In the knowledge society where individualism reigns supreme and ideology is dying, and where globalism and money have become the new frame of reference, helping the poor has become of no particular use to the rich. And because the poor can be isolated and are in fact being isolated everywhere, they are being ignored and largely forgotten; they no longer get the attention they deserve or the compassion they need.

Because the role of knowledge in life is on the rise, and since the association of wealth and power with knowledge is strong and getting stronger, the traditional industrial class has lost its ability to protect its interests, as well as the means to grow again and regain the confidence, independence and class consciousness it once had. As a consequence, the industrial class is no longer able to cause economic or political change in its favor. Meanwhile, the new emerging economy is creating jobs for the knowledge worker and the unskilled worker, but little for other workers. And because of its transitional nature, the new economy is causing job insecurity to increase and spread fear among workers. Promoters of market capitalism are promoting a new plan to make all jobs hourly, which, if implemented, would cause workers to lose health benefits, bonuses, vacations, sick leave and retirement benefits.

While land ownership defines the lines separating the rich from the poor in traditional agricultural society, income and the means to earn a good income define the lines separating social classes in industrial society. In the knowledge age, the fortunes of every individual, regardless of his social class, have become a function of his ability to recognize and exploit the educational, political and economic opportunities that society regularly creates. However, the requirements to recognize and exploit opportunities have grown more complex with every civilization; today, the ability to recognize and exploit opportunities needs skills, capital, experience, good education and awareness. The shift from manufacturing to services and the ever-changing nature of knowledge have caused opportunities open to members of the middle class to narrow, causing the size of the middle class to shrink and its power to wane. A knowledge barrier, as a result, was added to the old capital, skill and education barriers, causing upward mobility in all mature industrial societies to decline substantially.

The industrial society, I believe, was the only society in history that could and did produce a credible middle class. The tribal society, owing to the absence of a productive economy and private property, had one class; the agricultural society, owing to the institutionalization of private property, has two classes; and the knowledge society is clearly unable to sustain the middle class it has inherited from the industrial society. The middle class, which is hardly 150 years old, must therefore be considered an aberration in the history of societal development. Since history never repeats itself, we need to adjust our assumptions to reflect this reality in order to understand it and deal with its consequences rationally. I have no doubt that we can create a new middle class, but to do so we need to transform our business culture and the way we view and organize production relations.[3]

The transition from the twentieth-century industrial civilization to the twenty-first-century knowledge civilization is transforming people's cultures and ways of thinking and outlooks fundamentally and irreversibly, as well as the assumptions that form the foundations of political, economic and social systems. And as assumptions change, they invalidate the theories and analytical models built to understand and manage systems. Because of this transition, states are losing the organizing principles of their politics, cultures, societies and economies. In the meantime, societies are being divided into subsocieties along sociocultural lines that are value-oriented and need-related, and cultures are being fragmented into subcultures along religious and ideological lines.

Generally speaking, national politics is increasingly becoming the politics of subcultures and special interests, while international politics is increasingly becoming the politics of trade, finance, investment, security and environmental concerns. A new world is fast emerging where interests and economic advantage count much more than cultural values, traditional relationships, and national identities and loyalties. All issues related to national security, national interest, national sovereignty, national power, national industries and national politics are being quietly redefined and placed in different societal and global contexts that require a new class of leading thinkers and thinking leaders to deal with.

The chaotic situation created by the transition from the industrial to the knowledge age has caused the state and its agents to lose control of events and situations; but the loss of control has created a new space for freedom, initiative, creativity and innovation. As a consequence, the transition gives us, the people of the world, a historical opportunity to shape our history and destiny and create a just, peaceful and prosperous future for all. But to do so, we have to work together and believe that justice and fairness dictate that we share the sacrifices and rewards of change. National and global civil society organizations need to guide us through this transition, because neither political leaders nor ideologies can lead us to justice or peace. But for such organizations to do what they must do to help us create a better world for all, they need to commit themselves to the basic principles of honesty, decency and humanity. Outdated ideas and ideologies, and failed and failing states should not be allowed to shape the future; they are only able to cause more chaos and conflict and hinder our ability to move forward.

Today, values and ideologies for which people fought and died in the past are dying, and interests and pleasures for which people live and strive are blossoming. But when people are left alone to live in poverty and need, they feel oppressed and denied their legitimate rights; and that leaves them no choice but to fight for justice and dignity, and die for liberty and freedom. However, the times we live in are not suitable for launching revolutions and instigating drastic change; we therefore need to work peacefully to restructure or replace systems that oppressed us and denied us our legitimate rights for too long. The spirit of revolution that swept several Arab countries in 2011 proves that no nation or culture is immune to change, that no authoritarian regime is able to rule forever, that no ideology will die without a fight, and that no change is necessarily change for the better.

Every idea, theory, system and road map has a life of its own that could be interesting or dull, productive or unproductive, short or long, but never perpetual; eventually all ideas and systems will die. While most systems and road maps usually die a natural death through old age and gradual loss of energy and relevancy; others often die abruptly owing to transformational changes that overwhelm society and render old ideas and systems obsolete in a short time. Nevertheless, some systems, such as capitalism and democracy, possess a substantial capacity to adapt and prolong their productive lives. Others, such as dictatorships, are born sterile and live largely violent lives until their death. However, every system, roadmap and idea is a product of a particular time, place and civilization; and therefore it cannot have universal application or perpetual life and utility.

Throughout past history, knowledge was more spiritual than materialistic, more liberal than conservative and more pluralistic than ideological. Because of these characteristics, knowledge was able to play a constructive role in helping the poor and weak, developing and humanizing cultures, solving social and economic problems, causing change and making progress. In contrast, the bulk of knowledge in the new age is more materialistic than anything else; it is composed of scientific knowledge and technological innovations and information. Though such knowledge has high economic returns, it does not contribute to humanizing cultures or people. In fact, the new technologies which the knowledge age has been producing since the beginning of the twenty-first century have disrupted our lives and changed the way we think and view each other and the world around us; they have also made us feel less secure and less social.

Giving priority to material gain causes greed, jealousy and consumerism to spread and to undermine human values of fairness, honesty, justice and even rationality. On the other hand, information is vulnerable to manipulation by the media and other social actors to suit every strain of thought and the business activity they favor. As a consequence, knowledge and business elites have become less committed to causes that intellectuals and thinkers of the recent past fought for, causing our world to become more chaotic and less hospitable to free thinking and spiritualism. Therefore, we need to become conscious of the changing nature of knowledge, information and technologies and their consequences on our lives and social relationships; otherwise, we will fail to address the daunting challenges of tomorrow, strengthen our sense of humanity and protect our environment.

During the Arab Spring of 2011, small enlightened groups of young activists were able to use social media to mobilize millions of people in

Tunisia, Egypt, Libya and Yemen, and lead them to seek political change that ended the reign of the rulers of those countries. On the other hand, forces of darkness have been able to use social media, the Internet and the art of making videos to recruit, organize, indoctrinate and mobilize thousands of people worldwide to commit heinous crimes against humanity. And while the enlightened forces lost the battle, leaving behind a catastrophe of immense proportions, the forces of darkness have continued to expand their reach and criminal operations to many countries.

The transition from the tribal age to the agricultural age lasted about 3000 years, causing change to be incremental and very slow; as a result, no generation during that era was able to feel the impact of change on its life. The transition from the agricultural to the industrial age lasted about 300 years; as a result, most people at the time were able to see change and feel its impact on their lives. The current transition from the industrial to the knowledge age is expected to last about thirty years, ending around 2025. As a result, every person in every corner of the world is seeing change and feeling its profound impact on his life and the lives of people around him. If the speed of change during the first transition could be likened to the speed of an ant, the speed of change in the second transition would be equal to that of a horse competing in a race; as for the current transition, change is moving with the speed of an airplane flying nonstop to nowhere. Since the new knowledge age promises to live in a permanent state of change and transformation, future change is expected to be moving at the speed of sound.

The life we live is the time we spend enjoying what we love doing in life; the rest is a waste of life. The past is the moment we just left behind dying of old age, while worrying about its legacy. The present is what we experience in everyday life, as we try to face some challenges, enjoy others, avoid many and create many more to boast our egos and fulfill our desires. The future is what we dream of having the next day by doing what we can to make it happen. History is what we make of our life as we live, love, laugh, cry, sing, dance, read, learn, think, work, win, lose, imagine, build, destroy and dream again. Knowledge is the tools we must have to transform our reality in order to enjoy life and realize our dreams, and overcome the pain of failure and the indignity of poverty and need. Transformation is the continuous process of questioning our traditions, attitudes, ideas and convictions, as well as the wisdom of yesterday. And culture is what makes us human, able to live with one another and love each other, as we struggle individually and collectively to transform our world, make and remake our history, and shape our future.

Notes

1. Joel Rogers and Ruy Teixeira, "America's Forgotten Majority," *The Atlantic Monthly*, June 2000, 69.
2. Steven Weinberg, "Utopias," *The Atlantic Monthly*, June 2000, 109.
3. See, Mohamed Rabie; Saving Capitalism and Democracy, Palgrave Macmillan, 2013, chapter 8.

CHAPTER 14

A Peek at the Future

Though the global economic situation of today does not appear to be on the verge of a crisis, many reports suggest that the credit situation in the United States is as bad as it was at the time of the financial crisis of 2008. While a few countries were at the time able to ride out that crisis without being hurt, such as China and South Korea, the credit situation in both states today is not as good as it was in 2008. Mark O'Byrne, quoting a report issued by the McKinsey Institute, says, "China's debt has quadrupled since 2007 to $28 trillion. This represents 282% of GDP [gross domestic product]. Half of all loans are linked, directly or indirectly, to China's overheated real-estate market; unregulated shadow banking accounts for nearly half of new lending; and the debt of many local governments is probably unsustainable."[1]

Michael Snyder said in March 2016: "Corporate defaults [in the United States] are currently at the highest level that we have seen since 2009. In fact, the average credit rating for US corporations is now lower than it was at any point during the last recession … Big corporate giants all over America are in deep, deep financial trouble."[2] Matt Egan, commenting on the future of retail business in America, wrote in August 2016: "In a sign of how dramatically the retail shopping landscape is changing, Macy's is closing 100 of its stores nationwide, [which] represent about 15% of all Macy's department stores. The Macy's move is the latest in a wave of store closures. For instance, Walmart announced plans in January to shut down 269 stores this year. Sports Authority, once the nation's largest sporting goods retailer, is shutting all 450 of its stores after filing for bankruptcy. Other traditional

M. Rabie, *The Global Debt Crisis and Its Socioeconomic Implications*,
https://doi.org/10.1007/978-3-319-66215-2_14

retailers such as Target, JC Penney, Kmart, Sears and Kohl's have also pulled the plug on hundreds of stores in recent months."[3] As a consequence, around 44,000 retail layoffs were announced in the first half of 2016.

As for the Europeans, economic growth averaged about 1% over the last five years (2012–16). Meanwhile, unemployment in several countries has become structural, with millions of people needing to learn new skills to find decent jobs. The rate of unemployment in the Eurozone was 10.2% in 2016; three points higher than 2008; and for the EU as a whole, the unemployment rate is 9.8%. In addition, many countries have debts they cannot repay; such countries include Belgium, Britain, Cyprus, France, Greece, Ireland, Italy, Portugal and Spain. Therefore, finding solutions to stimulate these economies without going deeper into debt has become near impossible. If the numbers of the unemployed in Europe were to be added to the numbers of the unemployed in the United States, the result would be about 50 million, the equivalent of the populations of Austria, Greece, Holland, Ireland and Portugal put together. In fact, all reports of economic growth since 2008 talk about "recovery," which means that the European economies are yet to recover from the Great Recession.

As for the monetary policies of the American, European and Japanese central banks, their accomplishments are very modest indeed. Records of the Japanese monetary policy suggest that very low interest rates, coupled with a growing public debt borrowed almost exclusively from Japanese people, have not just failed to revive the economy, but probably caused it to stagnate, leading Japan to lose about two decades of growth, going back to the 1990s. The growth rate of Japan's economy for the last six years (2011–16) had averaged 0.8%.

As for the American and European central banks, they have adopted monetary policies to ease credit, reduce interest rates to near zero and create trillions of dollars to finance the ever-increasing public debts on both sides of the Atlantic. In Germany, the return on government bonds dropped in June 2016 to below zero. This monetary policy may have helped to stabilize the economic situation in America and Europe and calm the fears of the financial markets, but it has weakened the global economy while failing to restore economic vitality in America or Europe. On the other side, financing the debt in this manner has come at the expense of the middle class in all countries of the world, causing its size to shrink and its power to wane, and the income and wealth gaps separating the rich from the poor to widen further.

When interest rates on state bonds and saving accounts drop to near zero, they make it hard for people to consider investing in such financial instruments; and this causes government bonds to lose their role as investment options and tools to fight inflation. In fact, state bonds have become a means to cheat the public, and deny savers a fair return on their life savings, particularly members of the middle class who save for the education of their children and retirement. Even the one percentage point, which some US banks pay savers, is being confiscated by raising fees on financial transactions. Financial reports indicate that transaction fees have become a major source of income for American banks. As a result, the monetary policy of the American and European central banks has become a scheme to create free money to strengthen banks and enrich the rich. Before the Great Recession, central banks' policies were meant to grow national economies, create jobs for the unemployed, control inflation and create national wealth for all citizens to benefit from. Not anymore.

In the process of implementing their policies, central banks have undermined the lives and future plans of millions of individuals and families, causing poverty to deepen its roots in almost every place. This has caused consumers to be more cautious and has thus complicated plans to revive the global economy and create new jobs for the world's unemployed, particularly the young. Today, as the rich get richer and the powerful gain more power, relative wages decline, the middle class shrinks, social mobility becomes less accessible and climbing the social ladder becomes a dream to entertain but not a promise to believe in.

According to the International Monetary Fund (IMF), "Growth is slowing for the fifth year in a row, as the commodity super cycle and unprecedented credit booms have come to an end. This is of special relevance given the large share of emerging markets in the world economy, as well as the role that global markets play in transmitting shocks to emerging markets and spillovers to advanced economies. The IMF is especially concerned because corporations and banks in some emerging economies continue to rely on massive debt financing to maintain growth; and this makes them vulnerable to further falls in commodity prices and declines in global trade."[4] The *Guardian* reported in October 2015 that José Viñals, the IMF's financial counselor, said: "The threat of instability and recession hanging over economies including China, Brazil, Turkey and Malaysia was one of a "triad of risks" that could knock 3% off global GDP. The second was the legacy of debt and disharmony in Europe, while the third is centered on battered global markets that are more likely to transmit shocks rather than cushion the blow. In the absence of action, the global economy was at risk of losing 2.4 percentage points from growth, effectively pushing it into recession."[5] It is obvious that neither the IMF nor the World Bank nor central banks have concrete ideas about how to repay the global debt, revive the middle class, contain poverty or avert a seemingly impending crisis.

For more than two years, the US Federal Reserve has been talking about raising interest rates. But despite the improvement in consumer confidence, declining unemployment and lower than expected inflation rates, it has failed to do his since 2006, except twice; a largely symbolic quarter of a point each time. Should we believe the claims made by the US Federal Reserve that it will continue to raise interest rates two or three times a year until they reach 3%? The answer is doubtful. Low interest rates reduce the cost of servicing the public debt and, as a consequence, slow down the growth of budget deficits. This, in turn, gives governments the opportunity to claim that they have managed to stabilize the size of the debt and the deficit relative to GDP, which helps them to stay in power longer, while most people continue to suffer loss of income, wealth and time. But no matter how high interest rates go, most indebted states will continue to borrow, because they cannot service their current debt without doing so. This simply means that there is a conflict of interest between states and citizens; what serves the interests of one party hurts the interests of the other, causing the state to become an enemy of its own citizens.

Generally speaking, lower interest rates are good for potential borrowers and all indebted individuals, organizations, corporations and nations because they reduce the cost of servicing the debt. However, lower interest rates eat the life savings of people who save to ensure a secured retirement and meet emergencies. Such people, whose numbers are in the hundreds of millions, are waiting patiently for interest rates to rise and to see returns on their life savings improve. Keeping interest rates as low as they are achieves two major objectives, neither of which is fair or moral: to deny savers the right to earn a decent return on their savings; and allow governments to borrow more and force future generations to pay for their financial management blunders.

Given the sheer size of the American debt of more than $20 trillion, if interest rates were to increase by one percentage point the federal budget deficit would increase by $200 billion in the first year. Two percentage points would cause the deficit to increase by more than $400 billion. The same increase also applies to the public debt. This is why the Federal Reserve and the European Central Bank (ECB) hesitate to raise interest rates, and why I believe that interest rates are not going to reach normal levels anytime soon; thus any increase in interest rates that might come in the near future will likely be incremental and very slow.

Therefore, the longer it takes to solve the debt crisis, the more complicated other political and social matters will become; and this will increase the probability of getting hit by another global economic/financial crisis with far-reaching strategic implications that could undermine the major institutions of market capitalism. Mike O'Byrne says, "The attempt to solve what was essentially a global debt crisis with mountains of more debt means we will have another global financial crisis—the question is when rather than if."[6]

Having the experience to deal with strategic economic, social, political and security issues is a good thing at any time; nevertheless, all experience is limited in scope and time. If we were living in a traditional society in Africa where cultures and political, social and economic structures change little over time, past experience would be all that a leader needs to manage whatever challenges he may face. But in a world that lives a life of continuous change, experience rooted in the past is more of a liability than an asset. So-called experts tend to think of the future as an extension of the past, leading them to stick to outdated theories and ways of thinking. The records of the latest Federal Reserve meeting held before the financial crisis of 2008 indicate that the experts failed to foresee the housing bubble. "The Federal Open Market Committee members weren't stupid, lazy or uninformed. They could draw on a massive staff of economists for analysis. And yet, they were clueless."[7]

Since we have never lived in a world as complicated, integrated and transient as the one we live in today, tools used in the past have become dysfunctional and therefore largely useless. Putting the experts in charge to deal with an evolving crisis in a shifting situation is a serious mistake, because the knowledge they have is rooted in the past, rather than in the future. In fact, putting experts in charge of an evolving crisis amounts to an attempt to recycle unrecyclable ideas and human talent, and use unusable tools. Global challenges require global answers; and new times require new ideas.

Paul Kennedy, for example, bases his analysis regarding the future on the assumption that "the broad trends of the past five centuries are likely to continue."[8] Kennedy does not seem to have noticed that the transition from the industrial age to the knowledge age has put an end to the trends of the past five centuries, causing the trends that dominated change in the past to die and be replaced by new ones. Kennedy's thinking, which reflects the views common among Western strategic thinkers, misrepresents the nature of change, and therefore cannot produce anything but misconceptions of the future. The fact that humanity is in the middle of a transitional period leading to a new age and a new civilization makes all ideas based on past experience useless. Since the beginning of each civilization marks the end of its predecessor's history and logic, it invalidates the lessons of the past. Therefore, the forces, institutions and road maps that managed the past have become part of a largely irrelevant legacy of that past.

Until the end of the sixteenth century, history was rather predictable because it was dominated by a sociocultural process that resists change. In the meantime, the political process was weak and dominated by the religious establishment, and therefore it had neither the power nor the freedom to influence change in a meaningful way. On the other hand, the economic process was still in its infancy, unable to comprehend its environment and know its way; and the infomedia process was still being born. So the sociocultural process was the only process that was able to cause change and influence its direction; however, the change it had caused was in place rather than in time. Today, the four societal processes with their contradictory interests and goals are competing and collaborating to change reality in place, time and space at once, creating a dynamic, largely chaotic situation where history moves in all directions without a sense of direction, trying to find its way to an unknown future.

When systems and road maps die naturally because of old age, strategic thinkers are usually able to track the deteriorating health of such systems and make suggestions to restructure them or replace them with new ones. But when systems and road maps die abruptly, it is difficult for most thinkers to realize the extent of change in time to develop new systems to replace the dying ones. During transitional periods that connect one civilization to another, an atmosphere of crisis usually clouds reality, causing people to become disoriented and lose their sense of direction; and this limits their capacity to think clearly or to develop new road maps to replace the dying ones. Transitional periods represent historical discontinuities that end the history of the passing civilization and the validity of its logic, and undermine the structure of its society.

Traditional thinkers, being a product of the dying times and ideas, usually devote a great deal of their energies to defending the failing systems and inventing information and arguments to prove that they are still alive and well. In such situations, the lag time between the death of a system and the birth of its replacement is prolonged, causing social and economic crises to be extra painful; it may even cause crises to take unexpected turns that could be catastrophic. The Arab Spring is an example of a social revolution with limited objectives that turned into a catastrophe. Responding to societal transformations requires new thinkers and new ways of viewing reality; these are times of evolving crises that cannot be managed by recycling outdated ideas and talent.

Because of all these facts, it is hard to imagine how market capitalism and democracy could be saved while the global economy continues to slow down and fast-growing public and private debt persists. Stubbornly high unemployment rates, widening income and wealth gaps, the shrinking middle class and spreading poverty and violence are clear signs that times are changing fundamentally. No nation can live on its past legacy, or borrowed money or time, forever; eventually, every nation will have to restructure its economy, transform its society and culture, create jobs for the unemployed and generate enough revenue to balance its budget and meet the expectations of its citizens.

Many economists, politicians, businessmen and experts in both the West and the East still believe that the current low economic growth rates are abnormalities, and that higher rates are not just possible, but inevitable. Contrary to this view, I have argued since the early 1990s that the economic, monetary and social policies of the major Western powers have eliminated the possibility of high growth rates; the current rates therefore must be considered the new normal. In addition, there are other forces that undermine the capacity of the global economy to grow faster:

1. Widening income and wealth gaps at national and global levels: these gaps prevent the incomes of the lower 90% of the world's population from growing, because all increase in income goes to the top 10%. Any increase in spending by the rich 10% is not nearly enough to compensate for the loss of spending by the other 90%. This in turn causes rates of increase in demand to remain low.
2. Large and growing public and private debts: these debts undermine the capacity of all states to borrow more money to stimulate lagging economies, because more borrowing increases the debt servicing burden and thus budget deficits; and this limits states capacity to borrow more and invest in social and public services.
3. Declining population growth rates in the world: as this trend causes the annual increase in population to slow down, it limits any increase in global demand for goods and jobs. For example, statistics indicate

that the world's population growth rate peaked in 1960 at 2.2% annually, declined to 1.3% in 2000 and 1.1% in 2016; it is projected to continue declining, reaching 1% in 2020 and 0.8% in 2030.[9]

4. Rising life expectancy: this causes the number and ratio of older people to rise everywhere; but their desires to consume and own more things are declining, causing any increase in global demand to be modest.
5. The spread and persistence of a mode of diminishing expectations: this causes people to expect less in the future, and leads them to accept the less that is expected to come. This limits their ambitions and aspirations for more goods and better jobs.

To restructure the major systems and institutions that manage our lives, and in order to adapt to the emerging realities and imperatives of our age, all nations need to do five things: first, repay their public debt in its entirety; second, expand consumption and investment markets in both rich and poor states; third, revitalize their shrinking middle classes; fourth, transform their cultures; and fifth, collaborate to narrow the wealth and income gaps within and between societies. Since these issues are connected and involve all nations, solutions have to be sought within a global context.

When the Occupy Wall Street movement came to Washington DC in 2011, I decided to join them. My brief participation in the movement's activities gave me an opportunity to meet a few members of its leadership. After several discussions, I told the movement leaders that their chances of success are near zero. The following factors explain why:

1. Lack of a well-defined objective: rejectionist forces throughout history, on the right as well as on the left, have always been able to define what they stand against, but have almost always failed to define what they stand for. The Occupy movement adopted several objectives that could not be molded into one strategy capable of convincing a large segment of the American people to support it.
2. The movement had no plan of action to change Wall Street or achieve its other goals.
3. Leaders of the movement assumed that it was possible to bring about the desired change by working through the existing democratic and capitalist systems, seemingly unaware that both systems have become largely corrupt and dysfunctional.

As programs outlined in the Ramo Plan begin to be implemented and start to produce tangible results, most developing nations will enter a stage of "rising expectations," causing demand to increase and markets to expand rapidly. In the meanwhile, spending some $10 trillion over twenty to twenty-five years should create hundreds of millions of jobs, reduce unemployment everywhere, invigorate the global economy and vastly reduce the chances of another economic recession. Millions of these jobs would go to European, American and Asian young men and women working for national and multinational corporations and not-for-profit organizations that help poor nations to develop and industrialize. The Sustainable Development Fund should lift hundreds of millions of people out of poverty, revitalize the middle classes everywhere, and train millions of farmers, teachers, scientists, physicians, engineers, professors, thinkers and artists to keep our economy growing and enrich our lives.

During the coming fifteen to twenty years, several industrial societies in the West and East are expected to reach a state of equilibrium, where national economies and domestic demand grow at a very slow pace. Several factors are contributing towards this eventuality: many states have already built the big national projects that had to be built, have population growth rates near zero and declining, and have aging populations that prefer leisure over work. In addition, I believe that within the same timespan a few other nations will enter a largely permanent state of diminishing expectations, where people expect less in the future and are resigned to accept the less that is expected to come. These anticipated developments will moderate global demand for all goods, particularly natural resources. Japan is a good example of a nation about to enter a permanent state of diminishing expectations; Germany is a good example of a nation approaching a state of equilibrium; Italy, France, Spain, the United States, China, Russia and many other states are not far behind.

By the time the Ramo Plan is fully implemented in the year 2040 or so, assuming that its implantation will start soon, the global population growth rate would have reached 0.8% or less, and high unemployment rates would have become a thing of the past. As a consequence, improvements in labor and machine productivity alone would be more than enough to meet any increase in global demand, and the need to create many new jobs and waste more natural resources would disappear. A new global culture bordering on contentment would emerge and prevail, causing our world to become more stable and truly sustainable.

As mentioned earlier, world society is passing through a transitional period from the industrial age to the knowledge age. Since every transition between two civilizations represents a historical discontinuity, it undermines the pillars of the old society, invalidates most systems that manage economic and social and political affairs, and creates chaotic situations that cause people to lose their sense of direction. The great political and economic and military powers of today do not seem to understand the nature of the transition; and, because of that, they are unable to deal with it or anticipate its consequences. Though it is hard to predict how change will unfold and affect our lives in the knowledge age, there are many signs that give us a fairly good idea about what to expect in the coming decade or two.

Following the introduction of the iPhone in 2007, software and apps to harness the potential of the new technology began to disrupt many traditional industries, ways of doing business, and how we behave, manage our lives and communicate and socialize with one another. For example, the business of Uber is built on an idea that needed certain software to become the world's largest taxi company within five years, without owning a single car. As the popularity of Uber grew, it expanded internationally and its value skyrocketed; in late 2015, Uber's value was estimated at $62.5 billion.[10] Airbnb is another simple idea that transformed the way people book rooms when they travel, staying at regular homes instead of hotels, and in the process has enabled homeowners to lease a room or two, and make money. Within ten years, Airbnb has become the world's largest hotel company without owning a single hotel. In addition, many innovative ideas and apps are being developed to provide medical diagnosis and advice, prepare legal documents and provide legal advice in minutes. All of these ideas and systems save time and manpower and make results more accurate for less money. In the following few paragraphs, I shall comment on the probable consequences of self-driven cars and robots on taxi and truck drivers, car ownership and industrial jobs; and how this might affect employment and our cities and environment in a decade or two.

The GPS technology and the Internet have facilitated the birth of new enterprises such as Uber, Google, Yahoo, the smartphone industry, e-commerce, Facebook, Amazon, electronic libraries, publishing and much more. In fact, owing to the Internet and information technology, Amazon, Apple, Facebook, Google and Microsoft have become the largest companies in the world. And while making life easier and more productive and enjoyable for millions of people worldwide, these technologies have caused many companies to shrink in size or close, and millions of workers to lose their jobs, thereby disrupting the normal lives of millions more. For example, "since its peak in 1979, U.S. manufacturing employment has declined, with moderate losses through the late 1990s, mostly caused by higher manufacturing productivity relative to the rest of the economy. In the 2000s, with the rise of China and the new globalization, US manufacturing employment experienced a decade of unprecedented losses, shedding 5.8 million jobs, or about one-third of the workforce."[11]

"In the 1950s, the manufacturing sector accounted for almost 30 percent of total US employment. In 2002, however, the U.S. manufacturing sector accounted for 10.7% of the workforce only. As for other industrial countries, the manufacturing sector accounts for 19.8% of total jobs in Germany, 18.6% in Italy, and 16.6% in Japan and South Korea. But, as in the United States, these figures are all lower than they were a decade ago."[12] According to data from the Organisation for Economic Co-operation and Development (OECD), "the U.K. and Australia have seen their share of manufacturing drop by around two-thirds since 1971. Germany's share halved. In South Korea, the manufacturing share of employment rose from 13 percent in 1970 to 28 percent in 1991; it's fallen to 17 percent today."[13] The decline in manufacturing jobs is not confined to the rich countries; it includes Brazil, India and China. This means that manufacturing jobs are not expected to recover, making all talk about rebuilding the manufacturing sector in the United States and "making America great again" mere political slogans and far-fetched wishes.

In fact, I expect manufacturing jobs in all industrialized countries to decline by 50–60% in the next twenty to twenty-five years; robots and higher labor and machine productivity will compensate for job losses. Unlike human labor, robots do not sleep, do not need lunch breaks or vacations or sick leave, and do not ask for raises or social benefits; they are capable of working twenty-four hours a day, 365 days a year for no compensation. As a consequence, no man or women will be able to compete with robots in a decade or so, and no manufacturer will hesitate to replace machine power for manpower. If manufacturing jobs in all industrial countries were to be added together, the total would be close to 300 million; losing 50% of these jobs would add some 150 million to the unemployed worldwide, causing the size of the middle classes to shrink everywhere, wealth and income gaps to widen further, and global growth rates to decline. According to the National Association of Manufacturers, "In 2014, the average manufacturing worker in the United States earned $79,553 annually, including pay and benefits."[14] When this worker's job is gone, his income and social status, even his social existence, will go with it. Many of these workers will be forced by these circumstances to join the ranks of the poor, unless we transform our economies and cultures and social policies.

In seven to ten years from now, the self-driven car is expected to become a familiar object roaming the streets of American cities, as well as those in Europe, Japan and North Korea. The Ford Car Company announced on August 16, 2016 that it plans to begin mass producing self-driven cars in five years. As the first taxi company using self-driven cars begins regular operations, demand for cars will start declining fast, and taxi and truck drivers and chauffeurs will start losing their jobs. Meanwhile, our streets and cities will change in ways unknown before, causing the way we live our lives to change as well; streets will become wider, cities cleaner and traffic jams a thing of the past. And just as telephone booths disappeared with the appearance of the mobile phone, parking meters will disappear as most people start using self-driven cars. Since such cars are able to work day and night, they need no parking spaces in our cities or homes; moreover, they will use less energy, produce less pollution and enable passengers to work while travelling instead of driving. As a consequence, we will have more space and time to build parks and recreation centers and enjoy life.

However, cities and states will see revenues derived from cars decline by probably 30–40% in ten to twelve years: parking meter fees will disappear, licenses and tax fees will shrink substantially and fines collected from traffic violators will also decline substantially, because no self-driven car will violate traffic laws. As a result, cities and states will experience huge budget deficits that could force them to reduce services and the number of employees. Already, for most of the retired people in the industrial world, using Uber today for all purposes has become much cheaper, safer and more convenient than owning a car.

Therefore, it is expected that about 70% of all taxi and truck drivers will lose their jobs within the coming two decades; two or three of the largest car manufacturers are likely to go out of business; and the rest will be forced to restructure and change their business models to suit the new car market. In the meantime, the car insurance industry will lose most of its business. And owing to the shrinking car market, and electric cars, the oil industry will see its market shrink year after year. All car-related businesses such as car maintenance, car sales and production of spare parts will lose sales as well as manufacturing and service jobs, causing unemployment to increase and the size of the middle class to shrink further, unless we change our social and economic systems to build a new middle class along different lines.[15]

The global hospitality business, medical technicians, pharmaceutical and legal employees are also expected to lose jobs. In a year or two, an electronic device that works with smartphones is expected to be brought to market: you breathe into it, it scans your retina and takes a sample of your blood, then it analyses over fifty biomarkers that identify nearly every disease that you might have. Since all such devices tend to be inexpensive, everyone will have access to good medical and legal advice for little money. The numbers of people working in these fields, which have grown fast lately, are expected to start declining in a few years.

As scientific and technical knowledge undermines some professions, it opens new business opportunities for others, and helps more people to live longer and be more productive, but apparently less secure. As a result, new social, cultural and political, as well as economic and security challenges will be created, of which terrorism and unemployment are just two. A careful look at the global situation today reveals that most nations are not prepared to face the challenges of tomorrow.

Notes

1. Mark O'Byrne, Global Debt Now $200 Trillion!, May 14, 2015 (http://www.maxkeiser.com/2015/05/global-debt-now-200-trillion/#wmskZoHFm3JMujeU.99)
2. Michael Snyder, Corporate Debt Defaults Explode To Catastrophic Levels Not Seen Since the Last Financial Crisis, Washingtonsblog, March 31, 2016).
3. Matt Egan, Macy's is closing another 100 stores, CNN Money, August 11, 2016 http://money.cnn.com/2016/08/11/investing/macys-closes-100-stores/
4. Phillip Inman, Risk of global financial crash has increased, warns IMF, the Guardian, October 7, 2015.
5. Ibid.
6. Mark O'Byrne, Global Debt Now $200 Trillion, May 14, 2015 http://www.maxkeiser.com/2015/05/global-debt-now-200-trillion/#wmskZoHFm3JMujeU.99
7. Robert J. Samuelson, "Why the Fed slept?" *The Washington Post,* January, 23, 2012.
8. Kennedy, the Rise and Fall of the Great Powers, 439–40.

9. United States Census Bureau, US Census Bureau, July 2015 http://www.census.gov/population/international/data/idb/worldgrgraph.php
10. Eric Newcomer, Uber Raises Funding at $62.5 Billion Valuation, Bloomberg Technology, December 3, 2015 http://www.bloomberg.com/news/articles/2015-12-03/uber-raises-funding-at-62-5-valuation
11. International Labor Comparisons, 1970–2012, US Bureau of Labor Statistics, October 19, 2016 http://www.bls.gov/ilc/tables.htm
12. Where the Manufacturing Jobs Are, The Globalist, December 30, 2014 http://www.theglobalist.com/where-the-manufacturing-jobs-are/
13. Ibid.
14. Top 20 Facts About Manufacturing, National Association of Manufacturers http://www.nam.org/Newsroom/Top-20-Facts-About-Manufacturing/#sthash.actiLbEr.dpuf
15. See, Mohamed Rabie, Saving Capitalism and Democracy; Palgrave Macmillan, 2013; chapter 8.

CHAPTER 15

Concluding Remarks

During the latest era of rising expectations in America, which stretched from 2002 to 2007, the American people spent more and saved less; many in fact spent more than their incomes because they were able to borrow money using their homes and stock equities as collateral. For years, Americans as a nation spent and invested more than their gross domestic product (GDP), because foreign nationals sent billions of dollars to America every day. Former Federal Reserve Chairman Paul Volcker wrote in 2005 in the *Washington Post*: "We as a nation are consuming and investing about 6 percent more than we are producing ... What holds it all together is a massive and growing flow of capital from abroad, running to more than $2 billion every working day."[1]

In contrast, during the era of diminishing expectations which began in 2008, Americans spent less and saved more of their incomes. In light of the prevailing economic uncertainty, low wages and lack of confidence in the future, bringing the level of optimism to 2006 levels has become a daunting task. And without expanding consumer demand and restoring optimism, it is difficult to motivate investors to take the usual risks and invest in creating new jobs, particularly since the manufacturing sector in several countries has large unused and underused capacity. A vicious circle has thus been created, where producers wait for consumers to increase spending before investing in new projects, and where consumers wait for good paying jobs to get the money needed to increase spending and expand demand.

Published data indicate that the average growth rate of the world economy since the Great Recession has been about 3.4% annually; and that the

M. Rabie, *The Global Debt Crisis and Its Socioeconomic Implications*,
https://doi.org/10.1007/978-3-319-66215-2_15

average interest rate on the global debt has been about 3% per year. It ought to be noted, however, that rich nations, just like rich individuals, pay lower interest rates than poor nations. In 2015, the global GDP growth rate was 3.1%, and 2.7% in 2016. Based on these numbers, the entire growth of the global economy in 2016 would not be enough to service the global debt. A 3% interest on the global debt ($69 trillion) would be about $2.1 trillion, while a 2.7% increase in GDP ($75.5 trillion) would produce about $2 trillion in extra income, not enough to service the debt or reduce its size to GDP. Nevertheless, only about 20–40% of this money is collected as taxes to finance state budgets, and only a fraction of such budgets goes to service the debt.

Since money to service the national debt comes from states' budgets, which are financed by taxes people and corporations pay, all rich and poor taxpayers in every country pay a share in servicing the public debt. However, interest payments go directly to the bank accounts of the rich people and financial institutions, because they are the ones who own the money and extend the loans, giving the rich more than they pay in taxes. So the continuation of the debt causes the rich to get richer and the poor to get poorer. Since the poor and the middle classes have gained almost no increase in their incomes or wealth over the last forty years, tax policies are forcing them to pay a price they cannot afford to service a debt they did not benefit from. As a consequence, the economic situation in most states has become oppressive, causing a social crisis to develop slowly in many countries, as reflected in the unprecedented support for Donald Trump and Bernie Sanders in America. "The popular rage that gave birth to Trump also gave birth to Sanders. Both express widespread social and political discontent, but they do it in opposite ways—one engaging in rightist populism and the other opting for the leftist call for justice."[2] Trump, riding the wave of discontent, was elected US president by largely white marginalized Americans. A 2012 poll conducted by the Pew Research Center indicated that over 60% of all Americans say they are poor or feeling poor, and about 66% see "strong" conflicts between rich and poor.[3]

Years ago, power was defined more in military terms and less in economic terms. Today, power is defined more in economic terms and less in military terms; in the meantime, the major centers of economic power are shifting fast from the West to the East, particularly to China and India. On the other hand, no military power can be built and sustained these days without an economy strong enough to finance its many needs and activities. Nevertheless, military power has lost its capacity to achieve strategic objectives using violence only over many years; American wars in Korea and Vietnam in the 1950s and 1960s, respectively, and in Afghanistan, Iraq, Syria, Libya and Yemen since 2001 prove this point.

Giovanni Arrighi says: "The Vietnam War had demonstrated that the most expensive, technologically advanced, and destructive military apparatus the world had ever seen was quite powerless in curbing the will of one of the poorest people on earth, the US government temporarily lost most, if not all of its credibility as the policeman of the free world."[4]

Mike Roscoe says: "The wealth is increasingly concentrated in the hands of the very rich, to the detriment of society and, in the end, of civilization as a whole. The situation is unsustainable, and I think we might well be seeing the beginnings of the end of our current finance-dominated economic system, a system that depends on growth while at the same time killing the prospects of growth by increasing debt and inequality. We should be prepared for another major crisis."[5] The concentration of wealth in fewer hands causes most income to go to the rich who own the capital, leaving little or nothing for most workers and the poor; this means that the current distribution of income makes money flow from the poor to the rich; from people who have a higher propensity to spend to people who have a higher propensity to save—and this constrains consumption and causes economies to slow down.

Is there a real danger that our world might turn upside down suddenly and cause a new great recession or even a depression? And what are we supposed to do to face the seemingly looming danger? While no one knows the answers to these crucial questions, we can look at the factors that caused the Great Recession in order to determine the probability that something awful might happen and interrupt normal life in our world, driving many of us to seek comfort in rigid ideologies that have nothing to offer except more misery and violence. Though there are several forces that can affect the global economy and cause a recession, comparing the current situation with the pre-2008 one seems to suggest that we are unlikely to avoid another crisis in the coming few years.

The creation of credit bubbles encourages many unqualified individuals and businesses to borrow, which exposes them to the possibility of default and bankruptcy; bankruptcies and defaults affect the balance sheets of lending banks negatively, causing some banks to face serious problems or fail. During the few years that preceded the financial crisis of 2008, banks and mortgage companies extended credit and gave loans to people who did not have the financial resources to pay their monthly payments on a regular basis. Knowing this fact, lenders invented new ways to lessen their exposure by creating new financial products and selling them to foreign banks and hedge funds and regular investors. Therefore, when some borrowers failed to pay their mortgage payments in 2007, the entire credit structure began to crumble, causing the Great Recession that covered most parts of the world and affected all economies and nations. The factual information and expert analysis provided by the many international organizations, newspapers and economists quoted in this book suggest that the outlook now is rather gloomy.

If the entire public debt is not repaid now, it will never be paid back in the future, because the sheer size of the debt and interest payments have vastly reduced the capacity of all highly indebted nations to repay. As a consequence, the debt of such nations has caused their economies to slow down, stagnate or contract; it has also caused the populations of such nations to lose income and hope. This may be the last chance to solve this problem before we face wholesale defaults, and probably social revolutions no one can manage, or the consequences of which no nation can escape. The captains of the international monetary system at the International Monetary Fund (IMF) acknowledged during a closed meeting in January 2011 that they do not know how to deal with a new financial crisis, or what might trigger such a crisis, or how it might unfold. Nevertheless, they believed that mounting public debt is likely to instigate the next crisis. On the other hand, the new technologies and apps that are being developed at the speed of light are disrupting the way we do business and live our lives, and are causing most of us to get confused.

The Ramo Plan is an attempt to address the short-, medium- and long-term challenges of our times. The plan's main objective is to facilitate the transition of twentieth-century industrial society into twenty-first-century knowledge society. As the plan deals with the challenges and fears of change, it gives special attention to the opportunities change usually creates. Liberating rich and poor nations from the debt burden is meant to address the public debt crisis in the short term, and enable states to address other pressing economic, social and security concerns gradually. The sustainable development fund is designed to address the medium-term challenge of helping underdeveloped countries develop their economies and transform their cultures, alleviate poverty and unemployment in all states, and expand world markets; and this will enable industrial states to grow their economies without fear of a new financial crisis. And as the fund provides needed capital and technical assistance to help developing nations industrialize, it facilitates the transition of traditional agricultural societies into industrial ones, creates tens of millions of new jobs and causes poverty, ignorance, population growth rates and radicalism to recede.

As for the educational, humanitarian and environmental funds, they are meant to address the long-term issues related to creating a new world characterized by stability, fairness, peace, security, hope and respect for human rights. When people lose hope, they lose the incentive to work hard, seek good education and live productive, ethical lives. This is one reason why most economies have slowed down, and a large number of societies are experiencing racism, ideological revival and violence; ideological revival and radicalism and terrorism are consequences of places devoid of hope that lack good education. The average person in a country such as Greece, Egypt, Tunisia or Zimbabwe says, "We understand that there are no jobs today, but can anyone promise me a decent job next year or the year after?" The full implementation of the Ramo Plan is our only hope at this juncture in history to collectively deal with the challenges facing us and achieve our desired goal of transforming our world into a stable, sustainable, peaceful and enjoyable one in a matter of three decades.

Despite the fact that our world has never had a collective leadership with so many highly educated and intelligent people as we have today, we have never had a collective leadership that is so politically and economically corrupt and morally and intellectually bankrupt. The corruption and bankruptcy is not because they are stupid or born evil, but because many are blinded by greed, intoxicated by the lust for political and military power, and some even moved by a desire to exploit and dominate the poor and weak everywhere. As a consequence, all of us, rich and poor, strong and weak, young and old have lost a great deal of our humanity and sense of purpose. It is time that we join hands to regain our sense of humanity and purpose, and create a world we love and feel secure to live in.

Since all peoples are in one boat sailing against turbulent economic, financial, social, cultural, political and security winds, avoiding an impending global catastrophe demands that all nations and powers cooperate with each other and share sacrifices and rewards; and that all thinking leaders and leading thinkers of our times work collectively, creatively and humanely to guide our boat to safety.

Notes

1. Paul A. Volcker: "An Economy on Thin Ice," *The Washington Post*, April 10, 2005, B 7.
2. Slavoj Zizek; Clinton, Trump and the triumph of global capitalism; In These Times, August 24, 2016 http://inthesetimes.com/article/19410/clinton-trump-and-the-triumph-of-ideology
3. Rich Morin, Rising share of Americans see conflict between rich and poor, *Pew Research Center*, January 11, 2012.
4. Giovanni Arrighi, The Longest Twentieth Century, Verso, 2010, p. 332.
5. Mike Roscoe, Money Creation, *Positive Money*, February 3, 2015 http://positivemoney.org/2015/02/200-trillion-debt/

Selected References

Adams, Robert. 1996. *Paths of Fire: An Anthropologist's Inquiry into Western Technology*. Princeton University Press.
Anderson, Benedict. 1991. *Imagined Communities*. Verso.
Armstrong, Karen. 1991. *A History of God*. Ballantine Books.
Arrighi, Giovanni. 1983. *The Geometry of Imperialism*. Verso.
———. 2010. *The Longest Twentieth Century*. Verso.
Balaam, David, and Michael Veseth. 2000. *Introduction to International Political Economy*. Prentice Hall.
Baldwin, Robert E. 1966. *Economic Development and Growth*. Wiley.
Barrat Brown, Michael. 1974. *The Economics of Imperialism*. Penguin Books.
Bartlett, Robert. 1993. *The Making of Europe: Conquest, Colonialism and Cultural Change 950–1350*. Penguin.
Bessie, Sophie. 1995. *From Social Exclusion to Social Cohesion: A Policy Agenda*. UNESCO.
Bloom, Howard. 1995. *The Lucifer Principle*. The Atlantic Monthly Press.
Blum, Jerome, Rondo Cameron, and Thomas Barnes. 1966. *The European World*. Little Brown.
Brecher, Jeremy, and Tim Costello. 1994. *Global Village or Global Pillage*. South End Press.
Brockway, George P. 1995. *The End of Economic Man: Principles of Any Future Economics*. W. W. Norton.
Burton, John, and Frank Dukes, eds. 1990. *Conflict: Readings in Conflict Management and Resolution*. St. Martin's Press.
Bushrui, Suheil, Iraj Ayman, and Ervin Laszlo, eds. 1993. *Transition to Global Society*. Oneworld Publications.
Carr, Edward Hallett. 1961. *What Is History?* Vintage Books.

M. Rabie, *The Global Debt Crisis and Its Socioeconomic Implications*,
https://doi.org/10.1007/978-3-319-66215-2

Cavanaugh, Anderson S., et al. 2008. *Executive Excess 2008: How Average Taxpayers Subsidize Runaway Pay*. Institute for Policy Studies.
Chase, Stewart. 1962. *The Proper Study of Mankind*. Harper & Row.
Chase-Dun, Christopher. 1989. *Global Formation: Structures of the World Economy*. Basil Blackwell.
Chomsky, Noam. 2006. *Failed States: The Abuse of Power and the Assault on Democracy*. Henry Holt.
———. 2010. *Hope and Progress*. Haymarket Books.
———. 2015. *Rogue States*. Haymarket Books.
———. 2016. *Who Rules the World?* Metropolitan Books.
Cipolla, Carlo M. 1980. *Before the Industrial Revolution: European Society and Economy 1000–1700*. W. W. Norton.
Clark, Gregory. 2007. *A Farewell to Alms: A Brief Economic History of the World*. Princeton University Press.
Cook, Michael. 2003. *A Brief History of the Human Race*. W. W. Norton.
Crane, George, and Abla Amawi, eds. 1997. *The Theoretical Evolution of International Political Economy*. Oxford University Press.
Credit Suisse. 2015. *Global Wealth Report 2015*. Credit Suisse.
Damhoff, G. William. 1990. *The Power Elite and the State: How Policy Is Made in America*. Hawthorne.
———. 2006. *Who Rules America? Power, Politics, & Social Change*. McGraw-Hill.
Damhoff, G. William, and Michael J. Webber. 2011. *Class and Power in the New Deal: Corporate Moderates, Southern Democrats, and the Liberal-Labor Coalition*. Stanford University Press.
Davidson, Basil. 1992. *The Black's Man Burden: Africa and the Curse of the Nation State*. Random House.
Diamond, Stanley. 1974. *In Search of the Primitive: A Critique of Civilization*. Transaction Books.
Diamond, Jared. 1999. *Guns, Germs and Steel: The Fate of Human Societies*. W. W. Norton.
———. 2005. *Collapse: How Societies Choose to Fail or Succeed*. Viking.
Diggens, John Patrick. 1996. *Max Weber: Politics and the Spirit of Tragedy*. Basic Books.
Dray, William. 1980. *Perspectives on History*. Routledge and Kegan Paul.
Eriksen, Thomas Hylland. 1993. *Ethnicity and Nationalism*. Pluto Press.
Feuer, Lewis S., ed. 1959. *Marx and Engels: Basic Writings on Politics and Philosophy*. Anchor Books.
Frank, Andre Gunder. 1967. *Capitalism and Underdevelopment in Latin America*. Monthly Review Press.
Fukuyama, Francis. 1992. *The End of History and the Last Man*. The Free Press.
———. 1995. *Trust: The Social Virtues & the Creation of Prosperity*. The Free Press
Galbraith, John Kenneth. 1958. *The Affluent Society*. The New American Library.

———. 1987. *Economic Perspective: A Critical History*. Houghton Mifflin.
———. 1992. *The Culture of Contentment*. Houghton Mifflin.
———. 1997. *The Good Society*. Houghton Mifflin.
Gallagher, Winifred. 1993. *The Power of Place*. Poseidon Press.
Garraty, John A., and Peter Gay, eds. 1972. *The Columbia History of the World*. Harper & Row.
Gatlung, John. 1980. *The True World: A Transnational Perspective*. The Free Press.
Gellner, Ernest. 1988. *Plough, Sword and Book: The Structure of Human History*. Collins Harvill.
Gilbert, Christopher, and David Vines, eds. 2000. *The World Bank Structure and Policies*. Cambridge University Press.
Gough, Leo. 1998. *Asia Meltdown: The End of the Miracle?* Capstone.
Gramsci, Antonio. 1971. *Selections from the Prison Notebooks*. International Publishers.
Greenfeld, Liah. 1992. *Nationalism: Fire Roads to Modernity*. Harvard University Press.
Greif, Avner. 2006. *Institutions and the Path to the Modern Economy: Lessons from Medieval Trade*. Cambridge University Press.
Halliday, Fred. 1986. *The Making of the Second Cold War*. Verso.
Hardt, Michael, and Antonio Negri. 2000. *Empire*. Harvard University Press.
Harrison, Lawrence E., and Samuel Huntington, eds. 2000. *Culture Matters; How Values Shape Human Progress*. Basic Books.
Hawking, Stephen. 1988. *A Brief History of Time*. Bantam Books.
Hawking, Stephen, and Leonard Mlodinow. 2010. *The Grand Design*. Bantam Books.
Heaton, Herbert. 1958. *Economic History of Europe*. Harper & Row.
Hegel, Georg Wilhelm Friedrich. 1936. *The Philosophy of History*. Dover Publications.
Heilbroner, Robert. 1968. *The Making of Economic Society*. Prentice-Hall.
———. 1980. *Marxism, for and Against*. W. W. Norton.
———. 1985. *The Nature and Logic of Capitalism*. W. W. Norton and Company.
———. 1993. *21st Century Capitalism*. W. W. Norton and Co.
———. 1994. *21st Century Capitalism*. W. W. Norton.
Hermann, Edward, and Noam Chomsky. 1988. *Manufacturing Consent: The Political Economy of the Mass Media*. Pantheon.
Hill, McKay. 2000. *A History of the World Societies*. Houghton Mifflin Company.
Hill, Steven. 2002. *Fixing Elections*. Routledge.
Himmelfarb, Gertrude. 1994. *On Looking into the Abyss*. Vintage Books.
Hopkins, A.G., ed. 2002. *Globalization in World History*. W. W. Norton.
Hugh, Thomas. 1996. *World History*. Harper Collins.
Huntington, Samuel P. 1996. *The Clash of Civilizations and the Remaking of World History*. Simon & Schuster.

Jacob, Margaret C. 1997. *Scientific Culture and the Making of the Industrial West.* Oxford University Press.

Kaku, Machio. 1997. *Visions: How Science Will Revolutionize the 21st Century.* Anchor Books.

Kaplan, Robert. 1998. *An Empire Wilderness.* Random House.

Kaufman, Walter, ed. 1967. *Friedrich Nietzsche on the Genealogy of Morals.* Vintage Books.

Keister, L. 2005. *Getting Rich: A Study of Wealth Mobility in America.* Cambridge University Press.

Kennan, George. 1993. *Around the Cragged Hill.* W. W. Norton.

Kennedy, Paul. 1987. *The Rise and Fall of the Great Powers.* Vintage Books.

———. 1993. *Preparing for the Twenty-First Century.* Random House.

Kerr, Clark, and John T. Dunlop. 1964. *Industrialism and Industrial Man.* Oxford University Press.

Kitschelt, Herbert, Peter Lange, Gary Marks, and John D. Stephens, eds. 1999. *Continuity and Change in Contemporary Capitalism.* Cambridge University Press.

Korten, David. 2000. *The Post Corporate World: Life After Capitalism.* Berrett-Koehler.

———. 2001. *When Corporations Rule the World.* Berrett-Koehler.

———. 2006. *The Great Turning: From Empire to Earth Community.* Berrett-Koehler Publishers.

———. 2009. *Agenda for a New Economy: From Phantom Wealth to Real Wealth.* Berrett-Koehler.

Landes, David S. 1999. *The Wealth and Poverty of Nations.* W. W. Norton.

Lekachman, Robert, and David E. Novack, eds. 1964. *Development and Society: The Dynamics of Economic Change.* St. Martin's Press.

Lewis, Charles. 2005. The Buying of the President, Harper Perennial, 2004. In *Power: A Radical View*, ed. S. Lukes. Palgrave Macmillan.

Madoff, Ray. 2010. *Immortality and the Law: The Rising Power of the American Dead.* Yale University Press.

Marshall, Ray, and Marc Tucker. 1992. *Thinking for a Living: Education and the Wealth of Nations.* Basic Books.

Marx, Karl, and Friedrich Engels. 1937. *The Communist Manifesto.* Vanguard Publications.

McCoy, Alfred. 2009. *Policing America's Empire: The United States, the Philippines, and the Rise of the Surveillance State.* University of Wisconsin Press.

McMurtry, John. 1998. *Unequal Freedoms; The Global Market as an Ethical System.* Kumarian Press.

Mearsheimer, John, and Stephen Walt. 2007. *The Israeli Lobby and US Foreign Policy.* Farrar, Straus and Giroux.

Miles, Marc A., ed. 2004. *The Road to Prosperity.* Heritage Books.

Mills, John. 2003. *A Critical History of Economics*. Palgrave.
Mirsky, Yehuda, and Matt Ahren, eds. 1993. *Democracy in the Middle East*. Washington Institute for Near East Policy.
Modelski, George. 1987. *Long Cycles in World Politics*. University of Washington Press.
Ohmae, Lenichi. 1995. *The End of the Nation State*. The Free Press.
Panitch, Leo, and Sam Gindin. 2013. *The Making of Global Capitalism*. Verso.
Piketty, Thomas. 2015. *The Economics of Inequality*. The Belknap Press of Harvard University Press.
Pomeranz, Kenneth. 2000. *The Great Divergence: China, Europe, and the Making of the Modern World Economy*. Princeton University Press.
Pounds, Norman. 1974. *An Economic History of Medieval Europe*. Longmans.
Rabie, Mohamed. 1988. *The Politics of Foreign Aid*. Praeger.
———. 1992. *The New World Order*. Vantage Press.
———. 1994. *Conflict Resolution and Ethnicity*. Praeger Publishers.
———. 2001. *The Making of History*. Authors Choice Press.
———. 2013a. *Global Economic and Cultural Transformation*. Palgrave Macmillan.
———. 2013b. *Saving Capitalism and Democracy*. Palgrave Macmillan.
———. 2016. *A Theory of Sustainable Sociocultural and Economic Development*. Palgrave Macmillan.
Reich, Robert B. 1992. *The Work on Nations: Preparing Ourselves for the 21st Capitalism*. Random House.
———. 2010. *After-Shock*. Alfred A. Knopf.
Robbins, Richard. 1999. *Global Problems and the Culture of Capitalism*. Allyn and Bacon.
Roemer, J. 1996. *Theories of Distributive Justice*. Harvard University Press.
Ross, Alec. 2016. *The Industries of the Future*. Simon & Schuster.
Sachs, Jeffrey D. 2005. *The End of Poverty*. The Penguin Press.
Sandel, Michael. 1996. *Democracy's Discontent: America in Search of a Public Philosophy*. Belknap Press.
Scheuer, Michael. 2004. *Imperial Hubris: Why the West Is Losing the War on Terror*. Potomac Books.
Schlesinger, Arthur, Jr. 1958. *The Coming of the New Deal*. Houghton Mifflin.
———. 1992. *The Disuniting of America*. W. W. Norton.
Schumpeter, Joseph A. 1950. *Capitalism, Socialism and Democracy*. Harper Brothers.
Sen, Amartya. 1999. *Development as Freedom*. Anchor Books.
Smith, Adam. 1937. *The Wealth of Nations*. The Modern Library.
Smith, Huston. 1972. *The Religions of Man*. Harper & Row.
Sorkin, Andrew Ross. 2009. *Too Big to Fail*. Viking.
Soros, George. 2002. *On Globalization*. Public Affairs.
Sowell, Thomas. 1994. *Race and Culture*. Basic Books.

Stiglitz, Joseph E. 2003. *Globalization and Its Discontents.* W. W. Norton.
———. 2006. *Making Globalization Work.* W. W. Norton.
Thomas, Hugh. 1979. *World History.* Harper Collins.
Thurow, Lester. 2003. *Fortune Favors the Bold.* Harper Collins.
Tilly, Charles. 1984. *Big Structures, Large Processes, Hug Corporations.* Russell Sage.
Van Bilzen, Gerard. 2015. *The Development of Aid.* Cambridge Scholars Publishing.
Van Doren, Charles. 1991. *A History of Knowledge.* Ballantine Books.
Waldrop, Mitchell M. 1992. *Complexity: The Emerging Science at the Edge of Order and Chaos.* Simon & Schuster.
Wallerstein, Immanuel. 1991. *Geopolitics and Geoculture.* Cambridge University Press.
Walter, Andrew. 1991. *World Power and World Money: The Role of Hegemony and International Monetary Order.* St. Martin's Press.
Warde, Ibrahim. 2007. *The Price of Fear: The Truth Behind the Financial War on Terror.* University of California Press.
Weatherford, Jack. 1994. *Savages and Civilization.* Ballantine Books.
———. 2004. *Genghis Khan and the Making of the Modern World.* Three Rivers Press.
Weber, Max. 1930. *The Protestant Ethic and the Spirit of Capitalism.* Unwin.
Webster's Encyclopedic Unabridged Dictionary of English Language. 1989. Portland House.
Weisbrot, Mark, Dean Baker, Egor Kraev, and Judy Chen. 2001. *The Scorecard on Globalization 1980–2000: Twenty Years of Diminished Progress.* Center for Economic Policy and Research.
World Bank. 2016. *The World Bank.* Global Economic Prospects.
World Bank Development Indicators. 2008. World Bank.
Wright, Quincy. 1990. The Nature of Conflict. In *Conflict: Readings in Conflict Management and Resolution*, ed. John Burton and Frank Dukes. St. Martin's Press.
Zweigenhaft, Richard L., and G. William Damhoff. 2011. *The New CEOs: Women, African American, Latino, and Asian American Leaders of Fortune 500 Companies.* Rowman and Littlefield.

Other Sources

Center for Economic and Policy Research
Financial Times
Focus Economics
Foreign Affairs
Foreign Policy
Fortune
Mother Johns

Newsweek
OECD Data
The American Conservative
The Atlantic
The Economist
The Guardian
The Independent
The Nation
The New York Times
The Washington Post
Time
US Bureau of Labor Statistics
Wall Street

Websites

Congressional Budget Office.; https://www.cbo.gov
Council On Foreign Affairs.; http://www.cfr.org
Economic Policy Institute.; http://www.epi.org
http://www.inthesetimes.com
http://www.rationalwiki.org/wiki/American_exceptionalism
http://www.research.gavekal.com
http://www.abrahamlincolnonline.org/lincoln/speeches/gettysburg.htm
http://www.alternet.com
http://www.feedingamerica.org
http://www.gallup.com
http://www.goodreads.com/author/quotes/5001.Milton_Friedman
http://www.huffingtonpost.com
http://www.investopedia.com
http://www.people-press.org
http://www.pewresearch.org
http://www.politifact.com
http://www.salon.com
http://www.un-documents.net/ocf-02.htm
http://www.unicef.org
http://www.washingtonsblog.com
https://www.boundless.com
https://www.census.gov/foreign-trade/balance/c5700.html
https://www.thespainreport.com
The Globalist.; http://www.theglobalist.com
Trading Economics.; http://www.tradingeconomics.com
US Debt Clock; (http://www.usdebtclock.org/)

US National debt clock. http://www.usdebtclock.org/
World Economic Forum.; http://www.reports.weforum.org
www.census.gov/hhes/www/wealth/wealth.html; www.cia.gov/worldfactbook
www.faireconomy.org; www.globalissues.org; www.imf.org
www.org/publications; www.marketwatch.com; www.nytimes.com
www.oecd.org; www.politicalglobalization.com; www.repec.org
www.whorulesamerica.net; www.worldbankgroup.org; www.worldhunger.org

Index

Note: Page number followed by 'n' denotes end notes

M. Rabie, *The Global Debt Crisis and Its Socioeconomic Implications*, https://doi.org/10.1007/978-3-319-66215-2

Lightning Source UK Ltd.
Milton Keynes UK
UKHW02n1804290118
316776UK00019B/93/P

9 783319 662145